jaime hernandez

wigwam bam

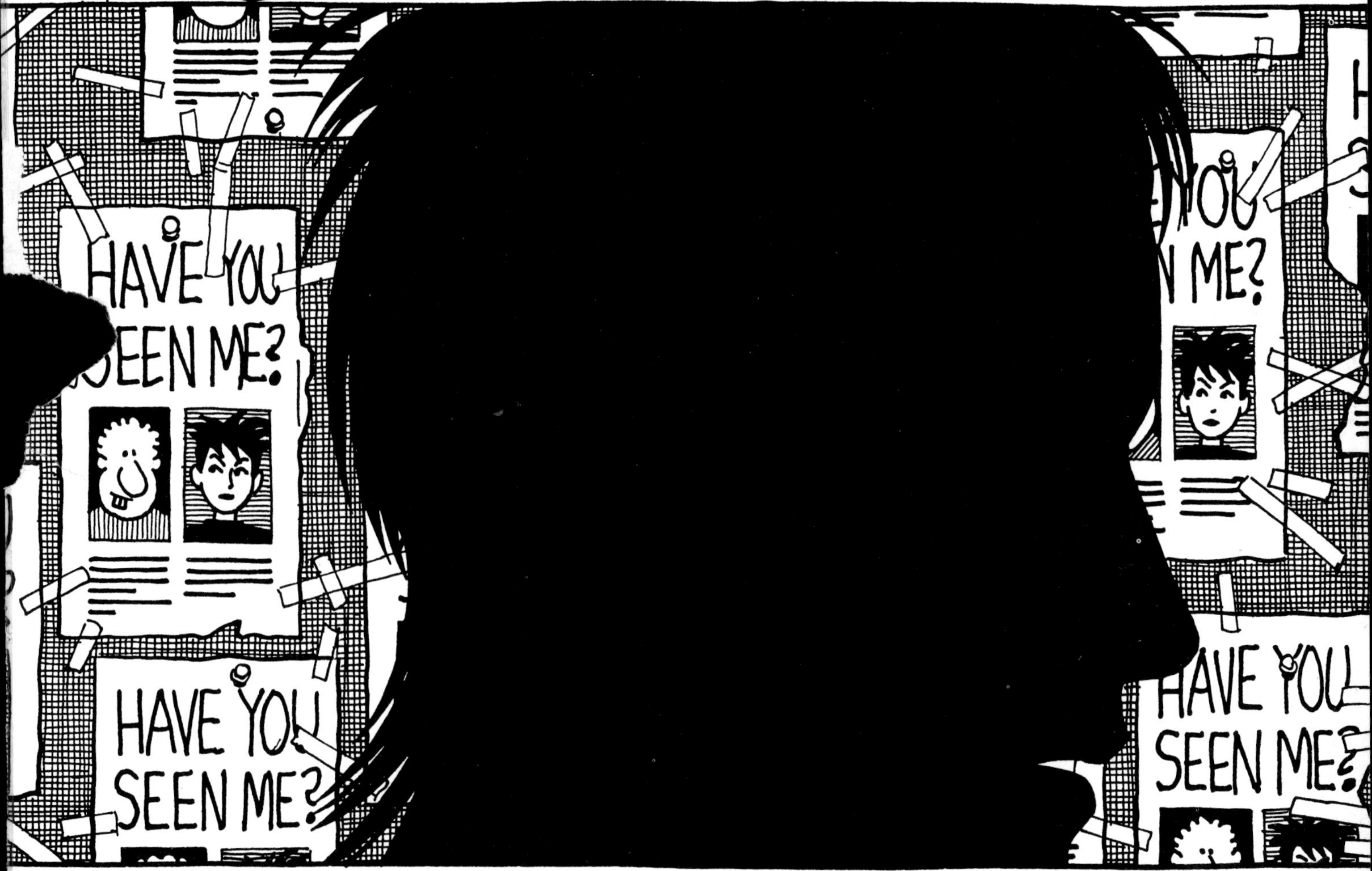
HAVE YOU SEEN ME?
HAVE YOU SEEN ME?
HAVE YOU SEEN ME?
HAVE YOU SEEN ME?

FANTAGRAPHICS BOOKS A Love and Rockets Collection

Fantagraphics Books
7563 Lake City Way Northeast
Seattle Washington 98115

Editor Gary Groth

Art Direction Dale Yarger

First Fantagraphics Books edition: March, 1994

ISBN (soft): 1 56097 120 7

ISBN (hard): 1 56097 121 5

Printed in Hong Kong

jaime hernandez

wigwam bam

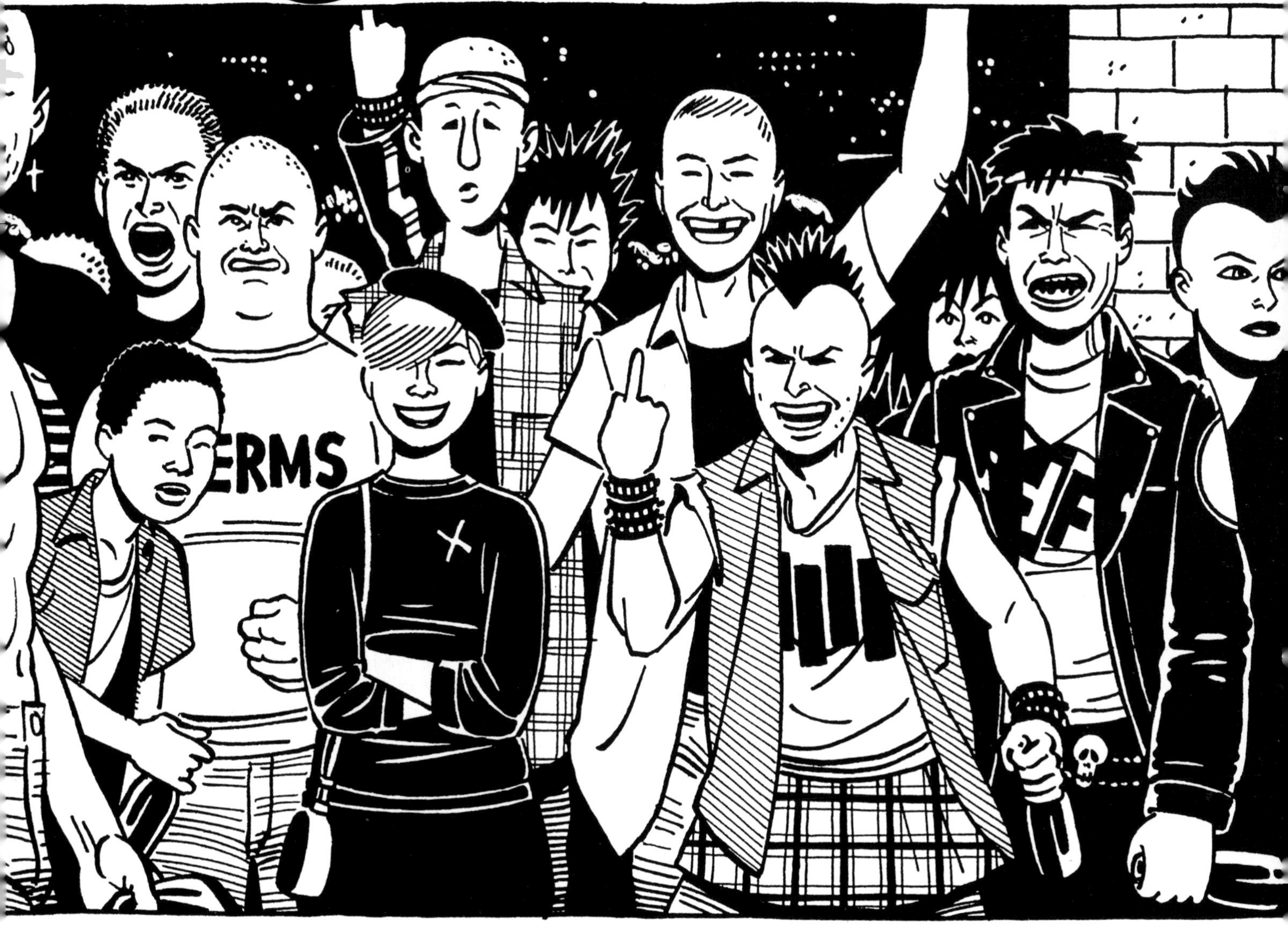
ERMS

FANTAGRAPHICS BOOKS A Love and Rockets Collection

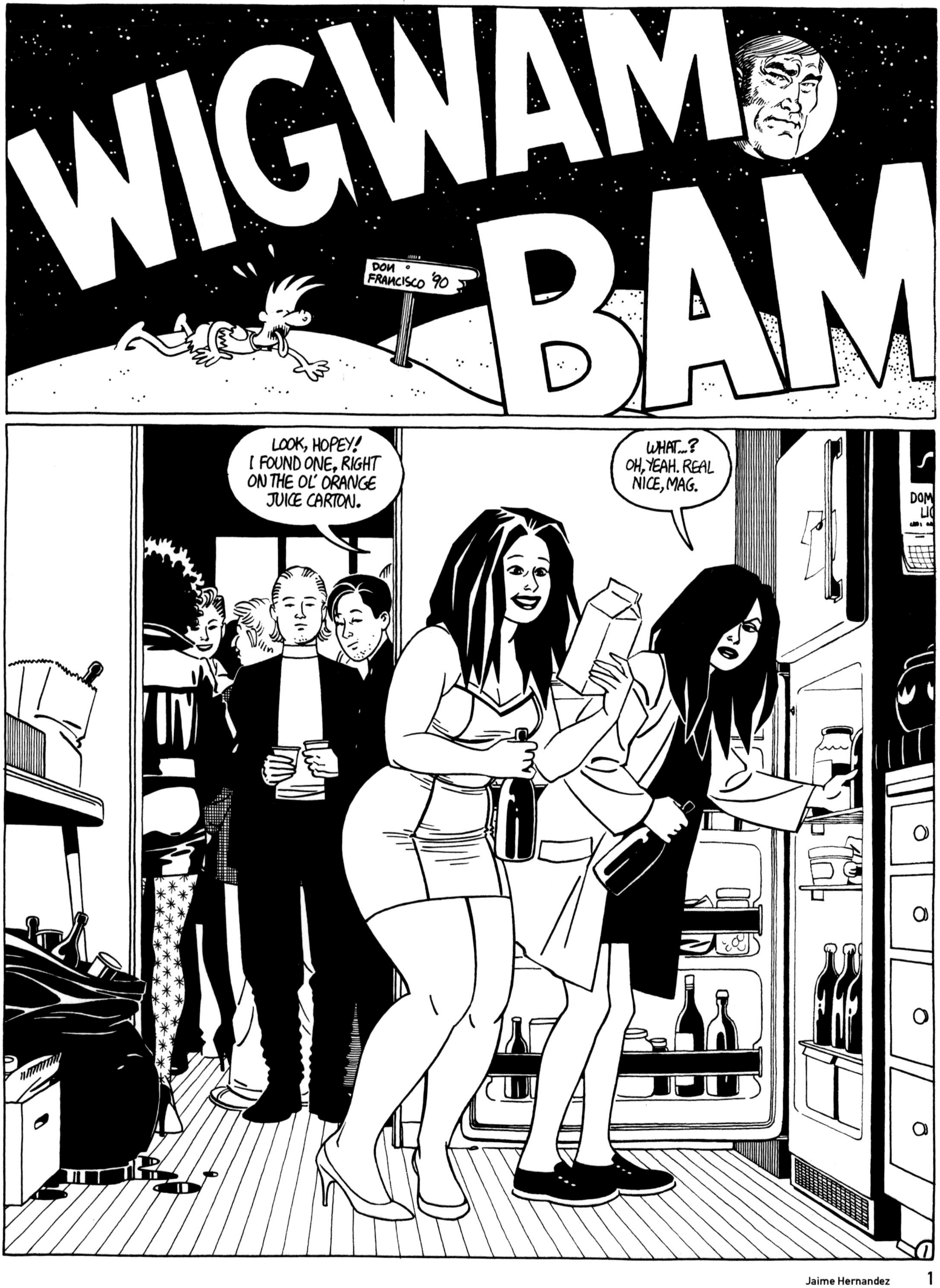
WIGWAM BAM
DON FRANCISCO '90
LOOK, HOPEY! I FOUND ONE, RIGHT ON THE OL' ORANGE JUICE CARTON.
WHAT...? OH, YEAH. REAL NICE, MAG.

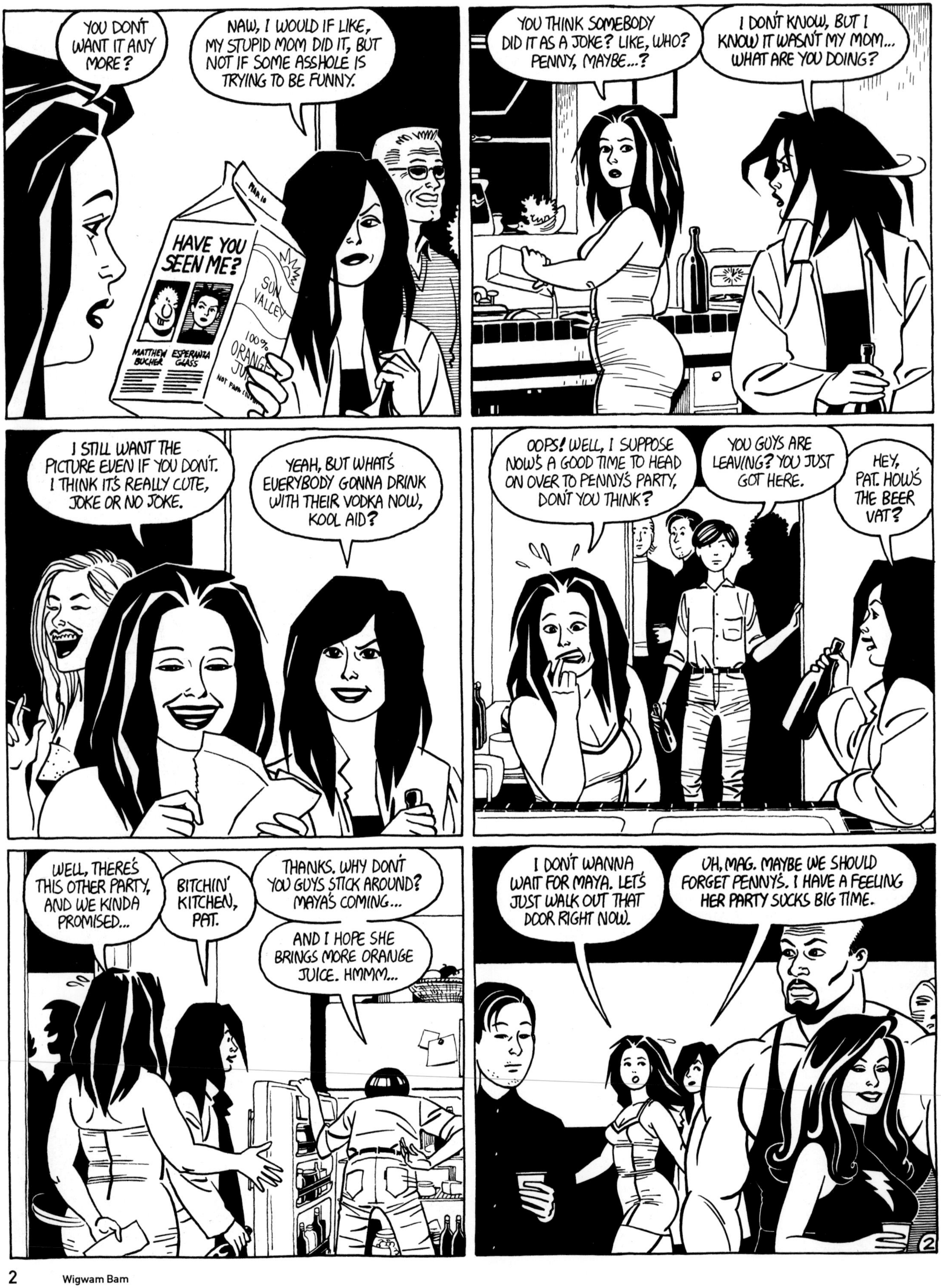
YOU DON'T WANT IT ANY MORE?
NAW, I WOULD IF LIKE, MY STUPID MOM DID IT, BUT NOT IF SOME ASSHOLE IS TRYING TO BE FUNNY.
HAVE YOU SEEN ME?
MATTHEW BUCHER
ESPERANZA GLASS
SUN VALLEY
100% ORANGE
YOU THINK SOMEBODY DID IT AS A JOKE? LIKE, WHO? PENNY, MAYBE...?
I DON'T KNOW, BUT I KNOW IT WASN'T MY MOM... WHAT ARE YOU DOING?
I STILL WANT THE PICTURE EVEN IF YOU DON'T. I THINK IT'S REALLY CUTE, JOKE OR NO JOKE.
YEAH, BUT WHAT'S EVERYBODY GONNA DRINK WITH THEIR VODKA NOW, KOOL AID?
OOPS! WELL, I SUPPOSE NOW'S A GOOD TIME TO HEAD ON OVER TO PENNY'S PARTY, DON'T YOU THINK?
YOU GUYS ARE LEAVING? YOU JUST GOT HERE.
HEY, PAT. HOW'S THE BEER VAT?
WELL, THERE'S THIS OTHER PARTY, AND WE KINDA PROMISED...
BITCHIN' KITCHEN, PAT.
THANKS. WHY DON'T YOU GUYS STICK AROUND? MAYA'S COMING...
AND I HOPE SHE BRINGS MORE ORANGE JUICE. HMMM...
I DON'T WANNA WAIT FOR MAYA. LET'S JUST WALK OUT THAT DOOR RIGHT NOW.
UH, MAG. MAYBE WE SHOULD FORGET PENNY'S. I HAVE A FEELING HER PARTY SUCKS BIG TIME.
2

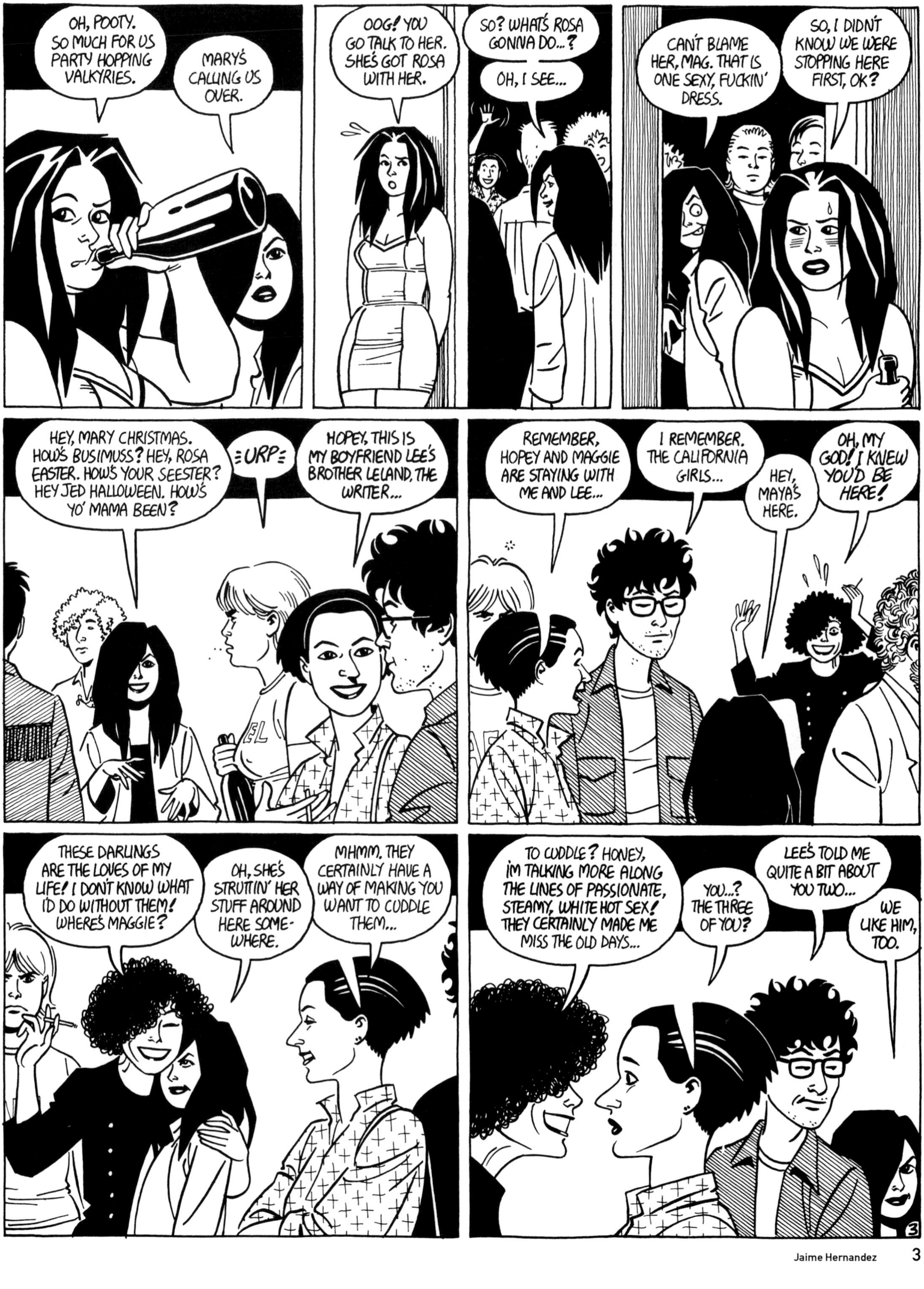
OH, POOTY. SO MUCH FOR US PARTY HOPPING VALKYRIES.
MARY'S CALLING US OVER.
OOG! YOU GO TALK TO HER. SHE'S GOT ROSA WITH HER.
SO? WHAT'S ROSA GONNA DO...?
OH, I SEE...
CAN'T BLAME HER, MAG. THAT IS ONE SEXY, FUCKIN' DRESS.
SO, I DIDN'T KNOW WE WERE STOPPING HERE FIRST, OK?
HEY, MARY CHRISTMAS. HOW'S BUSIMUSS? HEY, ROSA EASTER. HOW'S YOUR SEESTER? HEY JED HALLOWEEN. HOW'S YO' MAMA BEEN?
URP
HOPEY, THIS IS MY BOYFRIEND LEE'S BROTHER LELAND, THE WRITER...
REMEMBER, HOPEY AND MAGGIE ARE STAYING WITH ME AND LEE...
I REMEMBER. THE CALIFORNIA GIRLS...
HEY, MAYA'S HERE.
OH, MY GOD! I KNEW YOU'D BE HERE!
THESE DARLINGS ARE THE LOVES OF MY LIFE! I DON'T KNOW WHAT I'D DO WITHOUT THEM! WHERE'S MAGGIE?
OH, SHE'S STRUTTIN' HER STUFF AROUND HERE SOME-WHERE.
MHMM. THEY CERTAINLY HAVE A WAY OF MAKING YOU WANT TO CUDDLE THEM...
TO CUDDLE? HONEY, I'M TALKING MORE ALONG THE LINES OF PASSIONATE, STEAMY, WHITE HOT SEX! THEY CERTAINLY MADE ME MISS THE OLD DAYS...
YOU...? THE THREE OF YOU?
LEE'S TOLD ME QUITE A BIT ABOUT YOU TWO...
WE LIKE HIM, TOO.
3

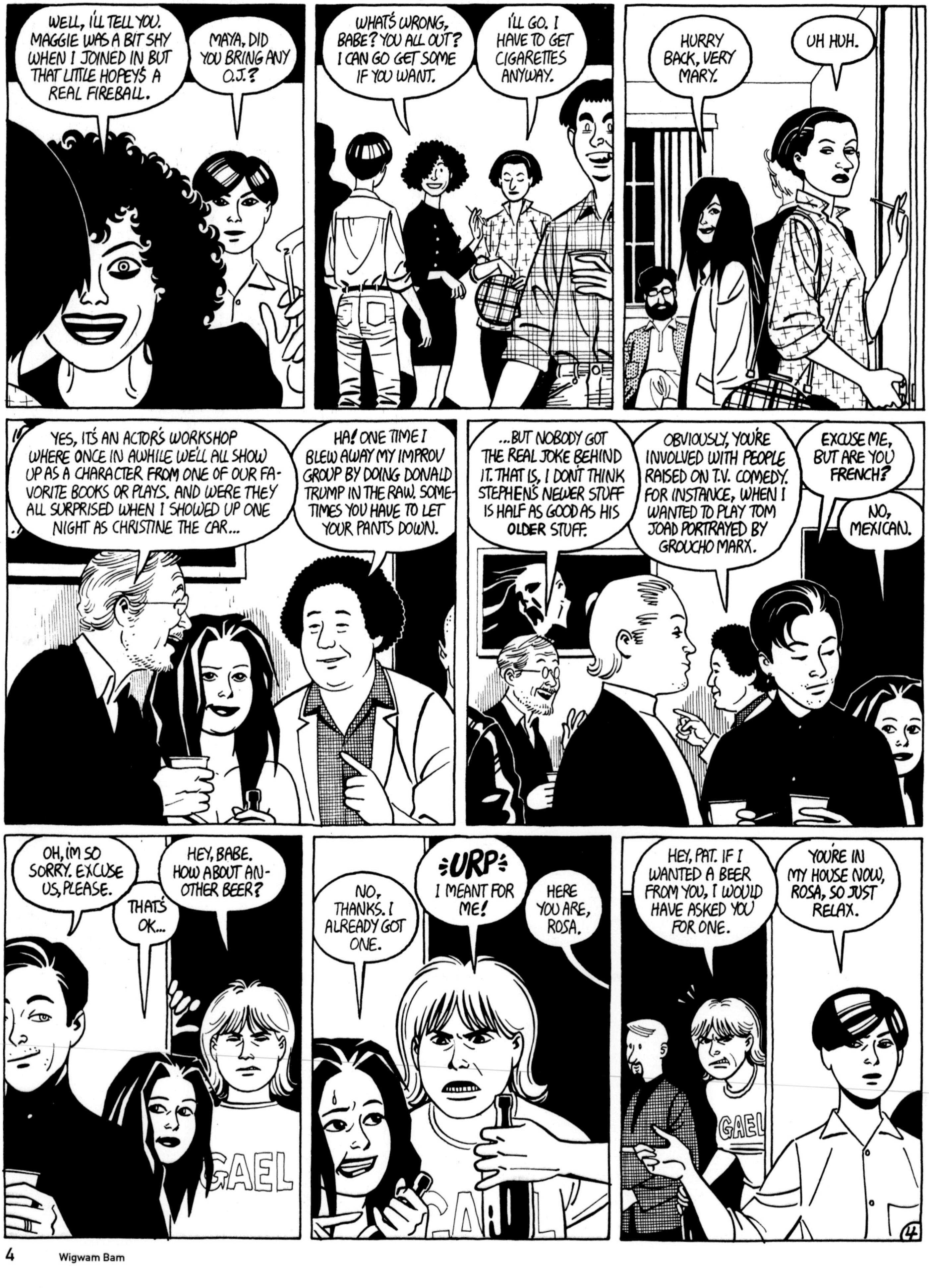
WELL, I'LL TELL YOU. MAGGIE WAS A BIT SHY WHEN I JOINED IN BUT THAT LITTLE HOPEY'S A REAL FIREBALL.
MAYA, DID YOU BRING ANY O.J.?
WHAT'S WRONG, BABE? YOU ALL OUT? I CAN GO GET SOME IF YOU WANT.
I'LL GO. I HAVE TO GET CIGARETTES ANYWAY.
HURRY BACK, VERY MARY.
UH HUH.
YES, IT'S AN ACTOR'S WORKSHOP WHERE ONCE IN AWHILE WE'LL ALL SHOW UP AS A CHARACTER FROM ONE OF OUR FAVORITE BOOKS OR PLAYS. AND WERE THEY ALL SURPRISED WHEN I SHOWED UP ONE NIGHT AS CHRISTINE THE CAR...
HA! ONE TIME I BLEW AWAY MY IMPROV GROUP BY DOING DONALD TRUMP IN THE RAW. SOMETIMES YOU HAVE TO LET YOUR PANTS DOWN.
...BUT NOBODY GOT THE REAL JOKE BEHIND IT. THAT IS, I DON'T THINK STEPHEN'S NEWER STUFF IS HALF AS GOOD AS HIS OLDER STUFF.
OBVIOUSLY, YOU'RE INVOLVED WITH PEOPLE RAISED ON T.V. COMEDY. FOR INSTANCE, WHEN I WANTED TO PLAY TOM JOAD PORTRAYED BY GROUCHO MARX.
EXCUSE ME, BUT ARE YOU FRENCH?
NO, MEXICAN.
OH, I'M SO SORRY. EXCUSE US, PLEASE.
THAT'S OK...
HEY, BABE. HOW ABOUT ANOTHER BEER?
GAEL
NO, THANKS. I ALREADY GOT ONE.
URP
I MEANT FOR ME!
HERE YOU ARE, ROSA.
GAEL
HEY, PAT. IF I WANTED A BEER FROM YOU, I WOULD HAVE ASKED YOU FOR ONE.
YOU'RE IN MY HOUSE NOW, ROSA, SO JUST RELAX.
GAEL
4

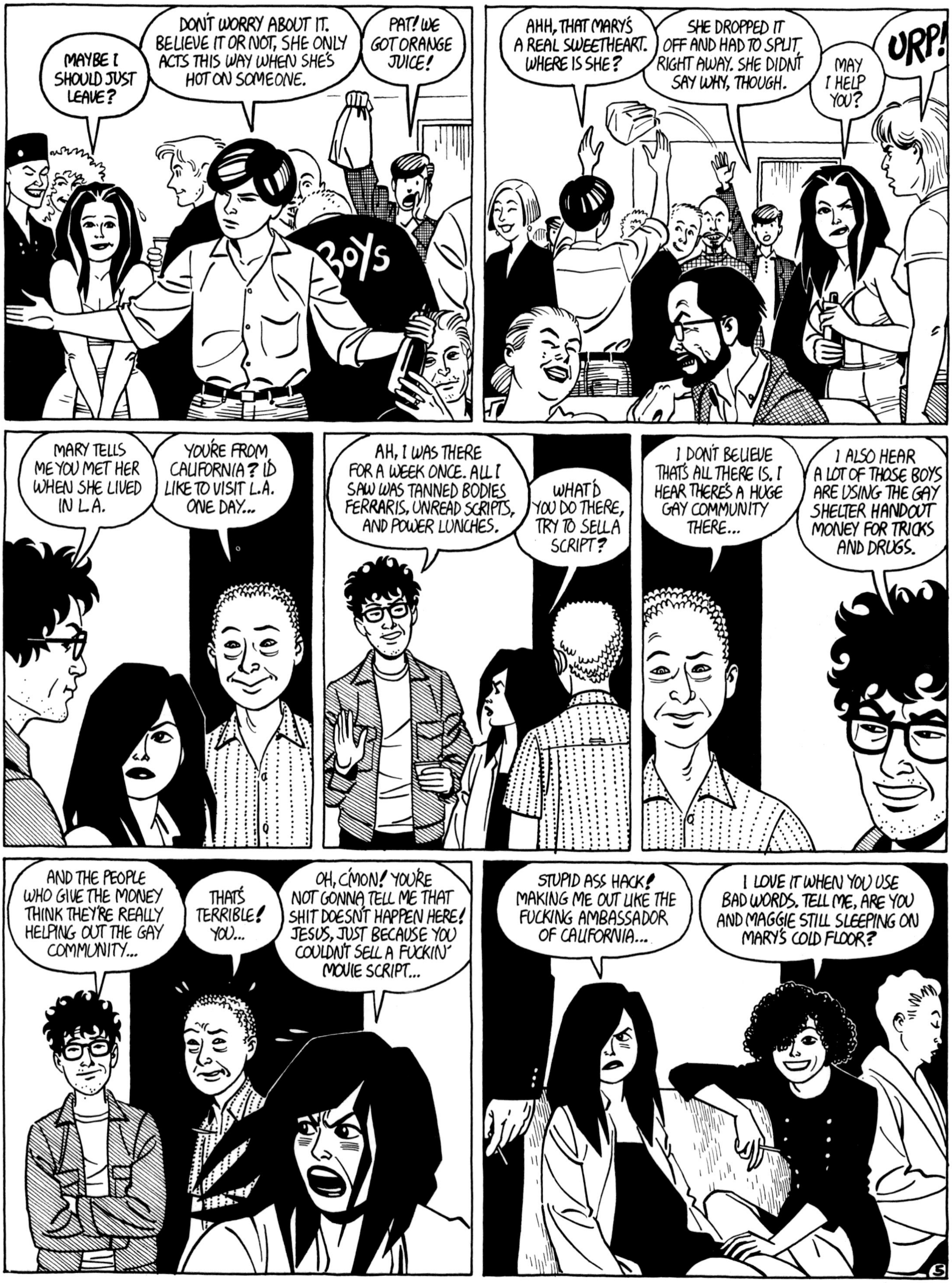
MAYBE I SHOULD JUST LEAVE?
DON'T WORRY ABOUT IT. BELIEVE IT OR NOT, SHE ONLY ACTS THIS WAY WHEN SHE'S HOT ON SOMEONE.
PAT! WE GOT ORANGE JUICE!
BOYS
AHH, THAT MARY'S A REAL SWEETHEART. WHERE IS SHE?
SHE DROPPED IT OFF AND HAD TO SPLIT RIGHT AWAY. SHE DIDN'T SAY WHY, THOUGH.
MAY I HELP YOU?
URP!
MARY TELLS ME YOU MET HER WHEN SHE LIVED IN L.A.
YOU'RE FROM CALIFORNIA? I'D LIKE TO VISIT L.A. ONE DAY...
AH, I WAS THERE FOR A WEEK ONCE. ALL I SAW WAS TANNED BODIES FERRARIS, UNREAD SCRIPTS, AND POWER LUNCHES.
WHAT'D YOU DO THERE, TRY TO SELL A SCRIPT?
I DON'T BELIEVE THAT'S ALL THERE IS. I HEAR THERE'S A HUGE GAY COMMUNITY THERE...
I ALSO HEAR A LOT OF THOSE BOYS ARE USING THE GAY SHELTER HANDOUT MONEY FOR TRICKS AND DRUGS.
AND THE PEOPLE WHO GIVE THE MONEY THINK THEY'RE REALLY HELPING OUT THE GAY COMMUNITY...
THAT'S TERRIBLE! YOU...
OH, C'MON! YOU'RE NOT GONNA TELL ME THAT SHIT DOESN'T HAPPEN HERE! JESUS, JUST BECAUSE YOU COULDN'T SELL A FUCKIN' MOVIE SCRIPT...
STUPID ASS HACK! MAKING ME OUT LIKE THE FUCKING AMBASSADOR OF CALIFORNIA...
I LOVE IT WHEN YOU USE BAD WORDS. TELL ME, ARE YOU AND MAGGIE STILL SLEEPING ON MARY'S COLD FLOOR?
S

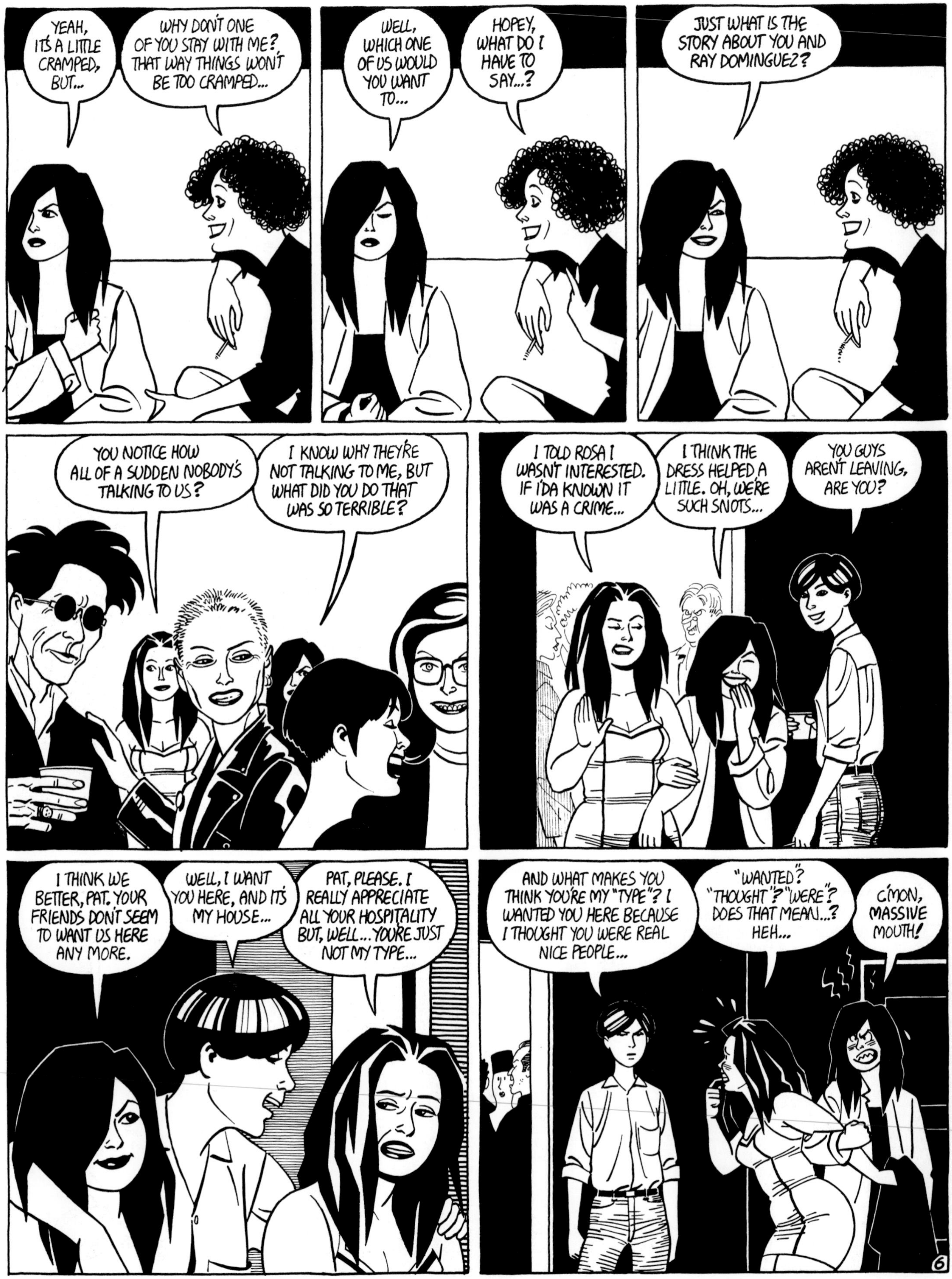

YEAH, IT'S A LITTLE CRAMPED, BUT...
WHY DON'T ONE OF YOU STAY WITH ME? THAT WAY THINGS WON'T BE TOO CRAMPED...
WELL, WHICH ONE OF US WOULD YOU WANT TO...
HOPEY, WHAT DO I HAVE TO SAY...?
JUST WHAT IS THE STORY ABOUT YOU AND RAY DOMINGUEZ?
YOU NOTICE HOW ALL OF A SUDDEN NOBODY'S TALKING TO US?
I KNOW WHY THEY'RE NOT TALKING TO ME, BUT WHAT DID YOU DO THAT WAS SO TERRIBLE?
I TOLD ROSA I WASN'T INTERESTED. IF I'DA KNOWN IT WAS A CRIME...
I THINK THE DRESS HELPED A LITTLE. OH, WE'RE SUCH SNOTS...
YOU GUYS AREN'T LEAVING, ARE YOU?
I THINK WE BETTER, PAT. YOUR FRIENDS DON'T SEEM TO WANT US HERE ANY MORE.
WELL, I WANT YOU HERE, AND IT'S MY HOUSE...
PAT, PLEASE. I REALLY APPRECIATE ALL YOUR HOSPITALITY BUT, WELL... YOU'RE JUST NOT MY TYPE...
AND WHAT MAKES YOU THINK YOU'RE MY "TYPE"? I WANTED YOU HERE BECAUSE I THOUGHT YOU WERE REAL NICE PEOPLE...
"WANTED"? "THOUGHT"? "WERE"? DOES THAT MEAN...? HEH...
C'MON, MASSIVE MOUTH!
6

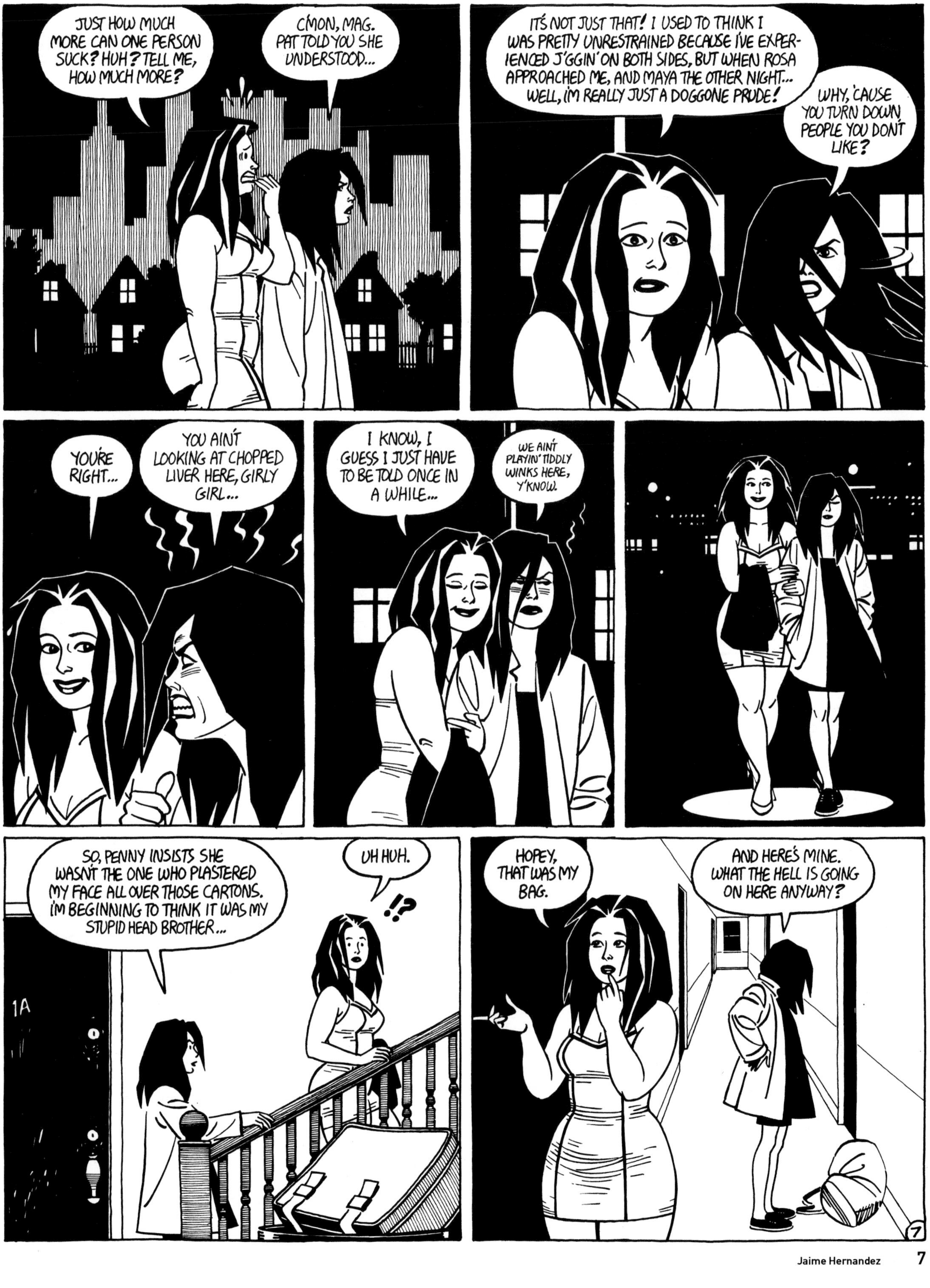
JUST HOW MUCH MORE CAN ONE PERSON SUCK? HUH? TELL ME, HOW MUCH MORE?
C'MON, MAG. PAT TOLD YOU SHE UNDERSTOOD...
IT'S NOT JUST THAT! I USED TO THINK I WAS PRETTY UNRESTRAINED BECAUSE I'VE EXPERIENCED J'GGIN' ON BOTH SIDES, BUT WHEN ROSA APPROACHED ME, AND MAYA THE OTHER NIGHT... WELL, I'M REALLY JUST A DOGGONE PRUDE!
WHY, 'CAUSE YOU TURN DOWN PEOPLE YOU DON'T LIKE?
YOU'RE RIGHT...
YOU AIN'T LOOKING AT CHOPPED LIVER HERE, GIRLY GIRL...
I KNOW, I GUESS I JUST HAVE TO BE TOLD ONCE IN A WHILE...
WE AIN'T PLAYIN' TIDDLY WINKS HERE, Y'KNOW.
SO, PENNY INSISTS SHE WASN'T THE ONE WHO PLASTERED MY FACE ALL OVER THOSE CARTONS. I'M BEGINNING TO THINK IT WAS MY STUPID HEAD BROTHER...
UH HUH.
!?
1A
HOPEY, THAT WAS MY BAG.
AND HERE'S MINE. WHAT THE HELL IS GOING ON HERE ANYWAY?
7

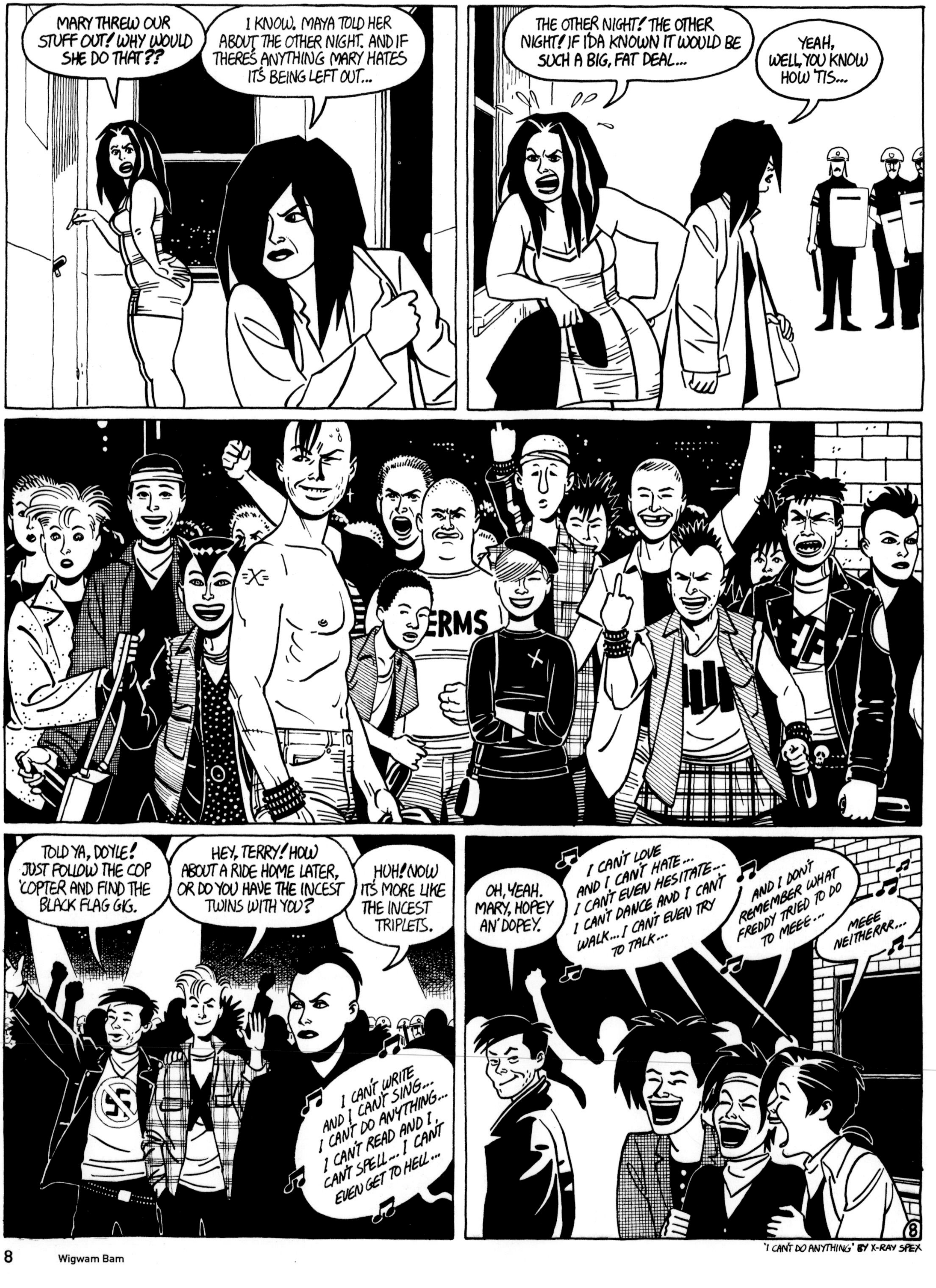
MARY THREW OUR STUFF OUT! WHY WOULD SHE DO THAT??
I KNOW. MAYA TOLD HER ABOUT THE OTHER NIGHT. AND IF THERE'S ANYTHING MARY HATES IT'S BEING LEFT OUT...
THE OTHER NIGHT! THE OTHER NIGHT! IF I'DA KNOWN IT WOULD BE SUCH A BIG, FAT DEAL...
YEAH, WELL, YOU KNOW HOW 'TIS...
ERMS
TOLD YA, DOYLE! JUST FOLLOW THE COP 'COPTER AND FIND THE BLACK FLAG GIG.
HEY, TERRY! HOW ABOUT A RIDE HOME LATER, OR DO YOU HAVE THE INCEST TWINS WITH YOU?
HUH! NOW IT'S MORE LIKE THE INCEST TRIPLETS.
I CAN'T WRITE AND I CAN'T SING... I CAN'T DO ANYTHING... I CAN'T READ AND I, CAN'T SPELL... I CAN'T EVEN GET TO HELL...
OH, YEAH. MARY, HOPEY AN' DOPEY.
I CAN'T LOVE AND I CAN'T HATE... I CAN'T EVEN HESITATE... I CAN'T DANCE AND I CAN'T WALK... I CAN'T EVEN TRY TO TALK...
AND I DON'T REMEMBER WHAT FREDDY TRIED TO DO TO MEEE...
MEEE NEITHERRR...
8
'I CAN'T DO ANYTHING' BY X-RAY SPEX

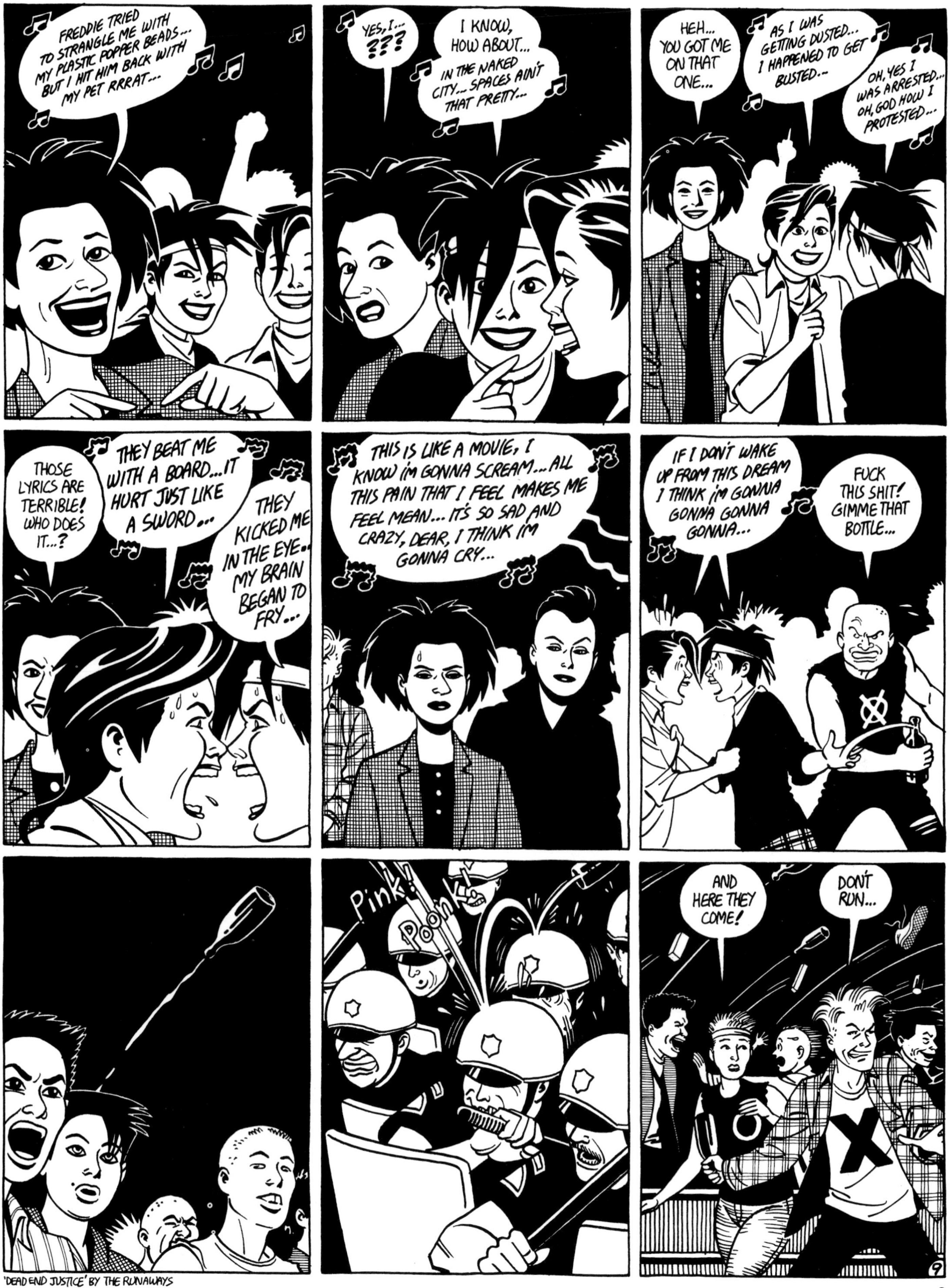
FREDDIE TRIED TO STRANGLE ME WITH MY PLASTIC POPPER BEADS... BUT I HIT HIM BACK WITH MY PET RRRAT...
YES, I... ???
I KNOW, HOW ABOUT...
IN THE NAKED CITY... SPACES AIN'T THAT PRETTY...
HEH... YOU GOT ME ON THAT ONE...
AS I WAS GETTING DUSTED... I HAPPENED TO GET BUSTED...
OH, YES I WAS ARRESTED... OH, GOD HOW I PROTESTED...
THOSE LYRICS ARE TERRIBLE! WHO DOES IT...?
THEY BEAT ME WITH A BOARD... IT HURT JUST LIKE A SWORD...
THEY KICKED ME IN THE EYE... MY BRAIN BEGAN TO FRY...
THIS IS LIKE A MOVIE, I KNOW I'M GONNA SCREAM... ALL THIS PAIN THAT I FEEL MAKES ME FEEL MEAN... IT'S SO SAD AND CRAZY, DEAR, I THINK I'M GONNA CRY...
IF I DON'T WAKE UP FROM THIS DREAM I THINK I'M GONNA GONNA GONNA GONNA...
FUCK THIS SHIT! GIMME THAT BOTTLE...
PINK!
POONK
AND HERE THEY COME!
DON'T RUN...
9

'DEAD END JUSTICE' BY THE RUNAWAYS

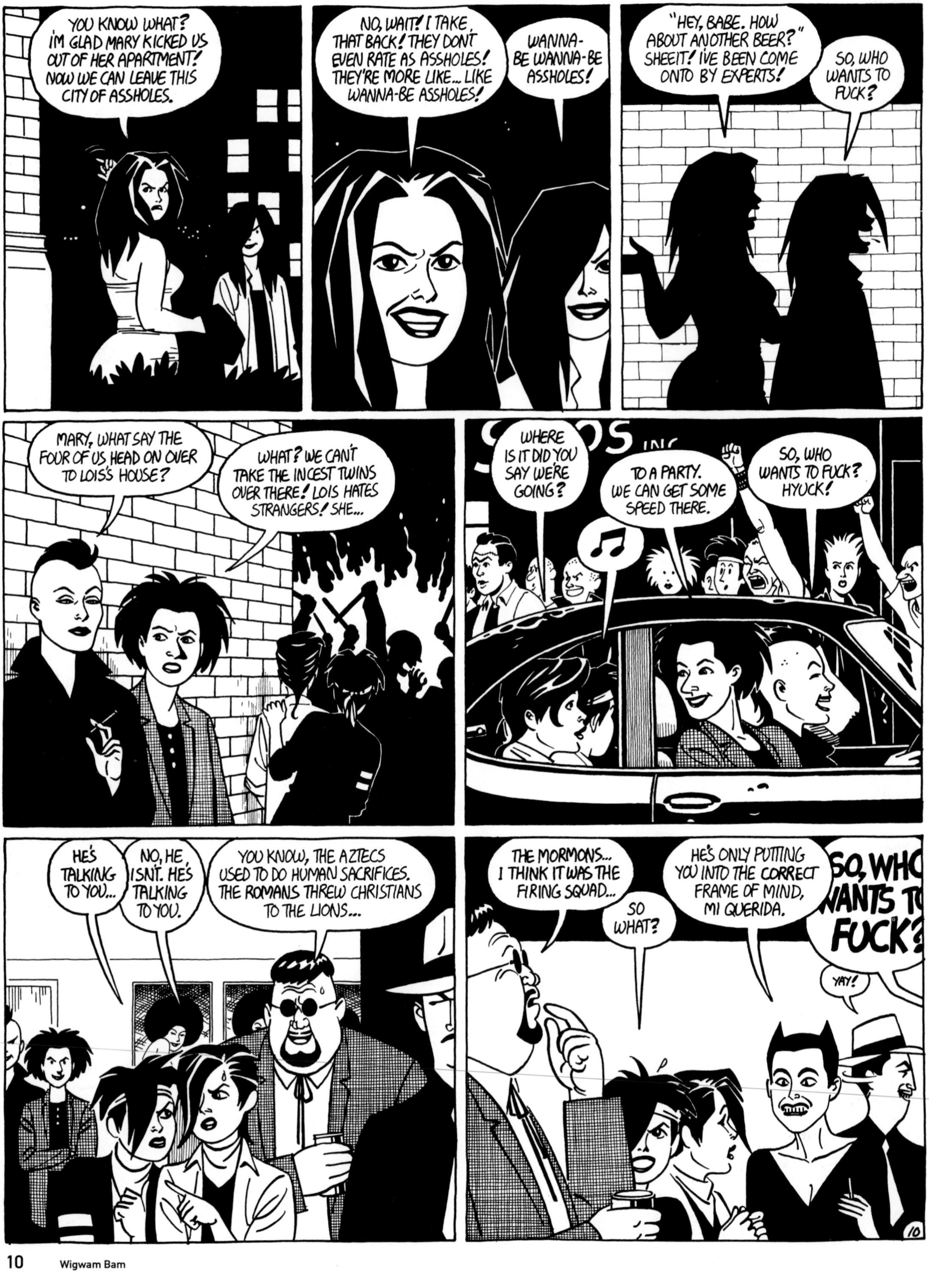

YOU KNOW WHAT? I'M GLAD MARY KICKED US OUT OF HER APARTMENT! NOW WE CAN LEAVE THIS CITY OF ASSHOLES.
NO, WAIT! I TAKE THAT BACK! THEY DON'T EVEN RATE AS ASSHOLES! THEY'RE MORE LIKE... LIKE WANNA-BE ASSHOLES!
WANNA-BE WANNA-BE ASSHOLES!
"HEY, BABE. HOW ABOUT ANOTHER BEER?" SHEEIT! I'VE BEEN COME ONTO BY EXPERTS!
SO, WHO WANTS TO FUCK?
MARY, WHAT SAY THE FOUR OF US HEAD ON OVER TO LOIS'S HOUSE?
WHAT? WE CAN'T TAKE THE INCEST TWINS OVER THERE! LOIS HATES STRANGERS! SHE...
WHERE IS IT DID YOU SAY WE'RE GOING?
TO A PARTY. WE CAN GET SOME SPEED THERE.
SO, WHO WANTS TO FUCK? HYUCK!
HE'S TALKING TO YOU...
NO, HE ISN'T. HE'S TALKING TO YOU.
YOU KNOW, THE AZTECS USED TO DO HUMAN SACRIFICES. THE ROMANS THREW CHRISTIANS TO THE LIONS...
THE MORMONS... I THINK IT WAS THE FIRING SQUAD...
SO WHAT?
HE'S ONLY PUTTING YOU INTO THE CORRECT FRAME OF MIND, MI QUERIDA.
SO, WHO WANTS TO FUCK?
YAY!
10

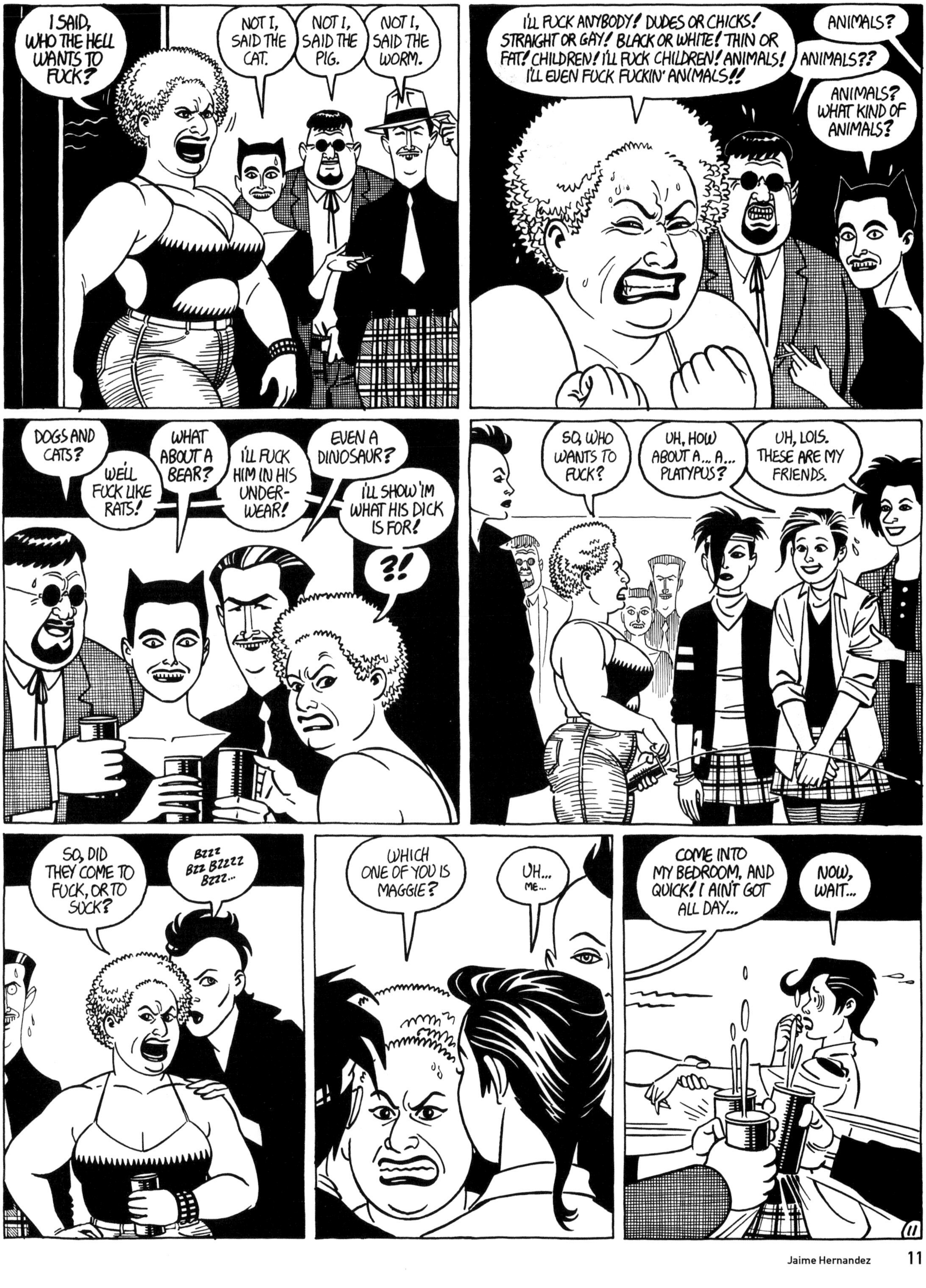
I SAID, WHO THE HELL WANTS TO FUCK?
NOT I, SAID THE CAT.
NOT I, SAID THE PIG.
NOT I, SAID THE WORM.
I'LL FUCK ANYBODY! DUDES OR CHICKS! STRAIGHT OR GAY! BLACK OR WHITE! THIN OR FAT! CHILDREN! I'LL FUCK CHILDREN! ANIMALS! I'LL EVEN FUCK FUCKIN' ANIMALS!!
ANIMALS?
ANIMALS??
ANIMALS? WHAT KIND OF ANIMALS?
DOGS AND CATS?
WE'LL FUCK LIKE RATS!
WHAT ABOUT A BEAR?
I'LL FUCK HIM IN HIS UNDER-WEAR!
EVEN A DINOSAUR?
I'LL SHOW 'IM WHAT HIS DICK IS FOR!
?!
SO, WHO WANTS TO FUCK?
UH, HOW ABOUT A... A... PLATYPUS?
UH, LOIS. THESE ARE MY FRIENDS.
SO, DID THEY COME TO FUCK, OR TO SUCK?
Bzzz Bzz Bzzzz Bzzz...
WHICH ONE OF YOU IS MAGGIE?
UH... ME...
COME INTO MY BEDROOM, AND QUICK! I AIN'T GOT ALL DAY...
NOW, WAIT...
11

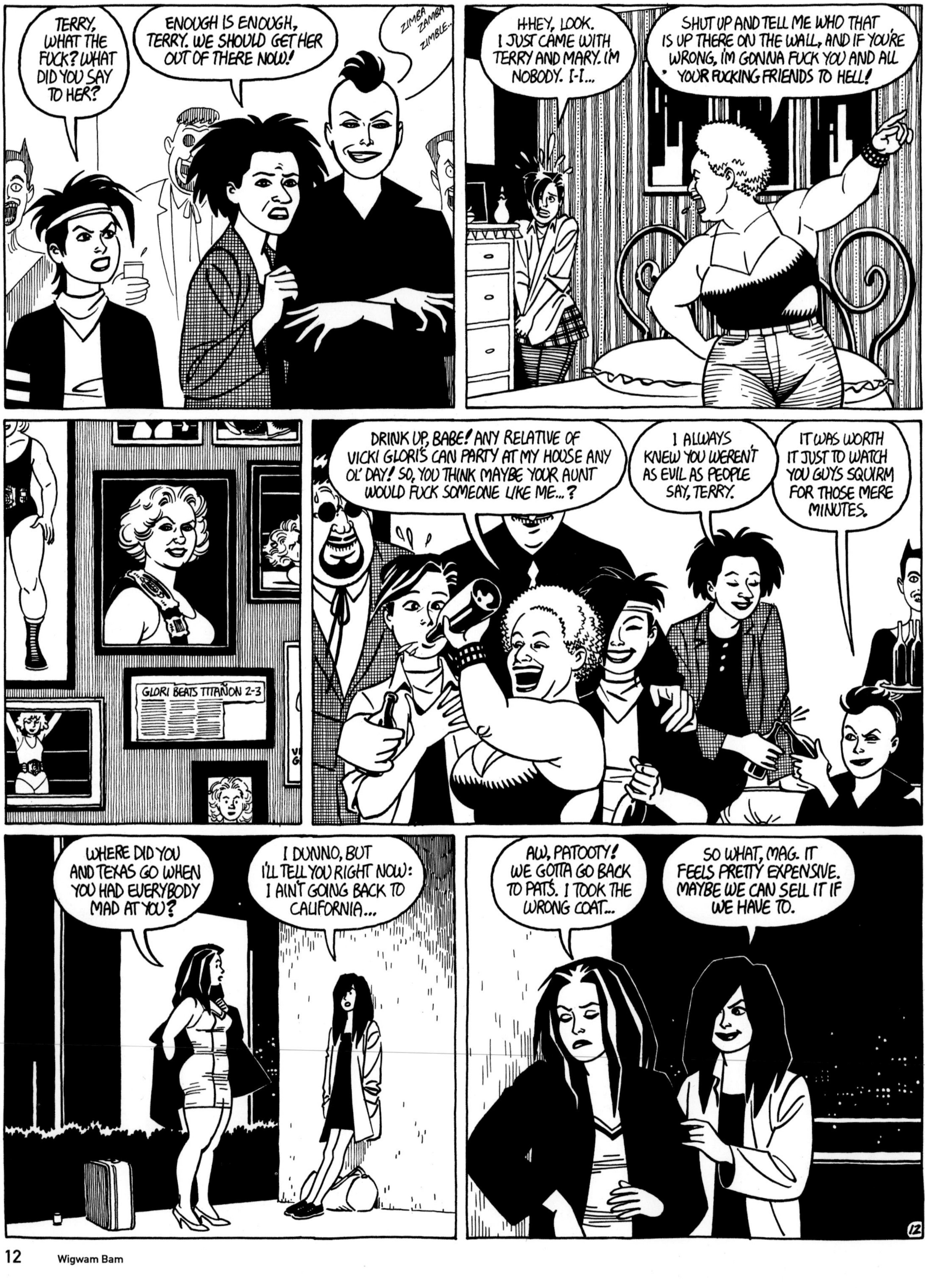
TERRY, WHAT THE FUCK? WHAT DID YOU SAY TO HER?
ENOUGH IS ENOUGH, TERRY. WE SHOULD GET HER OUT OF THERE NOW!
ZIMBA ZAMBA ZIMBLE...
H-HEY, LOOK. I JUST CAME WITH TERRY AND MARY. I'M NOBODY. I-I...
SHUT UP AND TELL ME WHO THAT IS UP THERE ON THE WALL, AND IF YOU'RE WRONG, I'M GONNA FUCK YOU AND ALL YOUR FUCKING FRIENDS TO HELL!
GLORI BEATS TITAÑON 2-3
DRINK UP, BABE! ANY RELATIVE OF VICKI GLORI'S CAN PARTY AT MY HOUSE ANY OL' DAY! SO, YOU THINK MAYBE YOUR AUNT WOULD FUCK SOMEONE LIKE ME...?
I ALWAYS KNEW YOU WEREN'T AS EVIL AS PEOPLE SAY, TERRY.
IT WAS WORTH IT JUST TO WATCH YOU GUYS SQUIRM FOR THOSE MERE MINUTES.
WHERE DID YOU AND TEXAS GO WHEN YOU HAD EVERYBODY MAD AT YOU?
I DUNNO, BUT I'LL TELL YOU RIGHT NOW: I AIN'T GOING BACK TO CALIFORNIA...
AW, PATOOTY! WE GOTTA GO BACK TO PAT'S. I TOOK THE WRONG COAT...
SO WHAT, MAG. IT FEELS PRETTY EXPENSIVE. MAYBE WE CAN SELL IT IF WE HAVE TO.
12

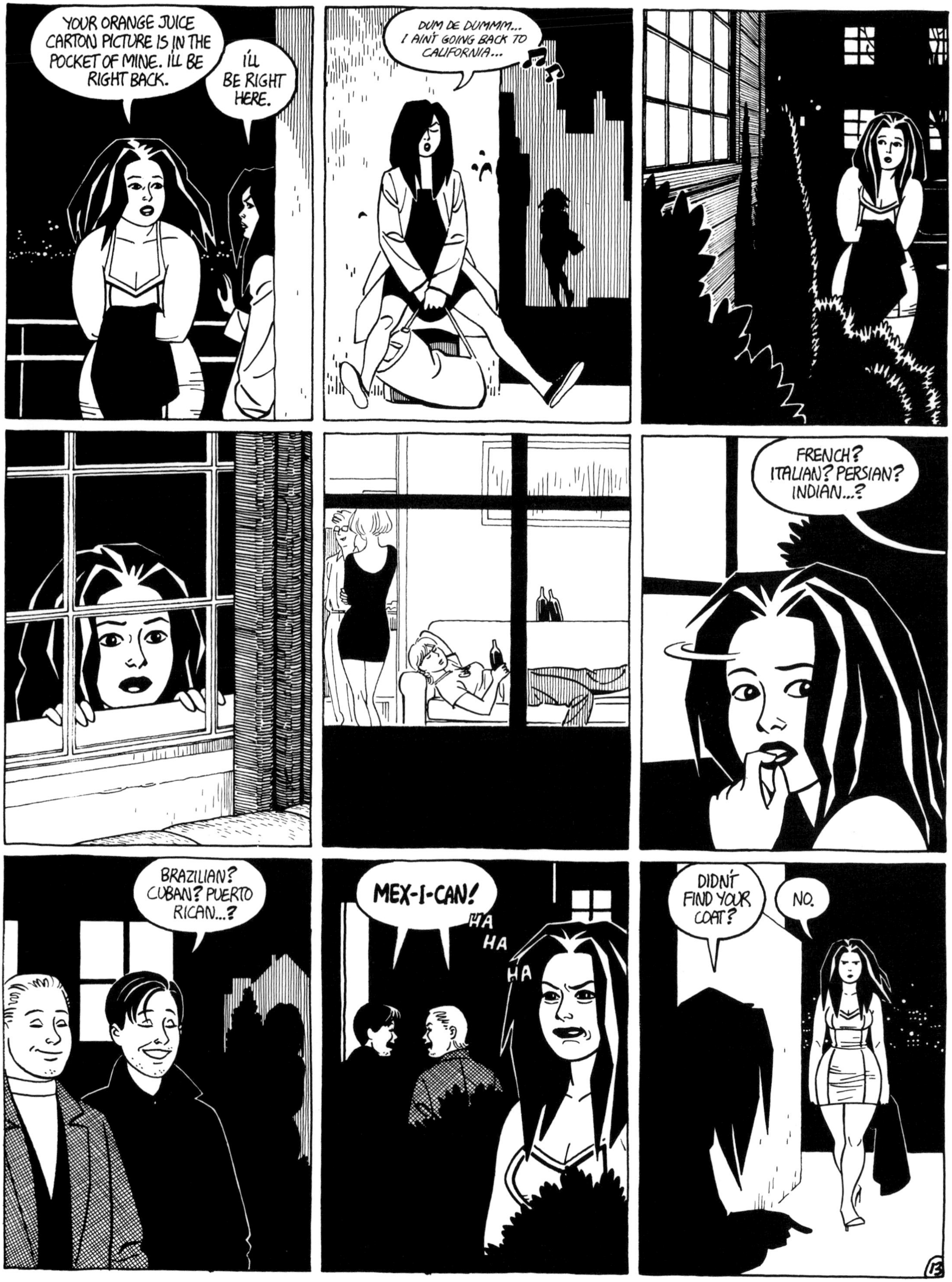
YOUR ORANGE JUICE CARTON PICTURE IS IN THE POCKET OF MINE. I'LL BE RIGHT BACK.
I'LL BE RIGHT HERE.
DUM DE DUMMM... I AIN'T GOING BACK TO CALIFORNIA...
FRENCH? ITALIAN? PERSIAN? INDIAN...?
BRAZILIAN? CUBAN? PUERTO RICAN...?
MEX-I-CAN!
HA HA HA
DIDN'T FIND YOUR COAT?
NO.
13

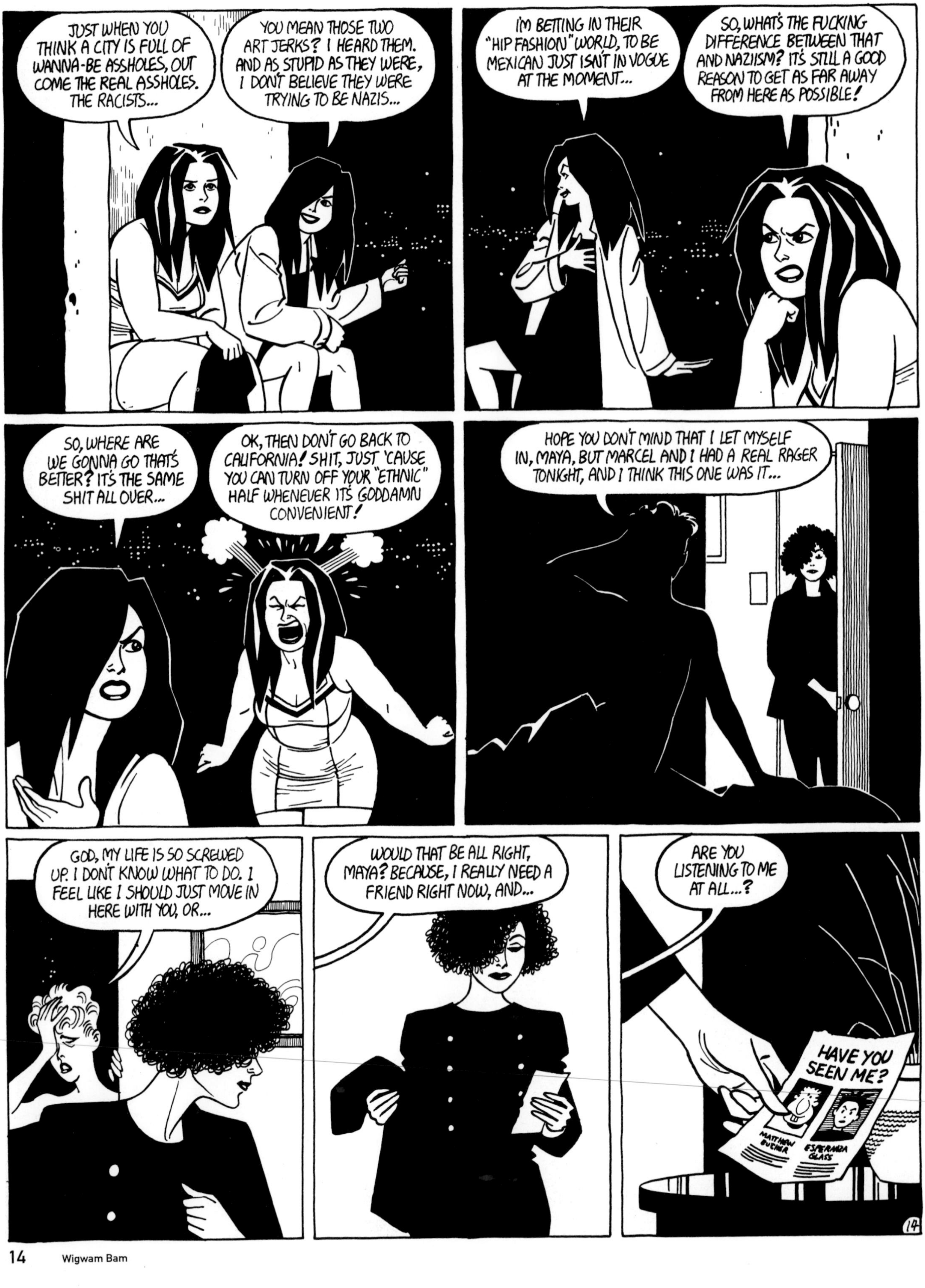
JUST WHEN YOU THINK A CITY IS FULL OF WANNA-BE ASSHOLES, OUT COME THE REAL ASSHOLES. THE RACISTS...
YOU MEAN THOSE TWO ART JERKS? I HEARD THEM. AND AS STUPID AS THEY WERE, I DON'T BELIEVE THEY WERE TRYING TO BE NAZIS...
I'M BETTING IN THEIR "HIP FASHION" WORLD, TO BE MEXICAN JUST ISN'T IN VOGUE AT THE MOMENT...
SO, WHAT'S THE FUCKING DIFFERENCE BETWEEN THAT AND NAZIISM? IT'S STILL A GOOD REASON TO GET AS FAR AWAY FROM HERE AS POSSIBLE!
SO, WHERE ARE WE GONNA GO THAT'S BETTER? IT'S THE SAME SHIT ALL OVER...
OK, THEN DON'T GO BACK TO CALIFORNIA! SHIT, JUST 'CAUSE YOU CAN TURN OFF YOUR "ETHNIC" HALF WHENEVER IT'S GODDAMN CONVENIENT!
HOPE YOU DON'T MIND THAT I LET MYSELF IN, MAYA, BUT MARCEL AND I HAD A REAL RAGER TONIGHT, AND I THINK THIS ONE WAS IT...
GOD, MY LIFE IS SO SCREWED UP. I DON'T KNOW WHAT TO DO. I FEEL LIKE I SHOULD JUST MOVE IN HERE WITH YOU, OR...
WOULD THAT BE ALL RIGHT, MAYA? BECAUSE, I REALLY NEED A FRIEND RIGHT NOW, AND...
ARE YOU LISTENING TO ME AT ALL...?
HAVE YOU SEEN ME?
MATTHEW BUCHER
ESPERANZA GLASS
14

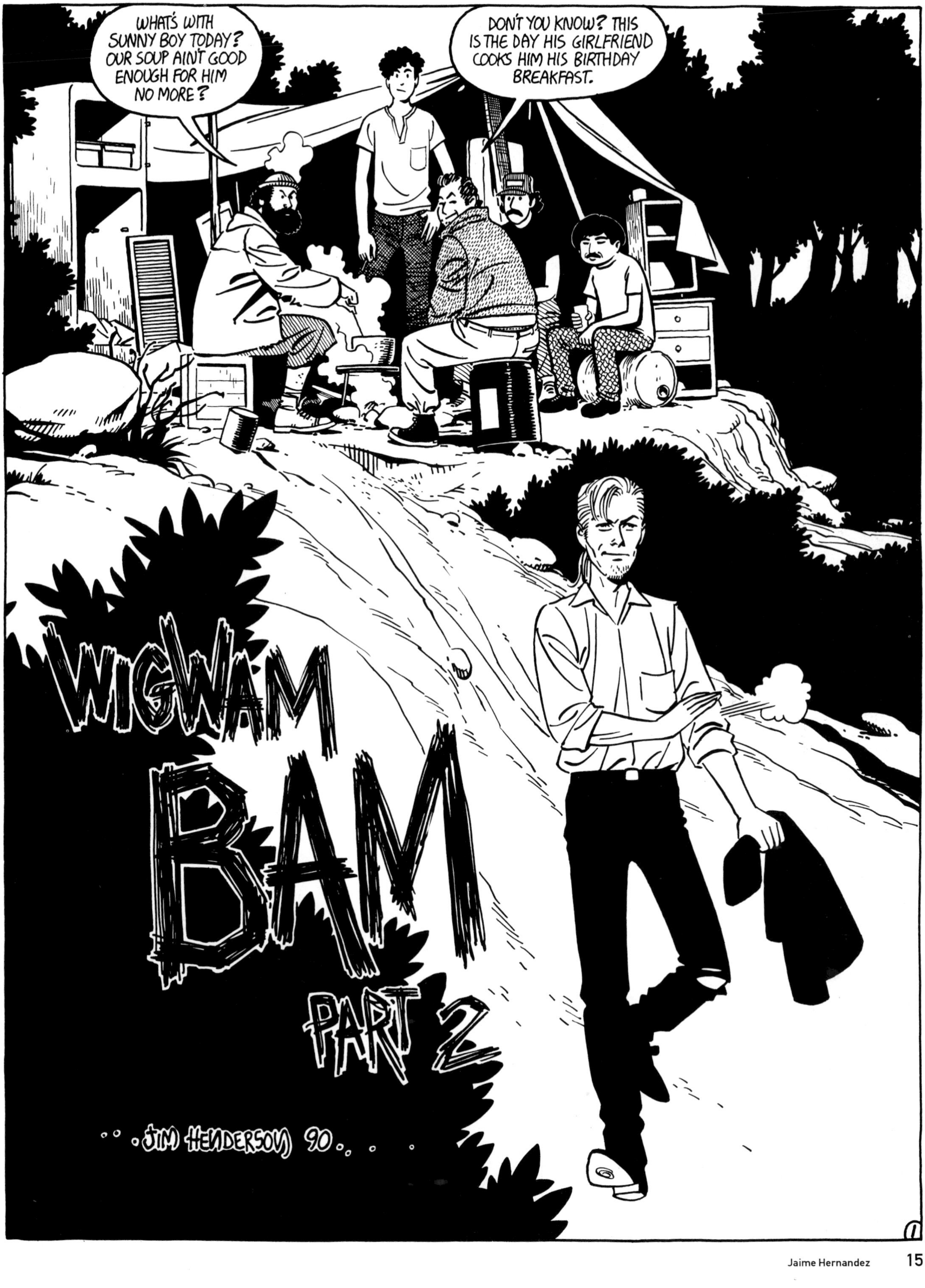
WHAT'S WITH SUNNY BOY TODAY? OUR SOUP AIN'T GOOD ENOUGH FOR HIM NO MORE?
DON'T YOU KNOW? THIS IS THE DAY HIS GIRLFRIEND COOKS HIM HIS BIRTHDAY BREAKFAST.
WIGWAM BAM
PART 2
..JIM HENDERSON 90..
1

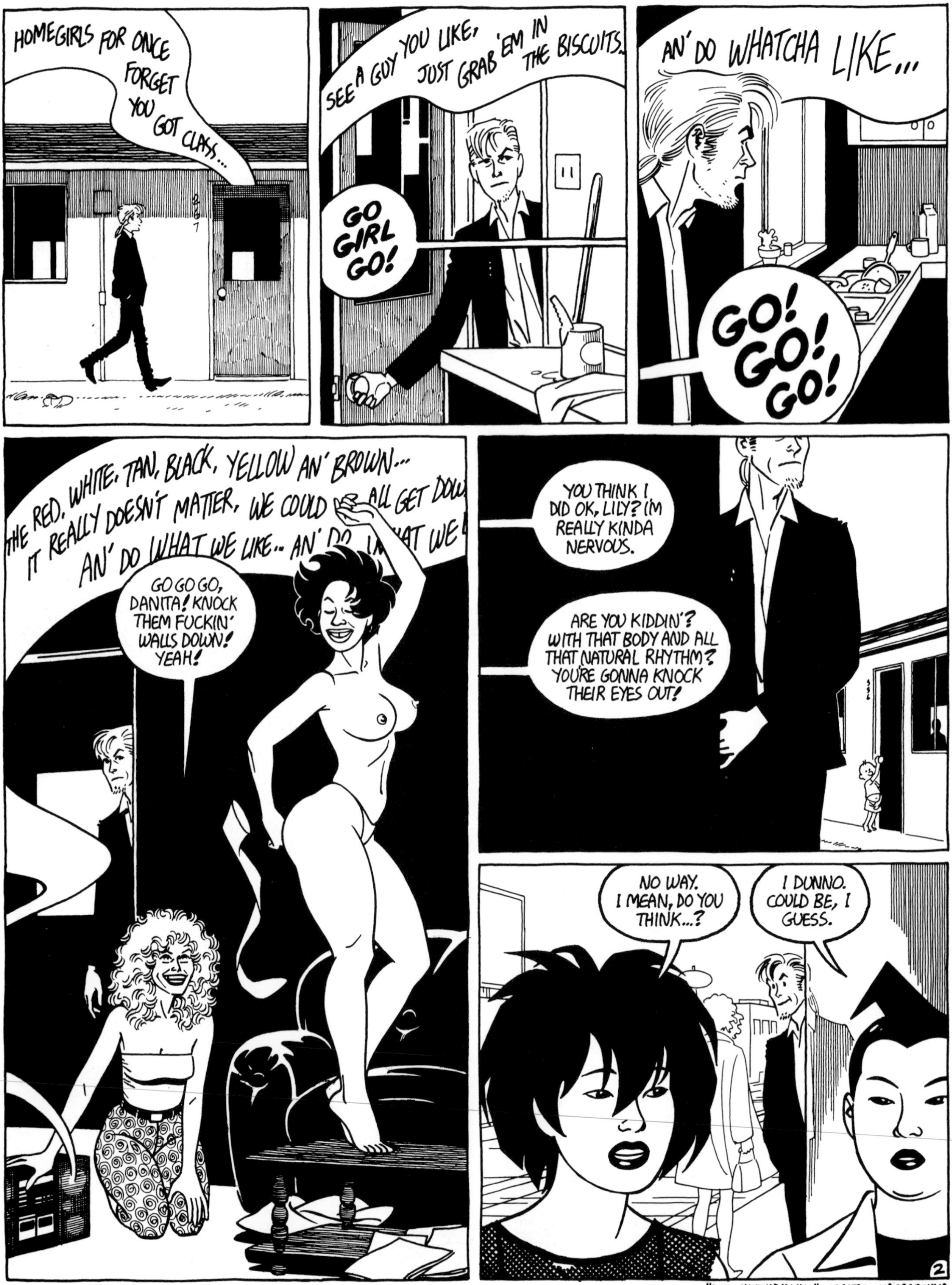
HOMEGIRLS FOR ONCE FORGET YOU GOT CLASS...
SEE A GUY YOU LIKE, JUST GRAB 'EM IN THE BISCUITS...
GO GIRL GO!
AN' DO WHATCHA LIKE...
GO! GO! GO!
THE RED, WHITE, TAN, BLACK, YELLOW AN' BROWN...
IT REALLY DOESN'T MATTER, WE COULD ALL GET DOW
AN' DO WHAT WE LIKE... AN' DO WHAT WE
GO GO GO, DANITA! KNOCK THEM FUCKIN' WALLS DOWN! YEAH!
YOU THINK I DID OK, LILY? I'M REALLY KINDA NERVOUS.
ARE YOU KIDDIN'? WITH THAT BODY AND ALL THAT NATURAL RHYTHM? YOU'RE GONNA KNOCK THEIR EYES OUT!
NO WAY. I MEAN, DO YOU THINK...?
I DUNNO. COULD BE, I GUESS.
2
"DOOWHUTCHYALIKE" - DIGITAL UNDERGROUND

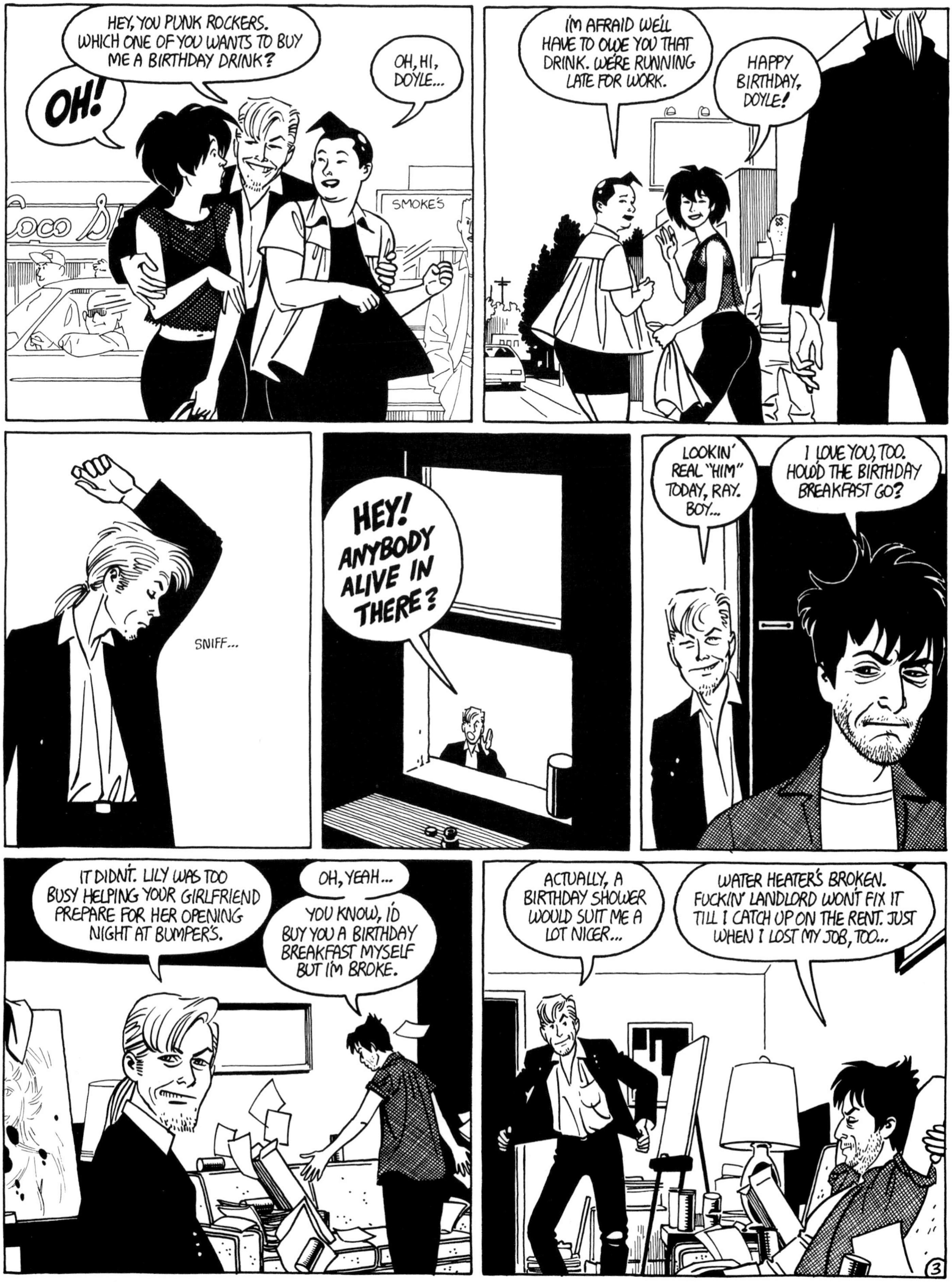
HEY, YOU PUNK ROCKERS. WHICH ONE OF YOU WANTS TO BUY ME A BIRTHDAY DRINK?
OH!
OH, HI, DOYLE...
SMOKE'S
I'M AFRAID WE'LL HAVE TO OWE YOU THAT DRINK. WE'RE RUNNING LATE FOR WORK.
HAPPY BIRTHDAY, DOYLE!
SNIFF...
HEY! ANYBODY ALIVE IN THERE?
LOOKIN' REAL "HIM" TODAY, RAY. BOY...
I LOVE YOU, TOO. HOW'D THE BIRTHDAY BREAKFAST GO?
IT DIDN'T. LILY WAS TOO BUSY HELPING YOUR GIRLFRIEND PREPARE FOR HER OPENING NIGHT AT BUMPER'S.
OH, YEAH...
YOU KNOW, I'D BUY YOU A BIRTHDAY BREAKFAST MYSELF BUT I'M BROKE.
ACTUALLY, A BIRTHDAY SHOWER WOULD SUIT ME A LOT NICER...
WATER HEATER'S BROKEN. FUCKIN' LANDLORD WON'T FIX IT TILL I CATCH UP ON THE RENT. JUST WHEN I LOST MY JOB, TOO...
3

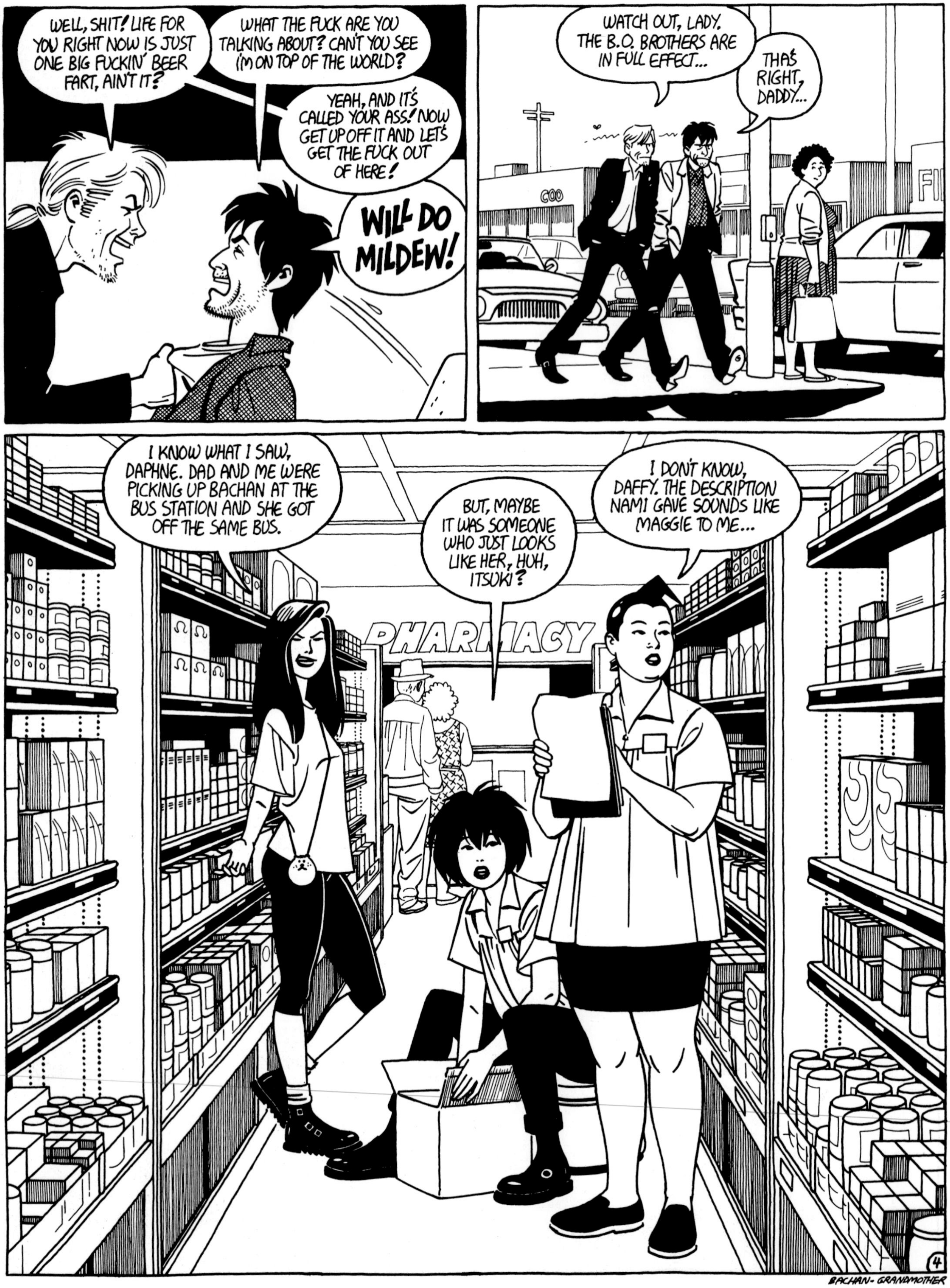
WELL, SHIT! LIFE FOR YOU RIGHT NOW IS JUST ONE BIG FUCKIN' BEER FART, AIN'T IT?
WHAT THE FUCK ARE YOU TALKING ABOUT? CAN'T YOU SEE I'M ON TOP OF THE WORLD?
YEAH, AND IT'S CALLED YOUR ASS! NOW GET UP OFF IT AND LET'S GET THE FUCK OUT OF HERE!
WILL DO MILDEW!
WATCH OUT, LADY. THE B.O. BROTHERS ARE IN FULL EFFECT...
THA'S RIGHT, DADDY...
I KNOW WHAT I SAW, DAPHNE. DAD AND ME WERE PICKING UP BACHAN AT THE BUS STATION AND SHE GOT OFF THE SAME BUS.
BUT, MAYBE IT WAS SOMEONE WHO JUST LOOKS LIKE HER, HUH, ITSUKI?
I DON'T KNOW, DAFFY. THE DESCRIPTION NAMI GAVE SOUNDS LIKE MAGGIE TO ME...
PHARMACY
4
BACHAN - GRANDMOTHER

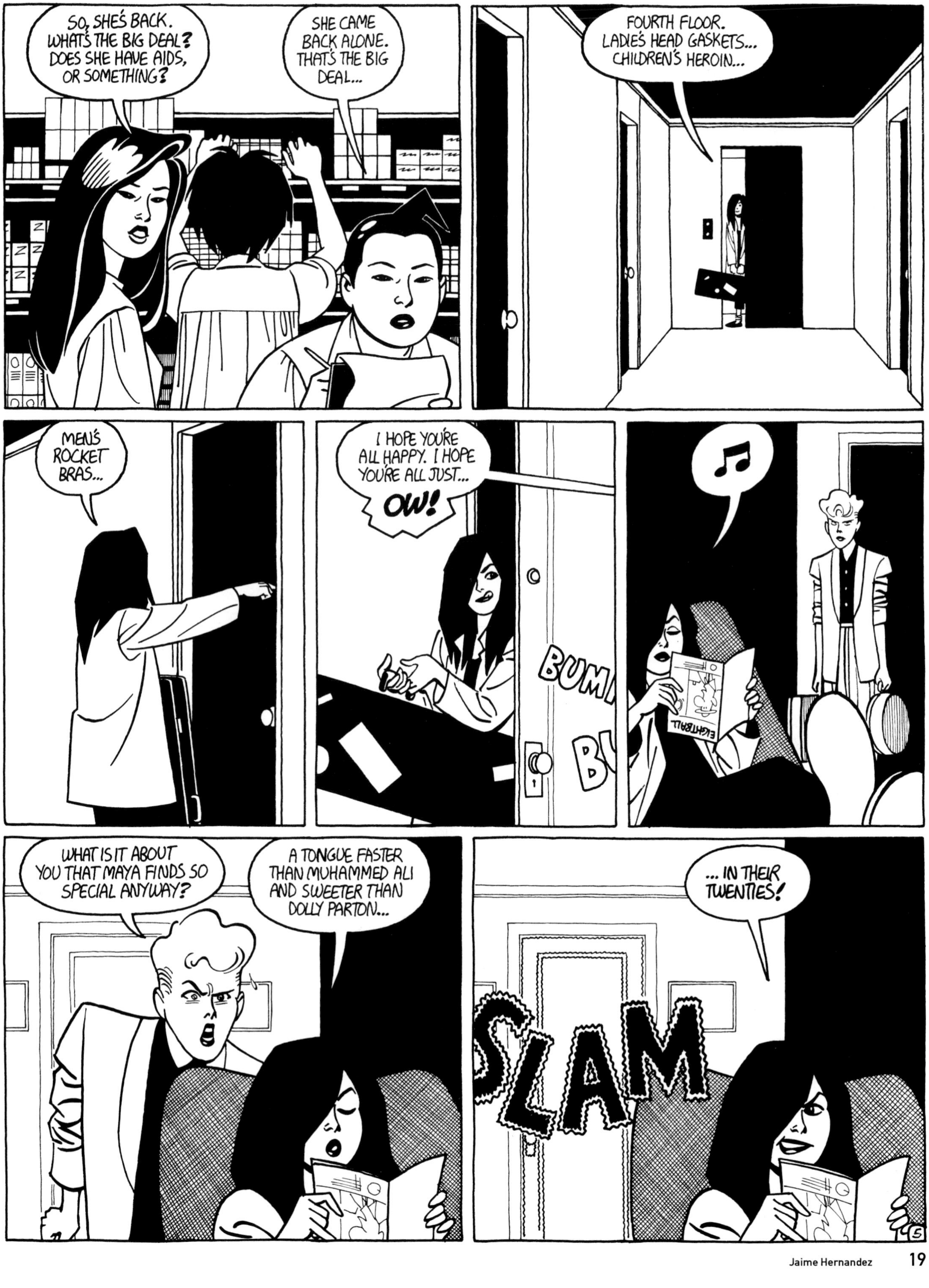

SO, SHE'S BACK. WHAT'S THE BIG DEAL? DOES SHE HAVE AIDS, OR SOMETHING?
SHE CAME BACK ALONE. THAT'S THE BIG DEAL...
FOURTH FLOOR. LADIE'S HEAD GASKETS... CHILDREN'S HEROIN...
MEN'S ROCKET BRAS...
I HOPE YOU'RE ALL HAPPY. I HOPE YOU'RE ALL JUST...
OW!
BUMI
BU
EIGHTBALL
WHAT IS IT ABOUT YOU THAT MAYA FINDS SO SPECIAL ANYWAY?
A TONGUE FASTER THAN MUHAMMED ALI AND SWEETER THAN DOLLY PARTON...
SLAM
... IN THEIR TWENTIES!
5

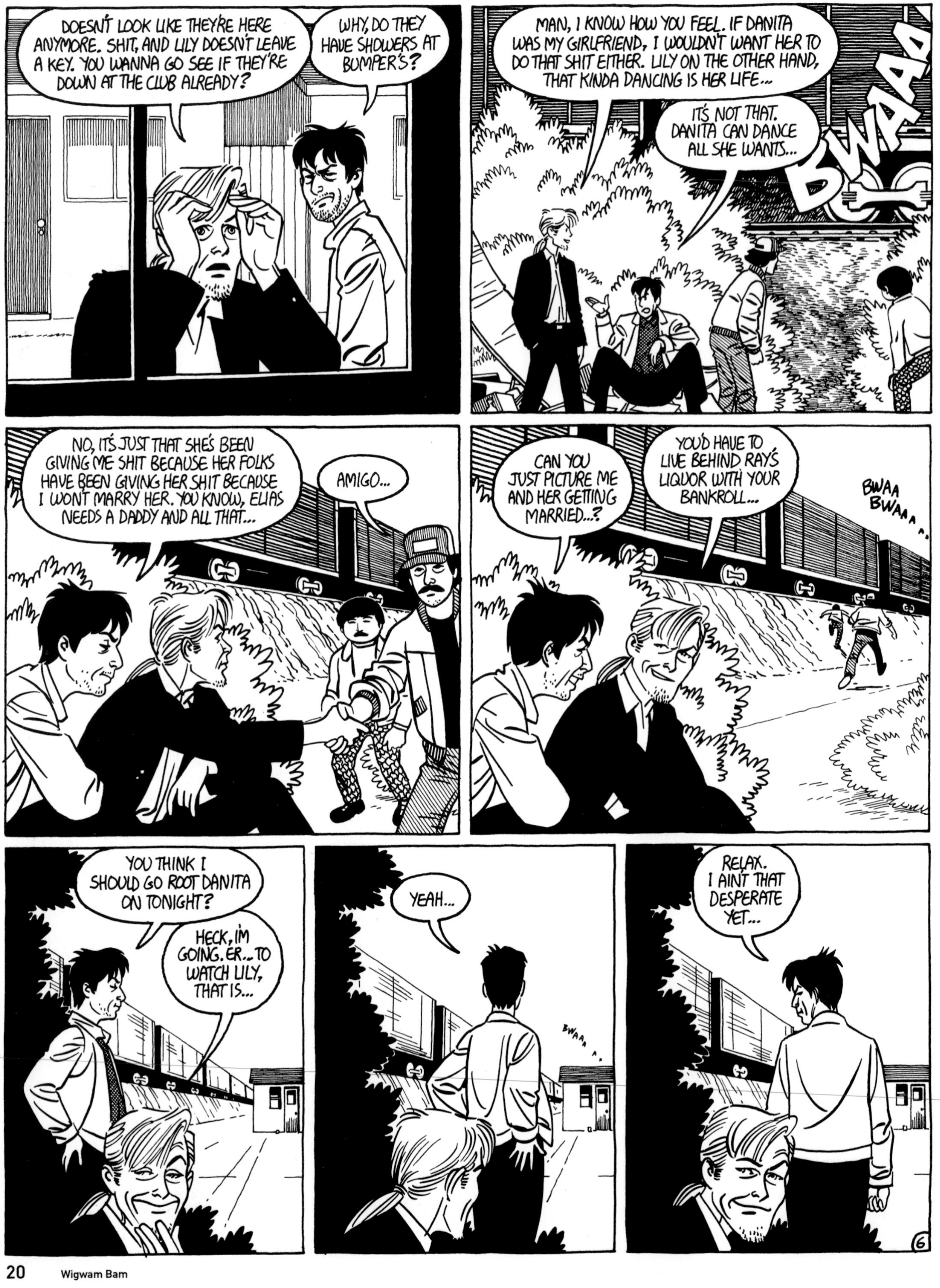
DOESN'T LOOK LIKE THEY'RE HERE ANYMORE. SHIT, AND LILY DOESN'T LEAVE A KEY. YOU WANNA GO SEE IF THEY'RE DOWN AT THE CLUB ALREADY?
WHY, DO THEY HAVE SHOWERS AT BUMPER'S?
MAN, I KNOW HOW YOU FEEL. IF DANITA WAS MY GIRLFRIEND, I WOULDN'T WANT HER TO DO THAT SHIT EITHER. LILY ON THE OTHER HAND, THAT KINDA DANCING IS HER LIFE...
IT'S NOT THAT. DANITA CAN DANCE ALL SHE WANTS...
BWAA
NO, IT'S JUST THAT SHE'S BEEN GIVING ME SHIT BECAUSE HER FOLKS HAVE BEEN GIVING HER SHIT BECAUSE I WON'T MARRY HER. YOU KNOW, ELIAS NEEDS A DADDY AND ALL THAT...
AMIGO...
CAN YOU JUST PICTURE ME AND HER GETTING MARRIED...?
YOU'D HAVE TO LIVE BEHIND RAY'S LIQUOR WITH YOUR BANKROLL...
BWAA BWAAAA..
YOU THINK I SHOULD GO ROOT DANITA ON TONIGHT?
HECK, I'M GOING. ER... TO WATCH LILY, THAT IS...
YEAH...
BWAAA A.
RELAX. I AINT THAT DESPERATE YET...
6

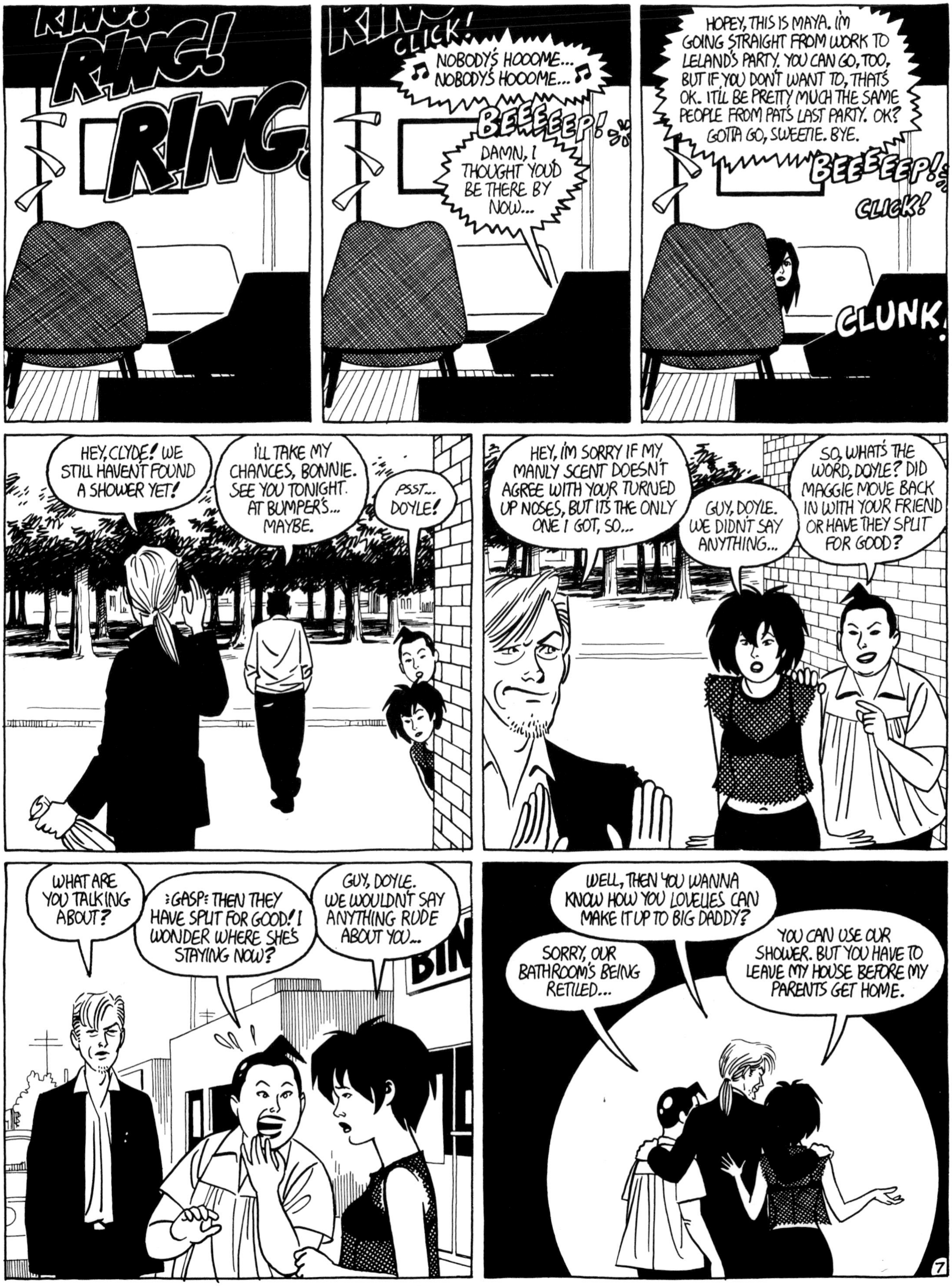
RING!
RING!
RING!
CLICK!
♫ NOBODY'S HOOOME... NOBODY'S HOOOME... ♫
BEEEEEP!
DAMN, I THOUGHT YOU'D BE THERE BY NOW...
HOPEY, THIS IS MAYA. I'M GOING STRAIGHT FROM WORK TO LELAND'S PARTY. YOU CAN GO, TOO, BUT IF YOU DON'T WANT TO, THAT'S OK. IT'LL BE PRETTY MUCH THE SAME PEOPLE FROM PAT'S LAST PARTY. OK? GOTTA GO, SWEETIE. BYE.
BEEEEEP!
CLICK!
CLUNK!
HEY, CLYDE! WE STILL HAVEN'T FOUND A SHOWER YET!
I'LL TAKE MY CHANCES, BONNIE. SEE YOU TONIGHT. AT BUMPER'S... MAYBE.
PSST... DOYLE!
HEY, I'M SORRY IF MY MANLY SCENT DOESN'T AGREE WITH YOUR TURNED UP NOSES, BUT IT'S THE ONLY ONE I GOT, SO...
GUY, DOYLE. WE DIDN'T SAY ANYTHING...
SO, WHAT'S THE WORD, DOYLE? DID MAGGIE MOVE BACK IN WITH YOUR FRIEND OR HAVE THEY SPLIT FOR GOOD?
WHAT ARE YOU TALKING ABOUT?
:GASP: THEN THEY HAVE SPLIT FOR GOOD! I WONDER WHERE SHE'S STAYING NOW?
GUY, DOYLE. WE WOULDN'T SAY ANYTHING RUDE ABOUT YOU...
WELL, THEN YOU WANNA KNOW HOW YOU LOVELIES CAN MAKE IT UP TO BIG DADDY?
SORRY, OUR BATHROOM'S BEING RETILED...
YOU CAN USE OUR SHOWER. BUT YOU HAVE TO LEAVE MY HOUSE BEFORE MY PARENTS GET HOME.
7

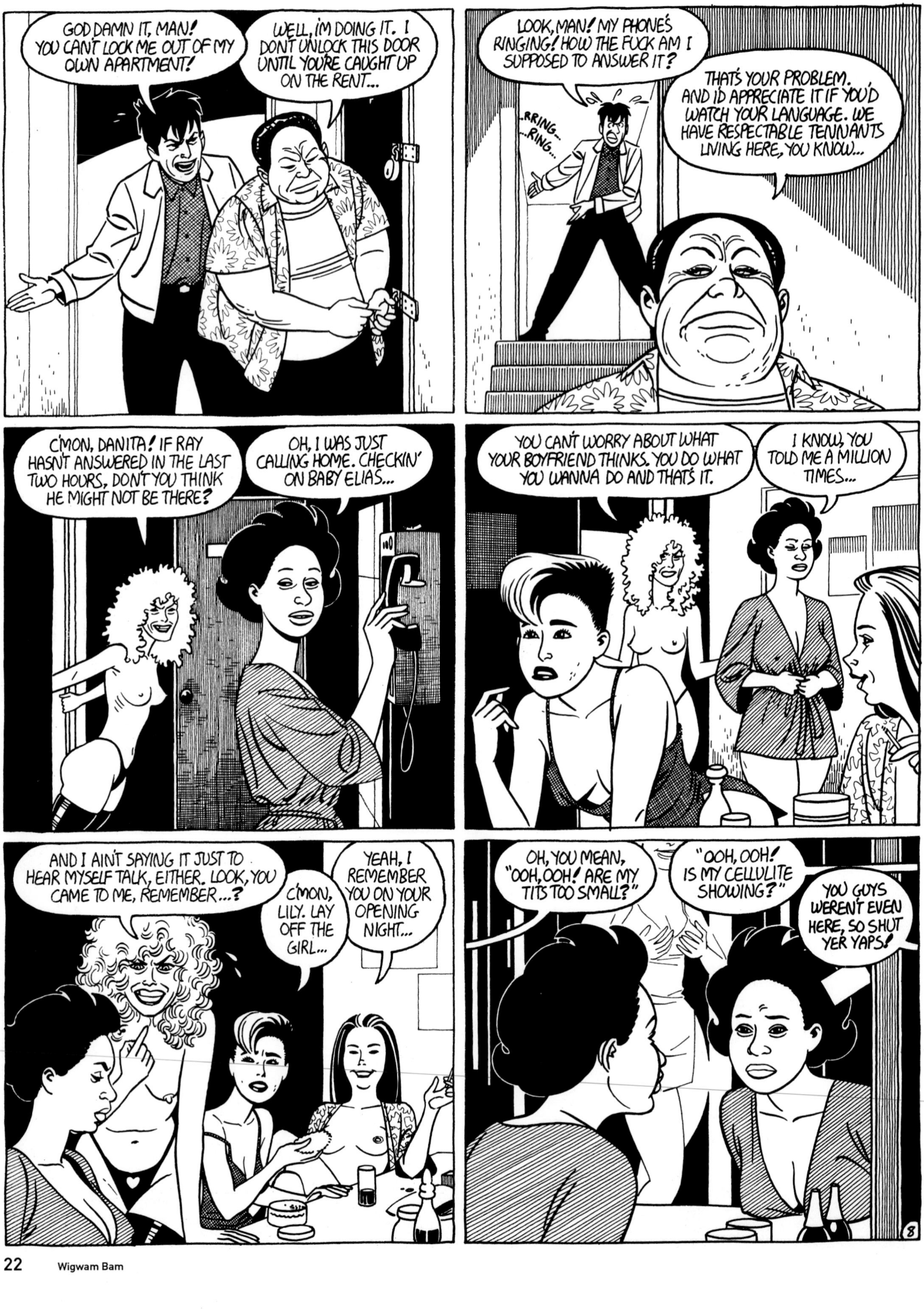
GOD DAMN IT, MAN! YOU CAN'T LOCK ME OUT OF MY OWN APARTMENT!
WELL, I'M DOING IT. I DON'T UNLOCK THIS DOOR UNTIL YOU'RE CAUGHT UP ON THE RENT...
LOOK, MAN! MY PHONE'S RINGING! HOW THE FUCK AM I SUPPOSED TO ANSWER IT?
..RRING... ..RING...
THAT'S YOUR PROBLEM. AND I'D APPRECIATE IT IF YOU'D WATCH YOUR LANGUAGE. WE HAVE RESPECTABLE TENNANTS LIVING HERE, YOU KNOW...
C'MON, DANITA! IF RAY HASN'T ANSWERED IN THE LAST TWO HOURS, DON'T YOU THINK HE MIGHT NOT BE THERE?
OH, I WAS JUST CALLING HOME. CHECKIN' ON BABY ELIAS...
YOU CAN'T WORRY ABOUT WHAT YOUR BOYFRIEND THINKS. YOU DO WHAT YOU WANNA DO AND THAT'S IT.
I KNOW, YOU TOLD ME A MILLION TIMES...
AND I AIN'T SAYING IT JUST TO HEAR MYSELF TALK, EITHER. LOOK, YOU CAME TO ME, REMEMBER...?
C'MON, LILY. LAY OFF THE GIRL...
YEAH, I REMEMBER YOU ON YOUR OPENING NIGHT...
OH, YOU MEAN, "OOH, OOH! ARE MY TITS TOO SMALL?"
"OOH, OOH! IS MY CELLULITE SHOWING?"
YOU GUYS WEREN'T EVEN HERE, SO SHUT YER YAPS!
8

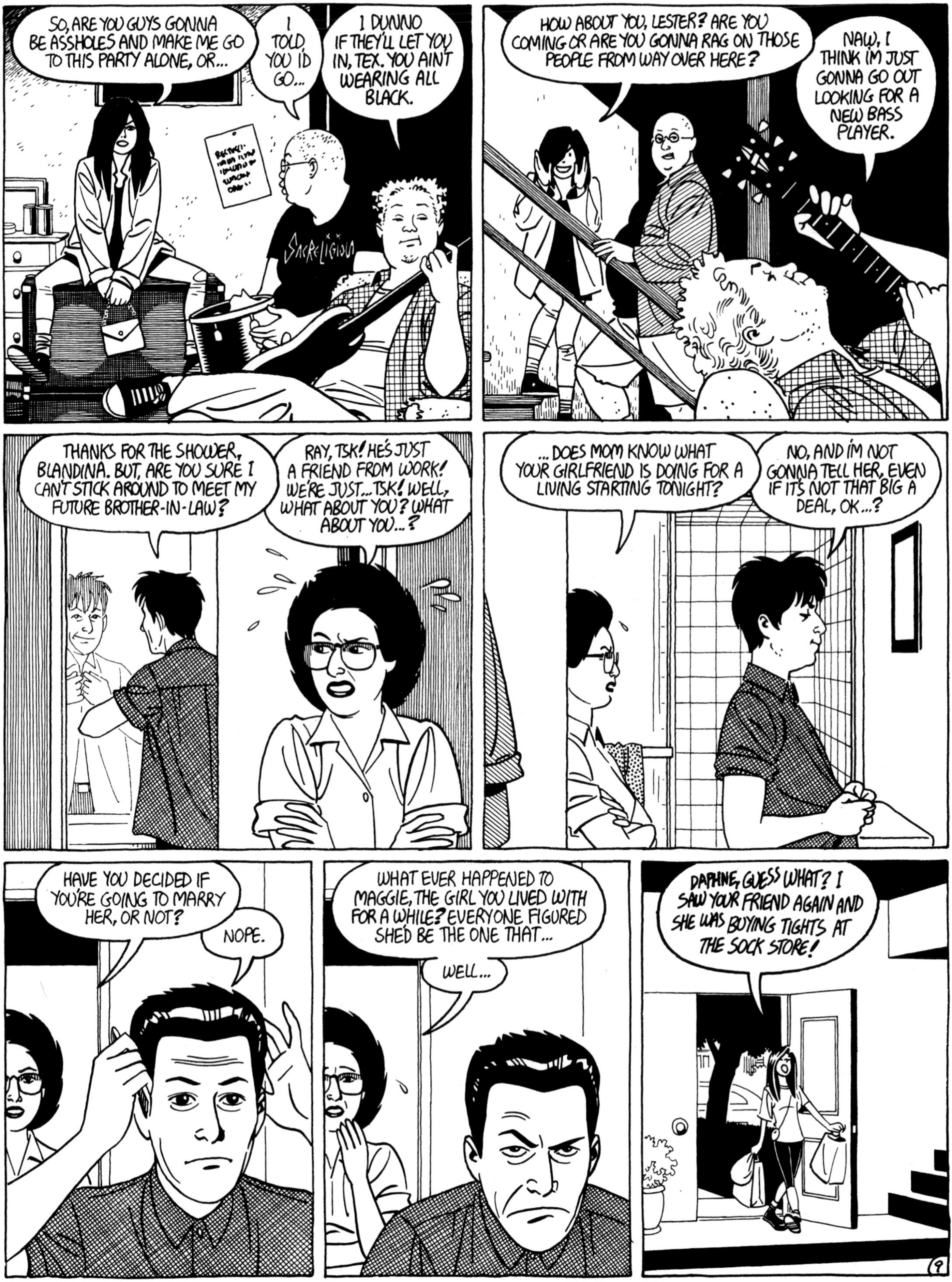
SO, ARE YOU GUYS GONNA BE ASSHOLES AND MAKE ME GO TO THIS PARTY ALONE, OR...
I TOLD YOU I'D GO...
I DUNNO IF THEY'LL LET YOU IN, TEX. YOU AIN'T WEARING ALL BLACK.
SACRELIGIOUS
HOW ABOUT YOU, LESTER? ARE YOU COMING OR ARE YOU GONNA RAG ON THOSE PEOPLE FROM WAY OVER HERE?
NAW, I THINK I'M JUST GONNA GO OUT LOOKING FOR A NEW BASS PLAYER.
THANKS FOR THE SHOWER, BLANDINA. BUT, ARE YOU SURE I CAN'T STICK AROUND TO MEET MY FUTURE BROTHER-IN-LAW?
RAY, TSK! HE'S JUST A FRIEND FROM WORK! WE'RE JUST... TSK! WELL, WHAT ABOUT YOU? WHAT ABOUT YOU...?
... DOES MOM KNOW WHAT YOUR GIRLFRIEND IS DOING FOR A LIVING STARTING TONIGHT?
NO, AND I'M NOT GONNA TELL HER, EVEN IF IT'S NOT THAT BIG A DEAL, OK...?
HAVE YOU DECIDED IF YOU'RE GOING TO MARRY HER, OR NOT?
NOPE.
WHAT EVER HAPPENED TO MAGGIE, THE GIRL YOU LIVED WITH FOR A WHILE? EVERYONE FIGURED SHE'D BE THE ONE THAT...
WELL...
DAPHNE, GUESS WHAT? I SAW YOUR FRIEND AGAIN AND SHE WAS BUYING TIGHTS AT THE SOCK STORE!
9

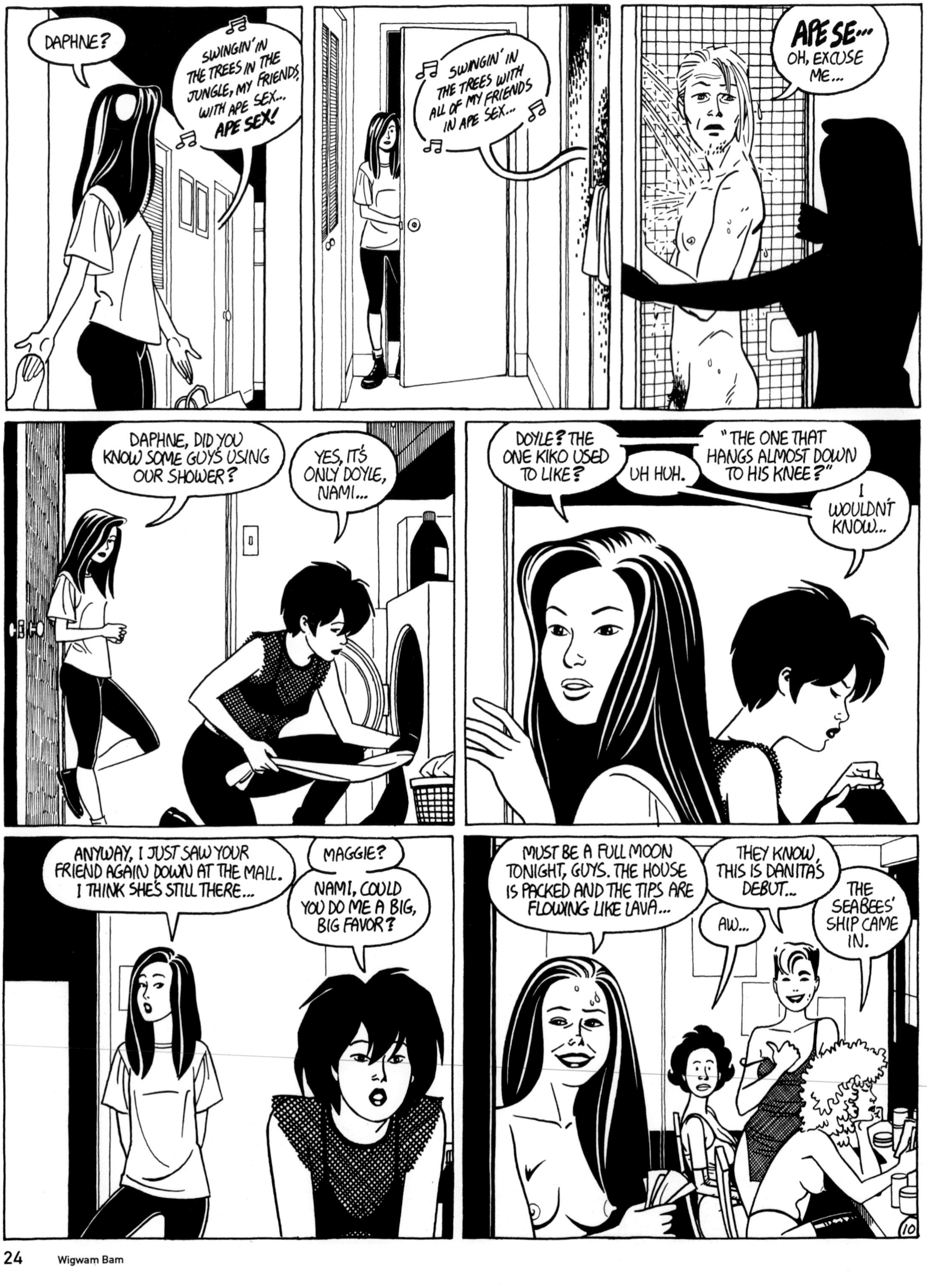
DAPHNE?
SWINGIN' IN THE TREES IN THE JUNGLE, MY FRIENDS, WITH APE SEX... APE SEX!
SWINGIN' IN THE TREES WITH ALL OF MY FRIENDS IN APE SEX...
APE SE... OH, EXCUSE ME...
DAPHNE, DID YOU KNOW SOME GUY'S USING OUR SHOWER?
YES, IT'S ONLY DOYLE, NAMI...
DOYLE? THE ONE KIKO USED TO LIKE?
UH HUH.
"THE ONE THAT HANGS ALMOST DOWN TO HIS KNEE?"
I WOULDN'T KNOW...
ANYWAY, I JUST SAW YOUR FRIEND AGAIN DOWN AT THE MALL. I THINK SHE'S STILL THERE...
MAGGIE?
NAMI, COULD YOU DO ME A BIG, BIG FAVOR?
MUST BE A FULL MOON TONIGHT, GUYS. THE HOUSE IS PACKED AND THE TIPS ARE FLOWING LIKE LAVA...
THEY KNOW, THIS IS DANITA'S DEBUT...
AW...
THE SEABEES' SHIP CAME IN.
10

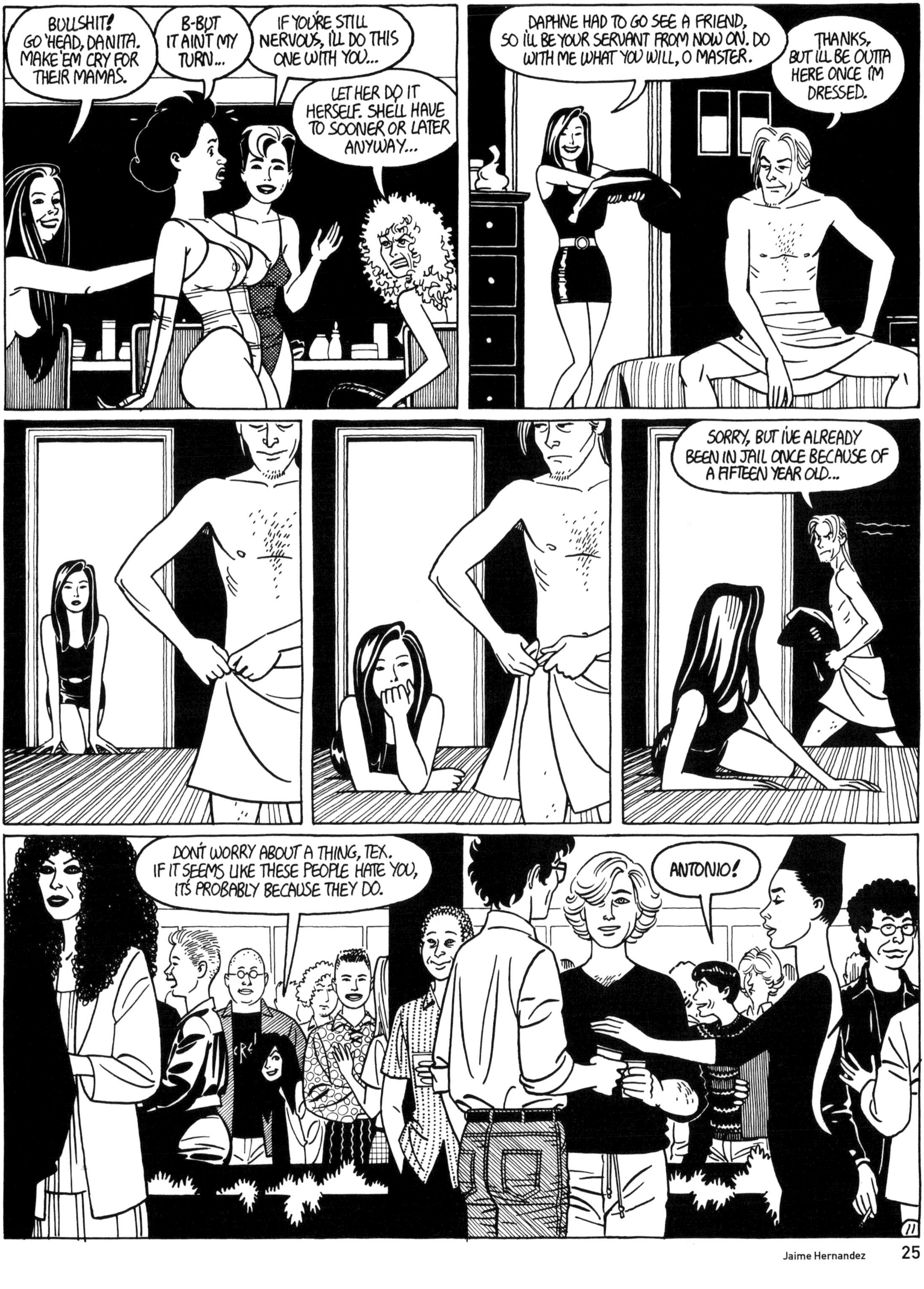
BULLSHIT! GO 'HEAD, DANITA. MAKE 'EM CRY FOR THEIR MAMAS.
B-BUT IT AINT MY TURN...
IF YOU'RE STILL NERVOUS, I'LL DO THIS ONE WITH YOU...
LET HER DO IT HERSELF. SHE'LL HAVE TO SOONER OR LATER ANYWAY...
DAPHNE HAD TO GO SEE A FRIEND, SO I'LL BE YOUR SERVANT FROM NOW ON. DO WITH ME WHAT YOU WILL, O MASTER.
THANKS, BUT I'LL BE OUTTA HERE ONCE I'M DRESSED.
SORRY, BUT I'VE ALREADY BEEN IN JAIL ONCE BECAUSE OF A FIFTEEN YEAR OLD...
DON'T WORRY ABOUT A THING, TEX. IF IT SEEMS LIKE THESE PEOPLE HATE YOU, IT'S PROBABLY BECAUSE THEY DO.
ANTONIO!
11

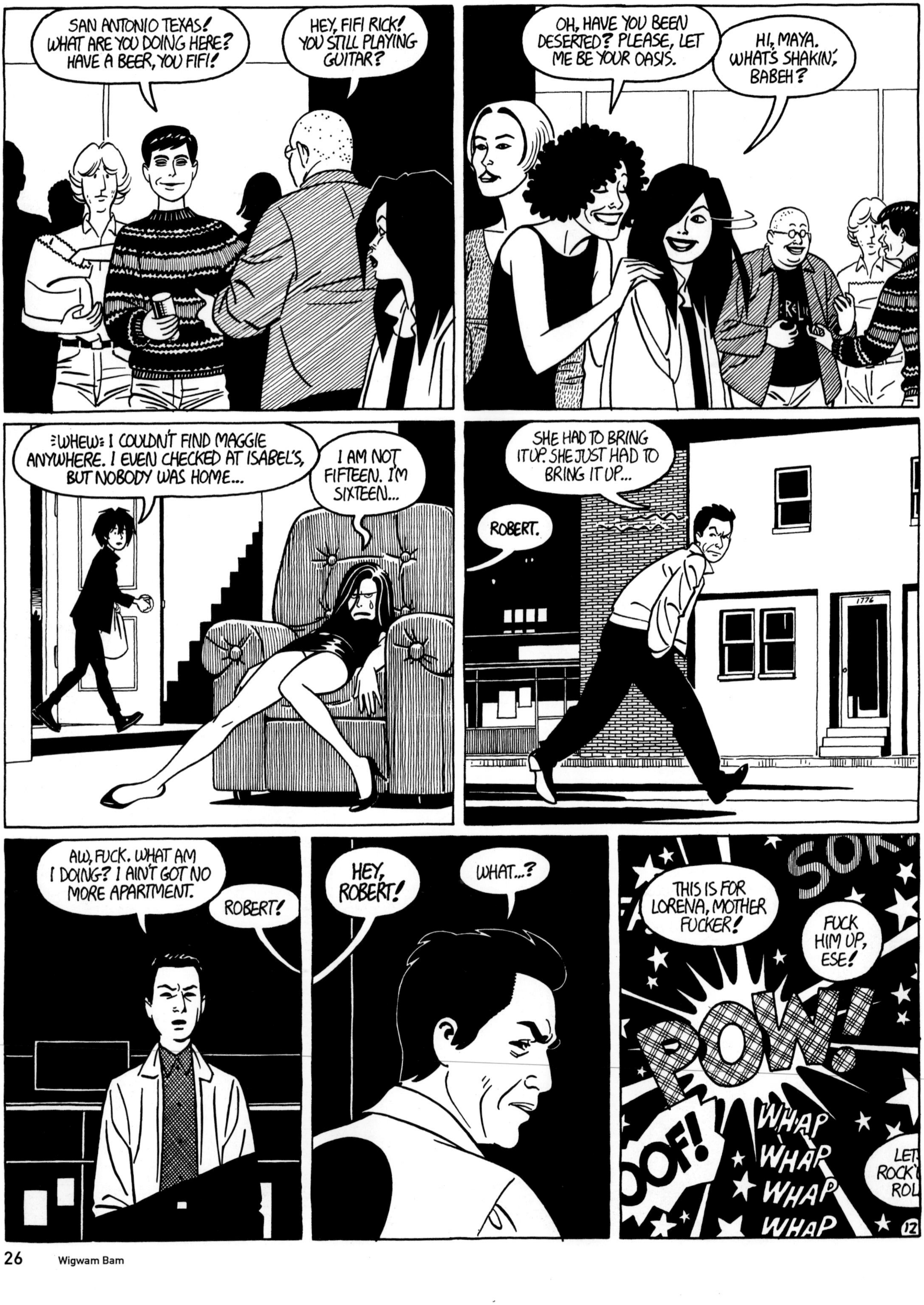
SAN ANTONIO TEXAS! WHAT ARE YOU DOING HERE? HAVE A BEER, YOU FIFI!
HEY, FIFI RICK! YOU STILL PLAYING GUITAR?
OH, HAVE YOU BEEN DESERTED? PLEASE, LET ME BE YOUR OASIS.
HI, MAYA. WHAT'S SHAKIN', BABEH?
=WHEW= I COULDN'T FIND MAGGIE ANYWHERE. I EVEN CHECKED AT ISABEL'S, BUT NOBODY WAS HOME...
I AM NOT FIFTEEN. I'M SIXTEEN...
SHE HAD TO BRING IT UP. SHE JUST HAD TO BRING IT UP...
ROBERT.
1776
AW, FUCK. WHAT AM I DOING? I AIN'T GOT NO MORE APARTMENT.
ROBERT!
HEY, ROBERT!
WHAT...?
THIS IS FOR LORENA, MOTHER FUCKER!
FUCK HIM UP, ESE!
POW!
OOF!
WHAP WHAP WHAP WHAP
12

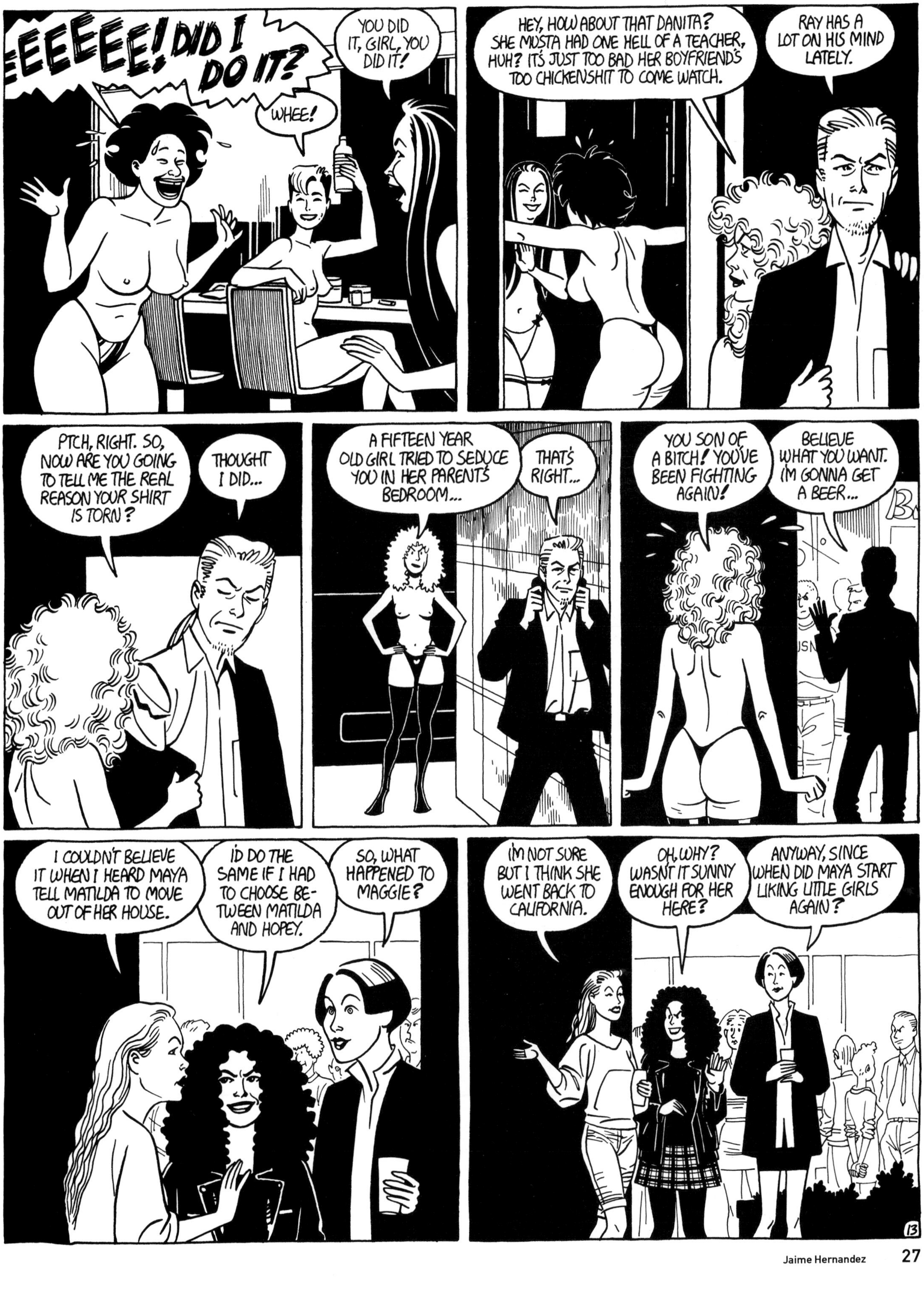
EEEEEE! DID I DO IT?
YOU DID IT, GIRL, YOU DID IT!
WHEE!
HEY, HOW ABOUT THAT DANITA? SHE MUSTA HAD ONE HELL OF A TEACHER, HUH? IT'S JUST TOO BAD HER BOYFRIEND'S TOO CHICKENSHIT TO COME WATCH.
RAY HAS A LOT ON HIS MIND LATELY.
PTCH, RIGHT. SO, NOW ARE YOU GOING TO TELL ME THE REAL REASON YOUR SHIRT IS TORN?
THOUGHT I DID...
A FIFTEEN YEAR OLD GIRL TRIED TO SEDUCE YOU IN HER PARENT'S BEDROOM...
THAT'S RIGHT...
YOU SON OF A BITCH! YOU'VE BEEN FIGHTING AGAIN!
BELIEVE WHAT YOU WANT. I'M GONNA GET A BEER...
I COULDN'T BELIEVE IT WHEN I HEARD MAYA TELL MATILDA TO MOVE OUT OF HER HOUSE.
I'D DO THE SAME IF I HAD TO CHOOSE BE-TWEEN MATILDA AND HOPEY.
SO, WHAT HAPPENED TO MAGGIE?
I'M NOT SURE BUT I THINK SHE WENT BACK TO CALIFORNIA.
OH, WHY? WASN'T IT SUNNY ENOUGH FOR HER HERE?
ANYWAY, SINCE WHEN DID MAYA START LIKING LITTLE GIRLS AGAIN?
13

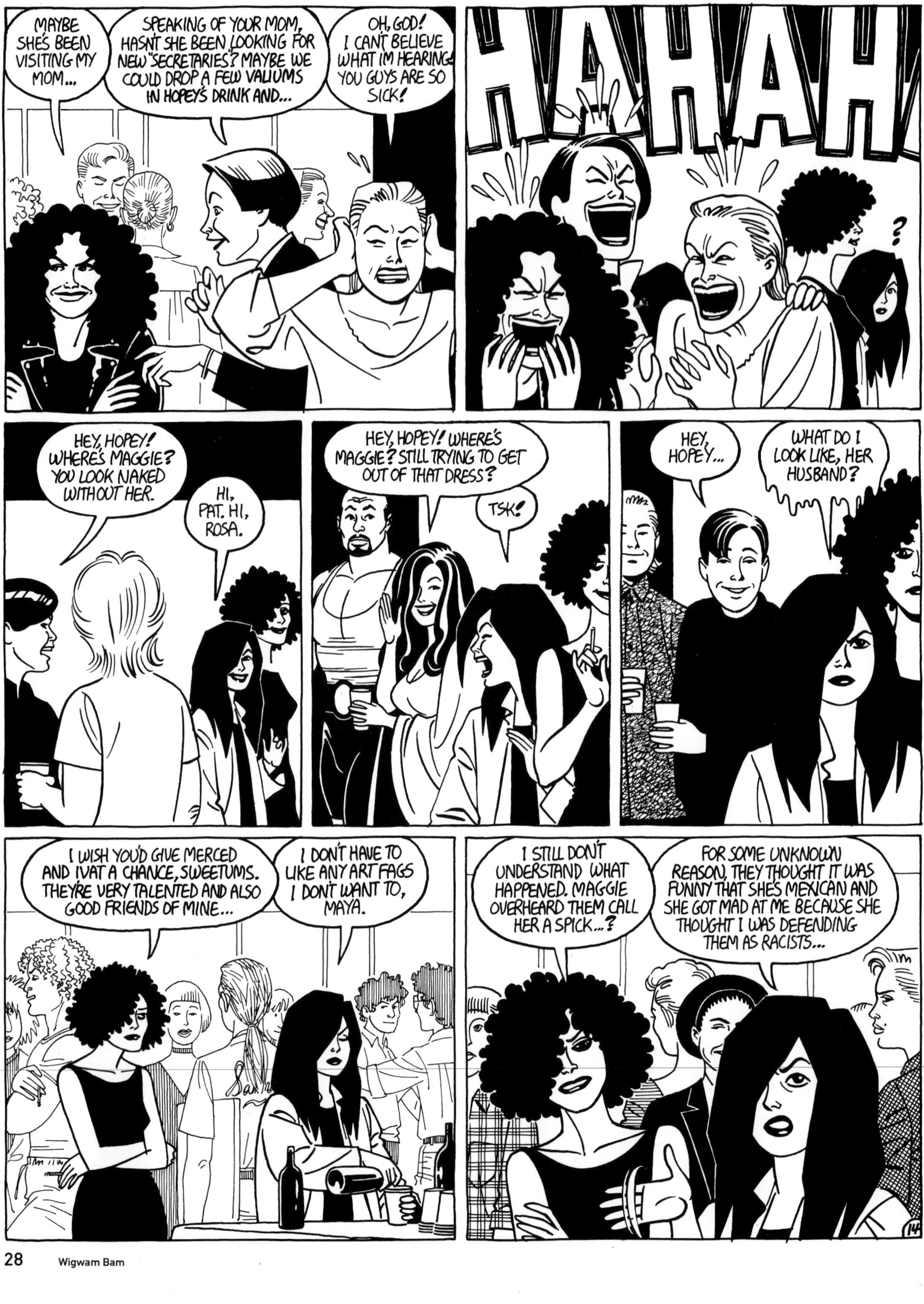
MAYBE SHE'S BEEN VISITING MY MOM...
SPEAKING OF YOUR MOM, HASN'T SHE BEEN LOOKING FOR NEW "SECRETARIES"? MAYBE WE COULD DROP A FEW VALIUMS IN HOPEY'S DRINK AND...
OH, GOD! I CAN'T BELIEVE WHAT I'M HEARING! YOU GUYS ARE SO SICK!
HAHAH
HEY, HOPEY! WHERE'S MAGGIE? YOU LOOK NAKED WITHOUT HER.
HI, PAT. HI, ROSA.
HEY, HOPEY! WHERE'S MAGGIE? STILL TRYING TO GET OUT OF THAT DRESS?
TSK!
HEY, HOPEY...
WHAT DO I LOOK LIKE, HER HUSBAND?
I WISH YOU'D GIVE MERCED AND IVAT A CHANCE, SWEETUMS. THEY'RE VERY TALENTED AND ALSO GOOD FRIENDS OF MINE...
I DON'T HAVE TO LIKE ANY ART FAGS I DON'T WANT TO, MAYA.
I STILL DON'T UNDERSTAND WHAT HAPPENED. MAGGIE OVERHEARD THEM CALL HER A SPICK...?
FOR SOME UNKNOWN REASON, THEY THOUGHT IT WAS FUNNY THAT SHE'S MEXICAN AND SHE GOT MAD AT ME BECAUSE SHE THOUGHT I WAS DEFENDING THEM AS RACISTS...
14

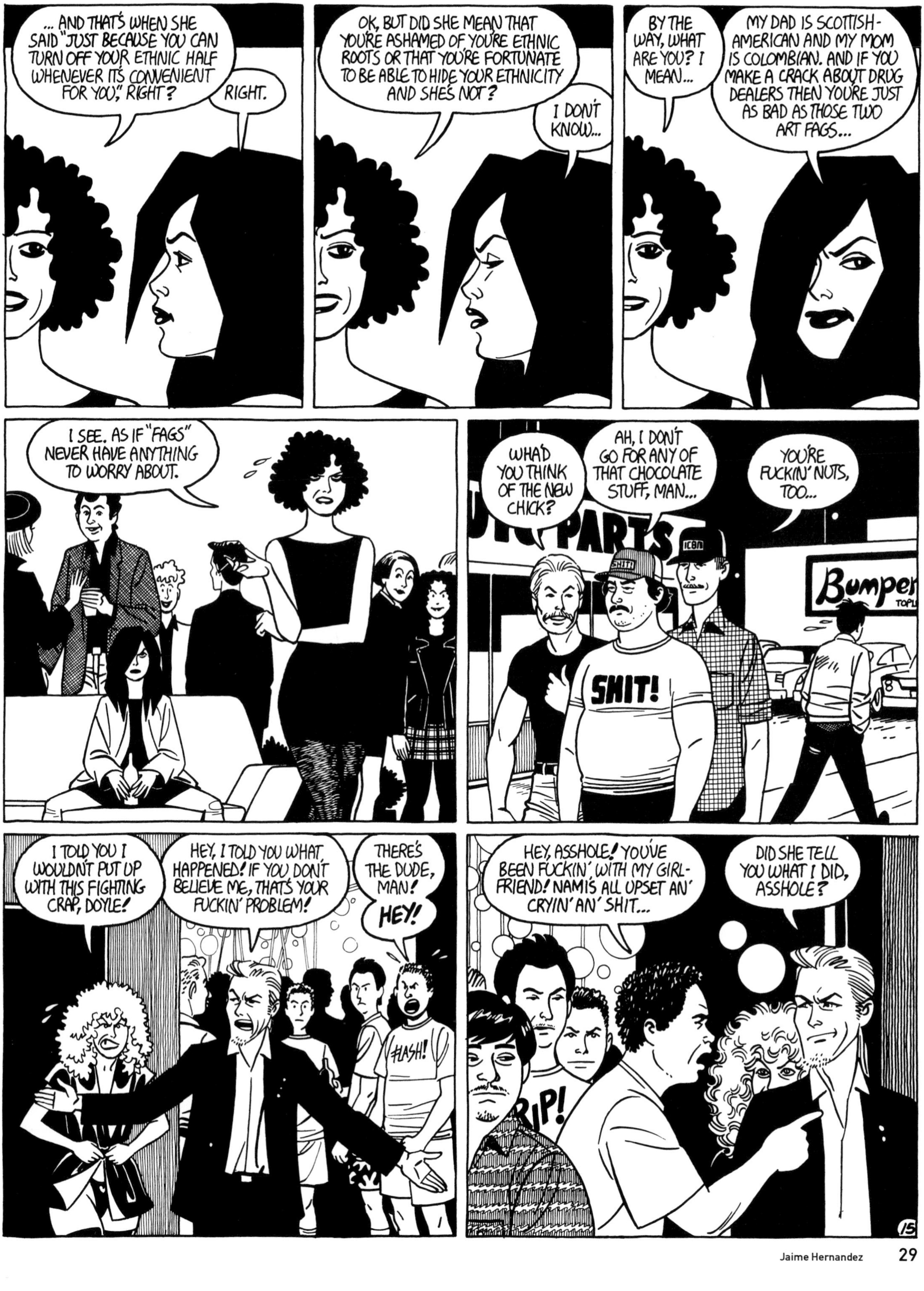
... AND THAT'S WHEN SHE SAID "JUST BECAUSE YOU CAN TURN OFF YOUR ETHNIC HALF WHENEVER IT'S CONVENIENT FOR YOU," RIGHT?
RIGHT.
OK, BUT DID SHE MEAN THAT YOU'RE ASHAMED OF YOU'RE ETHNIC ROOTS OR THAT YOU'RE FORTUNATE TO BE ABLE TO HIDE YOUR ETHNICITY AND SHE'S NOT?
I DON'T KNOW...
BY THE WAY, WHAT ARE YOU? I MEAN...
MY DAD IS SCOTTISH-AMERICAN AND MY MOM IS COLOMBIAN. AND IF YOU MAKE A CRACK ABOUT DRUG DEALERS THEN YOU'RE JUST AS BAD AS THOSE TWO ART FAGS...
I SEE. AS IF "FAGS" NEVER HAVE ANYTHING TO WORRY ABOUT.
WHA'D YOU THINK OF THE NEW CHICK?
AH, I DON'T GO FOR ANY OF THAT CHOCOLATE STUFF, MAN...
YOU'RE FUCKIN' NUTS, TOO...
PARTS
SHIT!
SHIT!
Bumper
I TOLD YOU I WOULDN'T PUT UP WITH THIS FIGHTING CRAP, DOYLE!
HEY, I TOLD YOU WHAT HAPPENED! IF YOU DON'T BELIEVE ME, THAT'S YOUR FUCKIN' PROBLEM!
THERE'S THE DUDE, MAN!
HEY!
FLASH!
HEY, ASSHOLE! YOU'VE BEEN FUCKIN' WITH MY GIRL-FRIEND! NAMI'S ALL UPSET AN' CRYIN' AN' SHIT...
DID SHE TELL YOU WHAT I DID, ASSHOLE?
RIP!
15

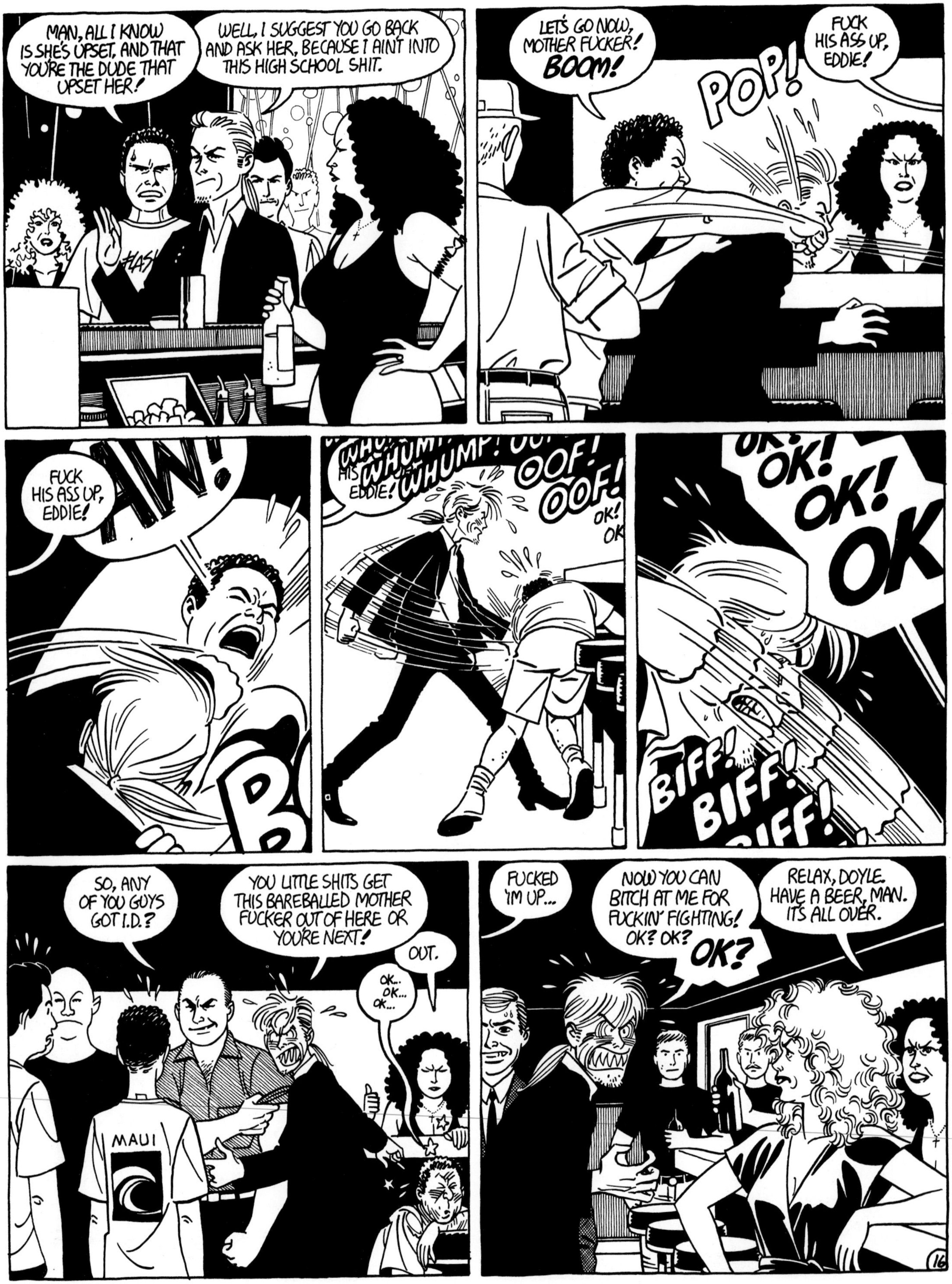
MAN, ALL I KNOW IS SHE'S UPSET, AND THAT YOU'RE THE DUDE THAT UPSET HER!
WELL, I SUGGEST YOU GO BACK AND ASK HER, BECAUSE I AIN'T INTO THIS HIGH SCHOOL SHIT.
LET'S GO NOW, MOTHER FUCKER! BOOM!
FUCK HIS ASS UP, EDDIE!
POP!
FUCK HIS ASS UP, EDDIE!
WHUMP! OOF! OOF! OK! OK
OK! OK! OK! OK
BIFF! BIFF! BIFF!
SO, ANY OF YOU GUYS GOT I.D.?
YOU LITTLE SHITS GET THIS BAREBALLED MOTHER FUCKER OUT OF HERE OR YOU'RE NEXT!
OUT.
OK.. OK... OK...
MAUI
FUCKED 'IM UP...
NOW YOU CAN BITCH AT ME FOR FUCKIN' FIGHTING! OK? OK? OK?
RELAX, DOYLE. HAVE A BEER, MAN. IT'S ALL OVER.
16

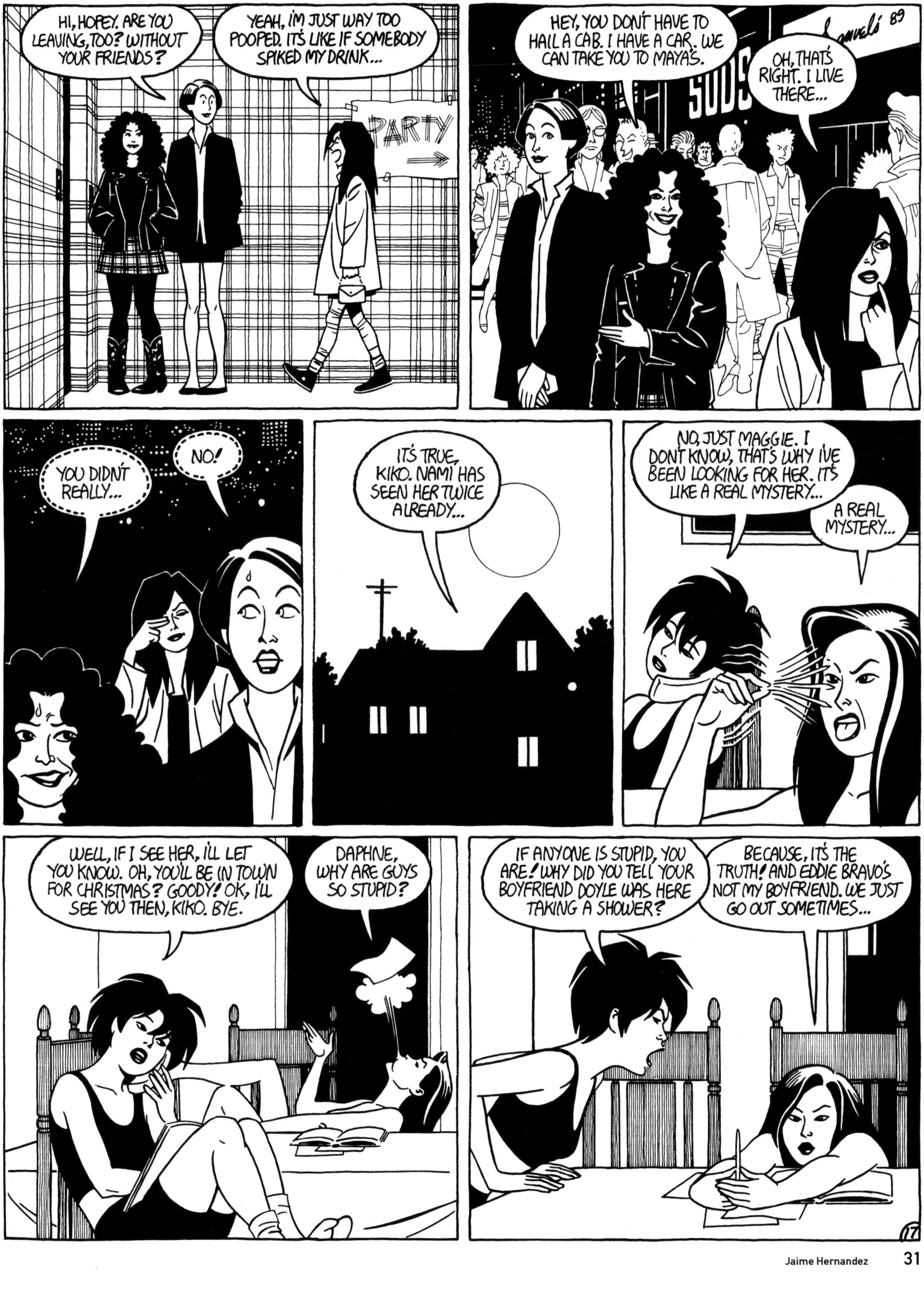
HI, HOPEY. ARE YOU LEAVING, TOO? WITHOUT YOUR FRIENDS?
YEAH, I'M JUST WAY TOO POOPED. IT'S LIKE IF SOMEBODY SPIKED MY DRINK...
PARTY
HEY, YOU DON'T HAVE TO HAIL A CAB. I HAVE A CAR. WE CAN TAKE YOU TO MAYA'S.
OH, THAT'S RIGHT. I LIVE THERE...
SUDS
YOU DIDN'T REALLY...
NO!
IT'S TRUE, KIKO. NAMI HAS SEEN HER TWICE ALREADY...
NO, JUST MAGGIE. I DON'T KNOW, THAT'S WHY I'VE BEEN LOOKING FOR HER. IT'S LIKE A REAL MYSTERY...
A REAL MYSTERY...
WELL, IF I SEE HER, I'LL LET YOU KNOW. OH, YOU'LL BE IN TOWN FOR CHRISTMAS? GOODY! OK, I'LL SEE YOU THEN, KIKO. BYE.
DAPHNE, WHY ARE GUYS SO STUPID?
IF ANYONE IS STUPID, YOU ARE! WHY DID YOU TELL YOUR BOYFRIEND DOYLE WAS HERE TAKING A SHOWER?
BECAUSE, IT'S THE TRUTH! AND EDDIE BRAVO'S NOT MY BOYFRIEND. WE JUST GO OUT SOMETIMES...
17

BUT, WHAT IF THEY FIND DOYLE? HE WAS IN JAIL, YOU KNOW...

HE WAS?? WAS THIS REAL JAIL OR OVERNIGHT JAIL? DID HE LIKE, KILL SOMEBODY, OR...?

NAN TUCKER IS YOUR MOM? "AMERICA'S NUMBER ONE FAVORITE COMEDIENNE?" "MY GAL NAN?" "NAN'S WORLD?" "WHERE'S NAN?"

SURE. YOU WANT TO MEET HER?

SURE, ANYTHING. JUST WAKE ME WHEN WE GET THERE...

SIT BACK, RELAX AND LEAVE THE DRIVING TO US, OL' GIRL...

VE YOU N ME?

MATTHEW BUCHER   ESP

HEW ER

ESPERANZA GLASS

HAVE YOU SEEN ME?

HOW ABOUT THAT? LET'S GIVE A BIG HAND TO OUR NEWEST SWEET SENSATION... DA-NI-TAAA...

⑱

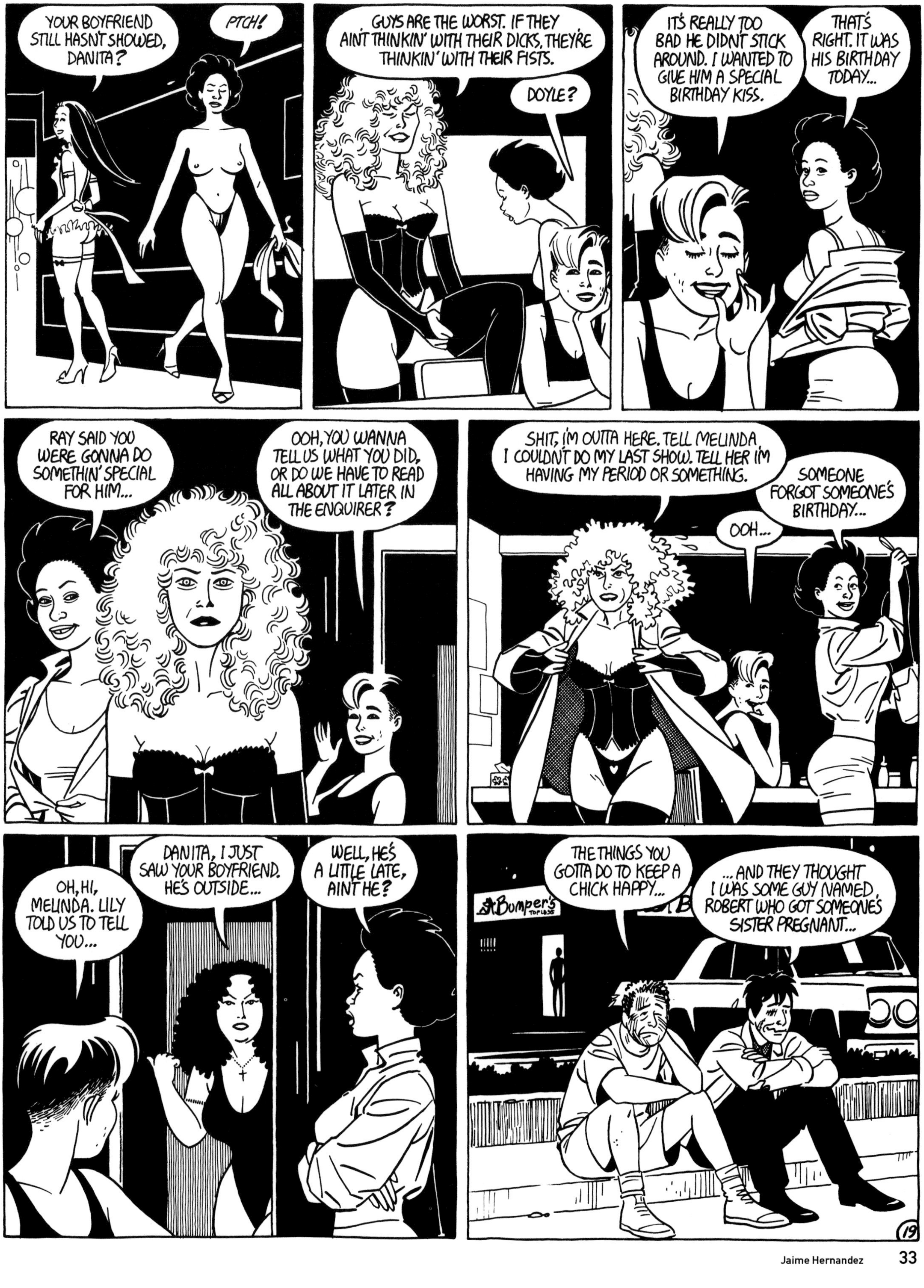
YOUR BOYFRIEND STILL HASN'T SHOWED, DANITA?
PTCH!
GUYS ARE THE WORST. IF THEY AIN'T THINKIN' WITH THEIR DICKS, THEY'RE THINKIN' WITH THEIR FISTS.
DOYLE?
IT'S REALLY TOO BAD HE DIDN'T STICK AROUND. I WANTED TO GIVE HIM A SPECIAL BIRTHDAY KISS.
THAT'S RIGHT. IT WAS HIS BIRTHDAY TODAY...
RAY SAID YOU WERE GONNA DO SOMETHIN' SPECIAL FOR HIM...
OOH, YOU WANNA TELL US WHAT YOU DID, OR DO WE HAVE TO READ ALL ABOUT IT LATER IN THE ENQUIRER?
SHIT, I'M OUTTA HERE. TELL MELINDA I COULDN'T DO MY LAST SHOW. TELL HER I'M HAVING MY PERIOD OR SOMETHING.
SOMEONE FORGOT SOMEONE'S BIRTHDAY...
OOH...
OH, HI, MELINDA. LILY TOLD US TO TELL YOU...
DANITA, I JUST SAW YOUR BOYFRIEND. HE'S OUTSIDE...
WELL, HE'S A LITTLE LATE, AIN'T HE?
Bumper's
THE THINGS YOU GOTTA DO TO KEEP A CHICK HAPPY...
...AND THEY THOUGHT I WAS SOME GUY NAMED ROBERT WHO GOT SOMEONE'S SISTER PREGNANT...
19

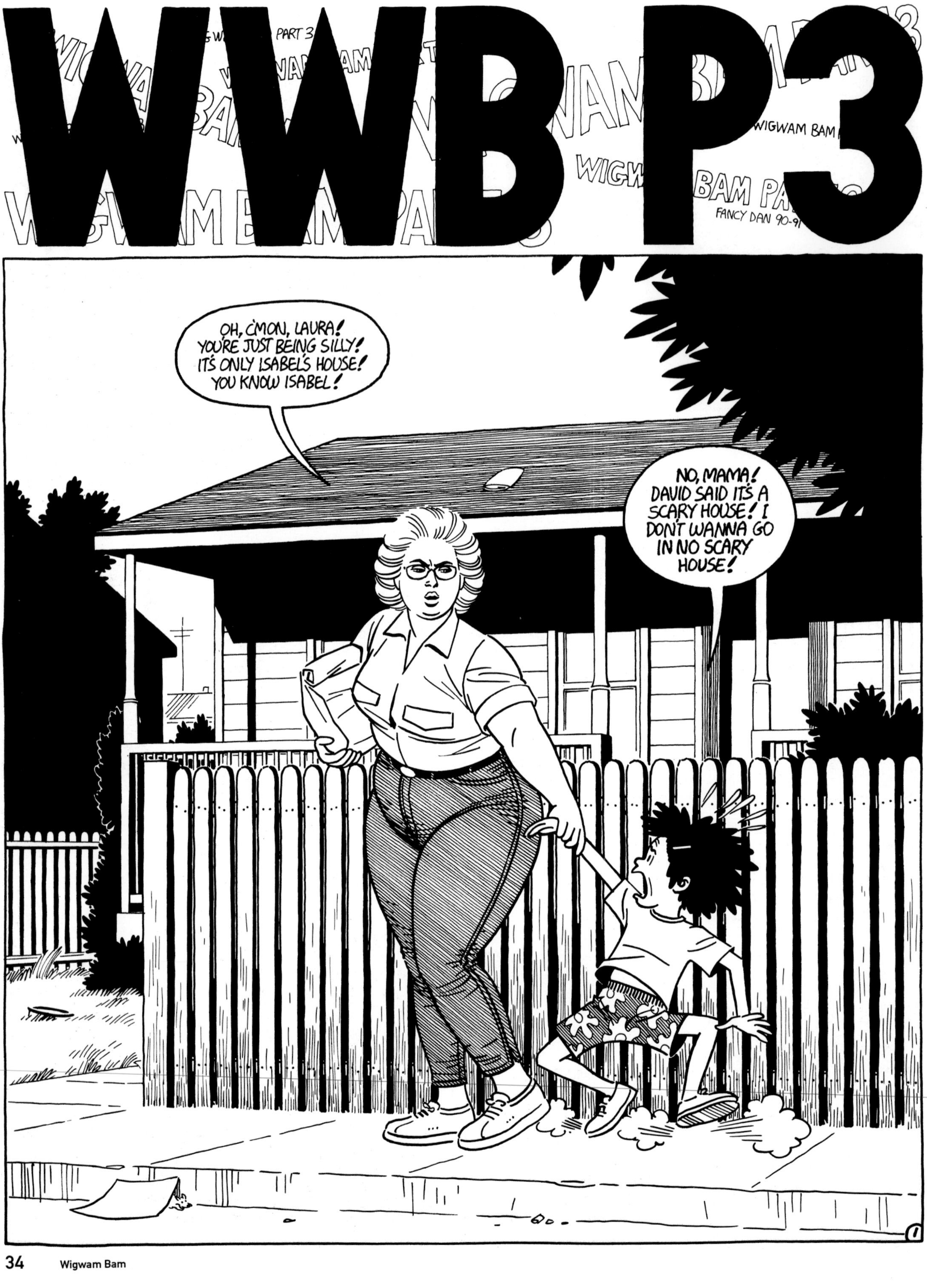
WWB P3
WIGWAM BAM PART 3
FANCY DAN 90-91
OH, C'MON, LAURA! YOU'RE JUST BEING SILLY! IT'S ONLY ISABEL'S HOUSE! YOU KNOW ISABEL!
NO, MAMA! DAVID SAID IT'S A SCARY HOUSE! I DON'T WANNA GO IN NO SCARY HOUSE!
1

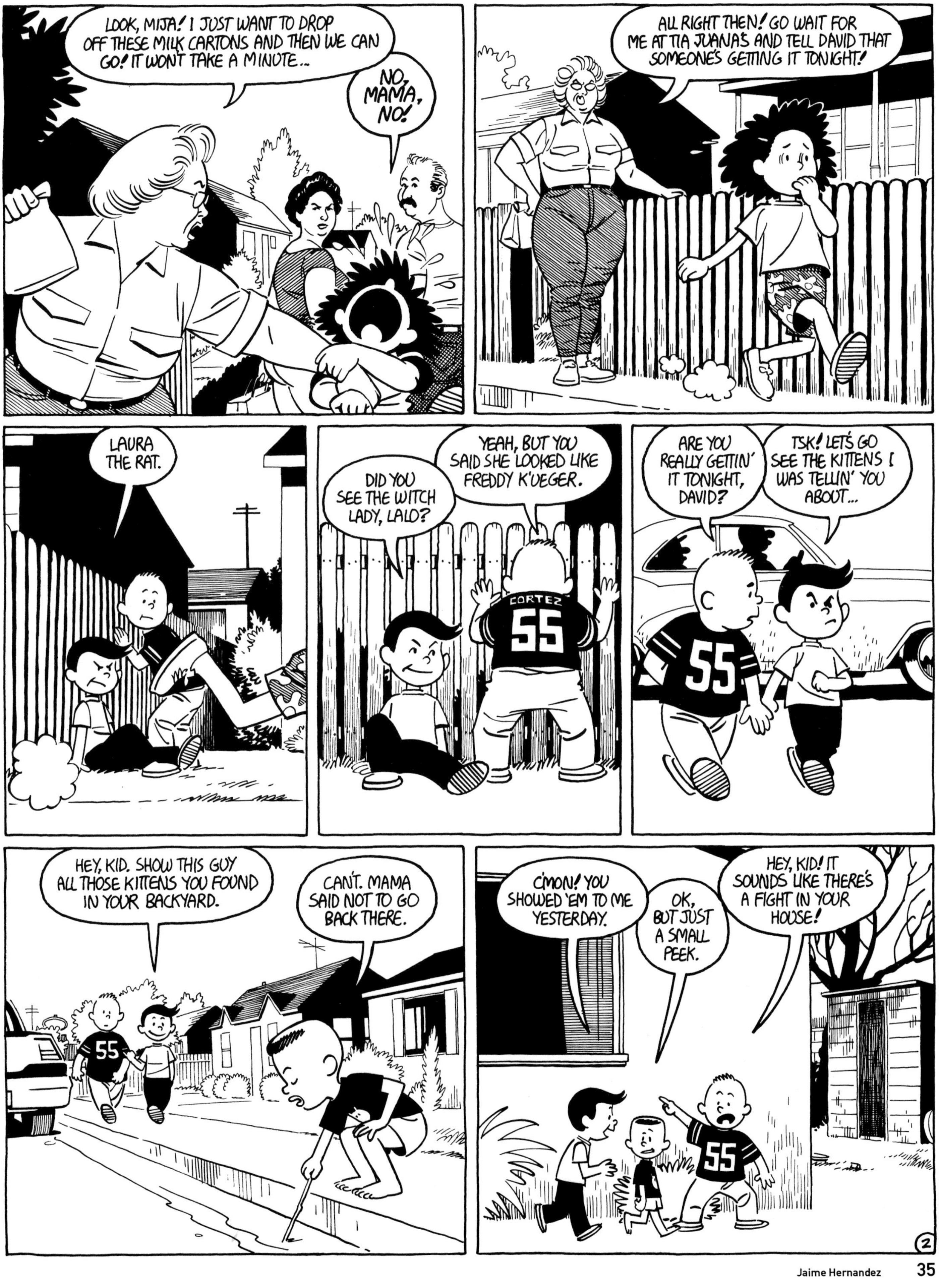
LOOK, MIJA! I JUST WANT TO DROP OFF THESE MILK CARTONS AND THEN WE CAN GO! IT WON'T TAKE A MINUTE...
NO, MAMA, NO!
ALL RIGHT THEN! GO WAIT FOR ME AT TIA JUANA'S AND TELL DAVID THAT SOMEONE'S GETTING IT TONIGHT!
LAURA THE RAT.
DID YOU SEE THE WITCH LADY, LALO?
YEAH, BUT YOU SAID SHE LOOKED LIKE FREDDY K'UEGER.
CORTEZ
55
ARE YOU REALLY GETTIN' IT TONIGHT, DAVID?
TSK! LET'S GO SEE THE KITTENS I WAS TELLIN' YOU ABOUT...
HEY, KID. SHOW THIS GUY ALL THOSE KITTENS YOU FOUND IN YOUR BACKYARD.
CAN'T. MAMA SAID NOT TO GO BACK THERE.
C'MON! YOU SHOWED 'EM TO ME YESTERDAY.
OK, BUT JUST A SMALL PEEK.
HEY, KID! IT SOUNDS LIKE THERE'S A FIGHT IN YOUR HOUSE!
2

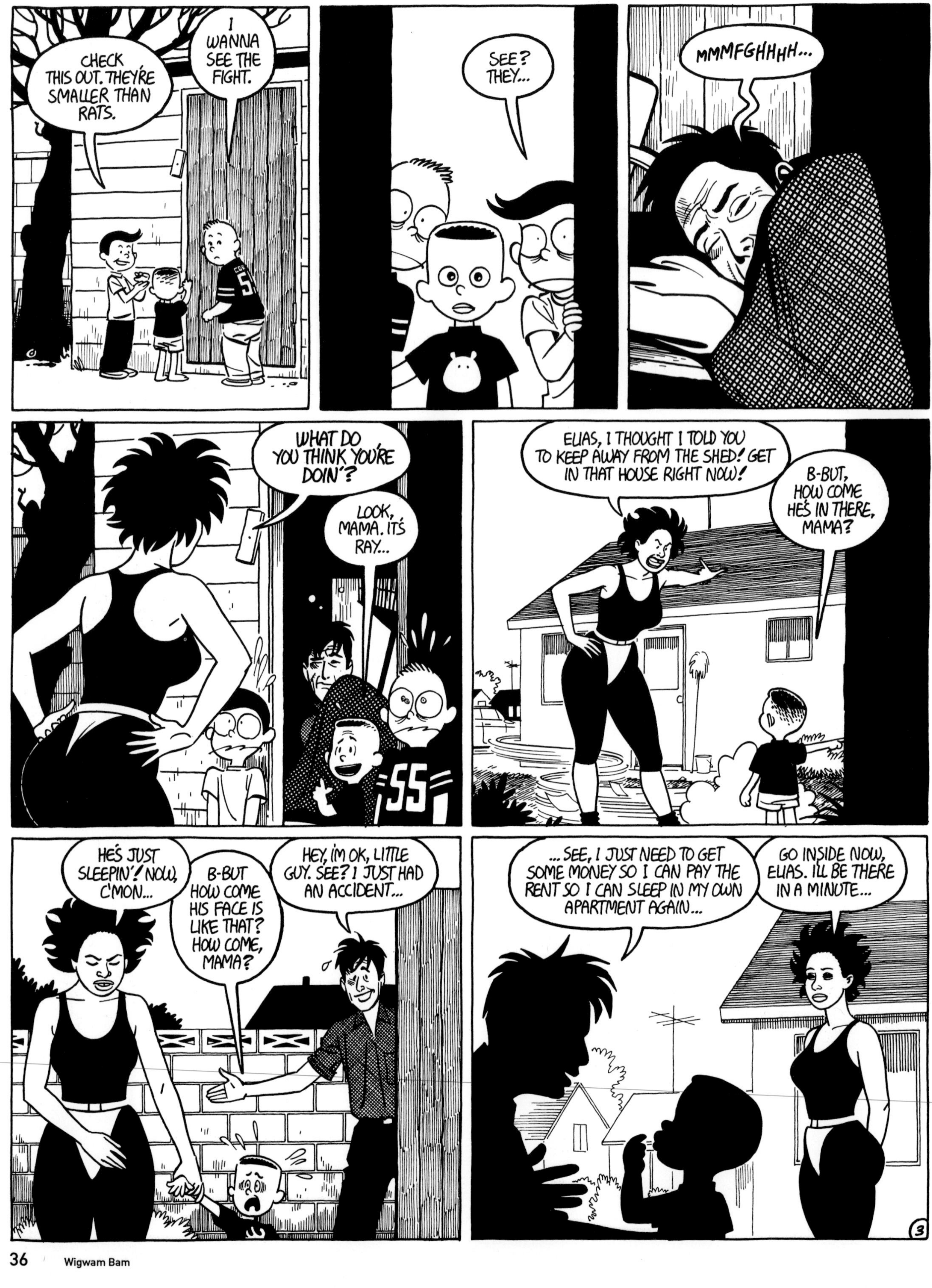
CHECK THIS OUT. THEY'RE SMALLER THAN RATS.
I WANNA SEE THE FIGHT.
SEE? THEY...
MMMFGHHHH...
WHAT DO YOU THINK YOU'RE DOIN'?
LOOK, MAMA. IT'S RAY...
ELIAS, I THOUGHT I TOLD YOU TO KEEP AWAY FROM THE SHED! GET IN THAT HOUSE RIGHT NOW!
B-BUT, HOW COME HE'S IN THERE, MAMA?
HE'S JUST SLEEPIN'! NOW, C'MON...
B-BUT HOW COME HIS FACE IS LIKE THAT? HOW COME, MAMA?
HEY, I'M OK, LITTLE GUY. SEE? I JUST HAD AN ACCIDENT...
...SEE, I JUST NEED TO GET SOME MONEY SO I CAN PAY THE RENT SO I CAN SLEEP IN MY OWN APARTMENT AGAIN...
GO INSIDE NOW, ELIAS. I'LL BE THERE IN A MINUTE...
3

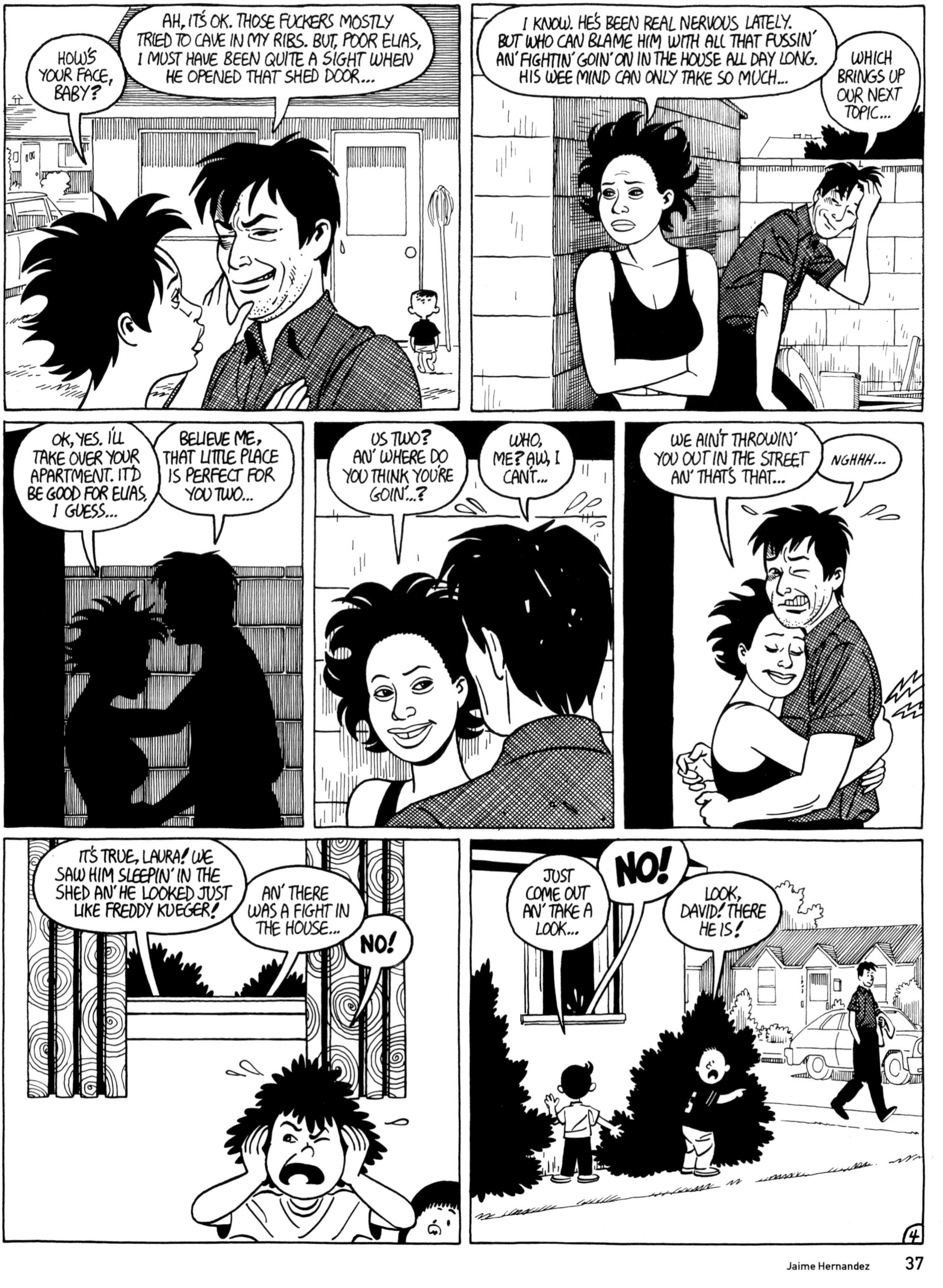
HOW'S YOUR FACE, BABY?
AH, IT'S OK. THOSE FUCKERS MOSTLY TRIED TO CAVE IN MY RIBS. BUT, POOR ELIAS, I MUST HAVE BEEN QUITE A SIGHT WHEN HE OPENED THAT SHED DOOR...
I KNOW. HE'S BEEN REAL NERVOUS LATELY. BUT WHO CAN BLAME HIM WITH ALL THAT FUSSIN' AN' FIGHTIN' GOIN' ON IN THE HOUSE ALL DAY LONG. HIS WEE MIND CAN ONLY TAKE SO MUCH...
WHICH BRINGS UP OUR NEXT TOPIC...
OK, YES. I'LL TAKE OVER YOUR APARTMENT. IT'D BE GOOD FOR ELIAS, I GUESS...
BELIEVE ME, THAT LITTLE PLACE IS PERFECT FOR YOU TWO...
US TWO? AN' WHERE DO YOU THINK YOU'RE GOIN'...?
WHO, ME? AW, I CAN'T...
WE AIN'T THROWIN' YOU OUT IN THE STREET AN' THAT'S THAT...
NGHHH...
IT'S TRUE, LAURA! WE SAW HIM SLEEPIN' IN THE SHED AN' HE LOOKED JUST LIKE FREDDY KUEGER!
AN' THERE WAS A FIGHT IN THE HOUSE...
NO!
JUST COME OUT AN' TAKE A LOOK...
NO!
LOOK, DAVID! THERE HE IS!
4

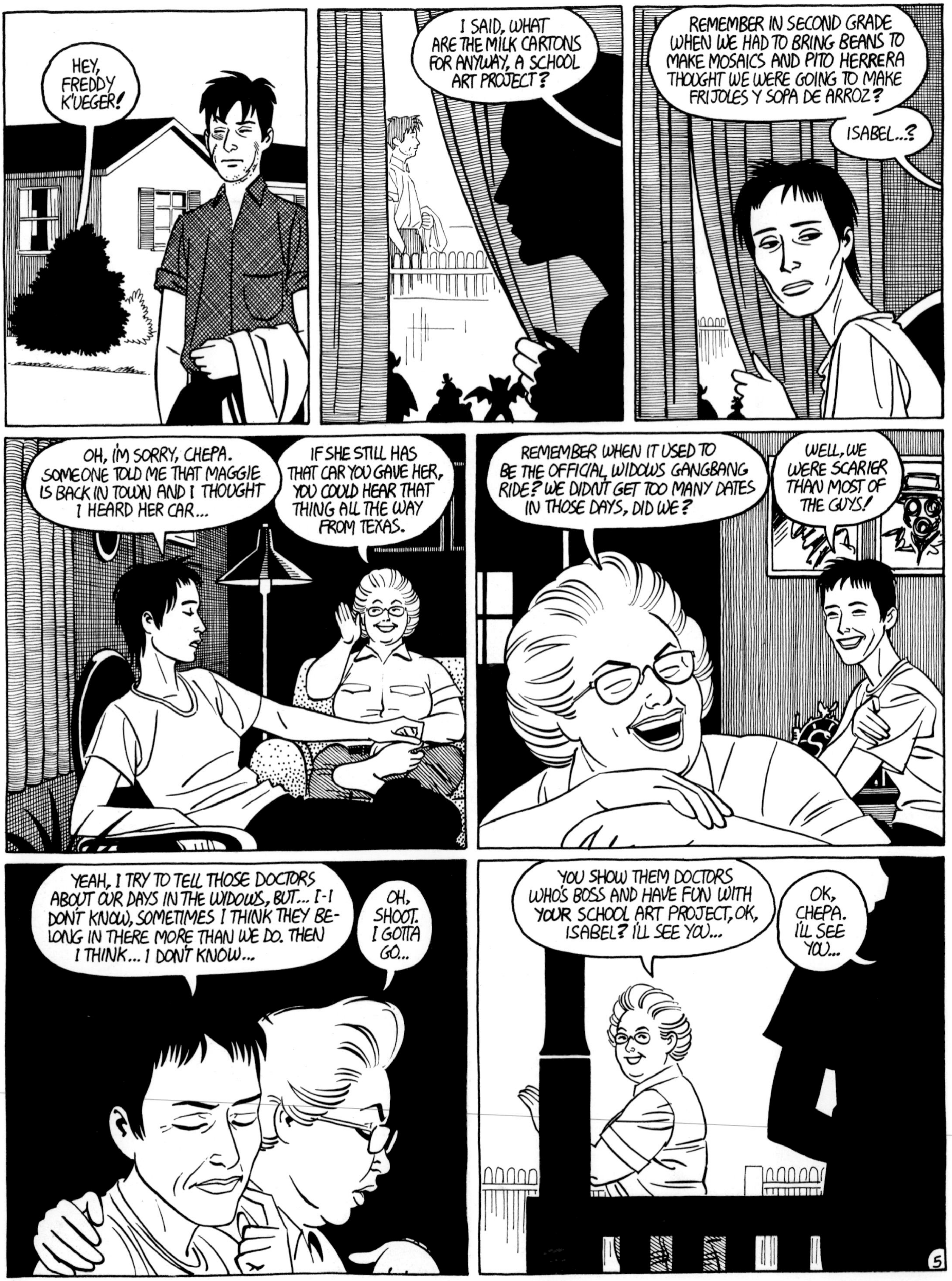
HEY, FREDDY K'UEGER!
I SAID, WHAT ARE THE MILK CARTONS FOR ANYWAY, A SCHOOL ART PROJECT?
REMEMBER IN SECOND GRADE WHEN WE HAD TO BRING BEANS TO MAKE MOSAICS AND PITO HERRERA THOUGHT WE WERE GOING TO MAKE FRIJOLES Y SOPA DE ARROZ?
ISABEL..?
OH, I'M SORRY, CHEPA. SOMEONE TOLD ME THAT MAGGIE IS BACK IN TOWN AND I THOUGHT I HEARD HER CAR...
IF SHE STILL HAS THAT CAR YOU GAVE HER, YOU COULD HEAR THAT THING ALL THE WAY FROM TEXAS.
REMEMBER WHEN IT USED TO BE THE OFFICIAL WIDOWS GANGBANG RIDE? WE DIDN'T GET TOO MANY DATES IN THOSE DAYS, DID WE?
WELL, WE WERE SCARIER THAN MOST OF THE GUYS!
YEAH, I TRY TO TELL THOSE DOCTORS ABOUT OUR DAYS IN THE WIDOWS, BUT... I-I DON'T KNOW, SOMETIMES I THINK THEY BELONG IN THERE MORE THAN WE DO. THEN I THINK... I DON'T KNOW...
OH, SHOOT. I GOTTA GO...
YOU SHOW THEM DOCTORS WHO'S BOSS AND HAVE FUN WITH YOUR SCHOOL ART PROJECT, OK, ISABEL? I'LL SEE YOU...
OK, CHEPA. I'LL SEE YOU...
5

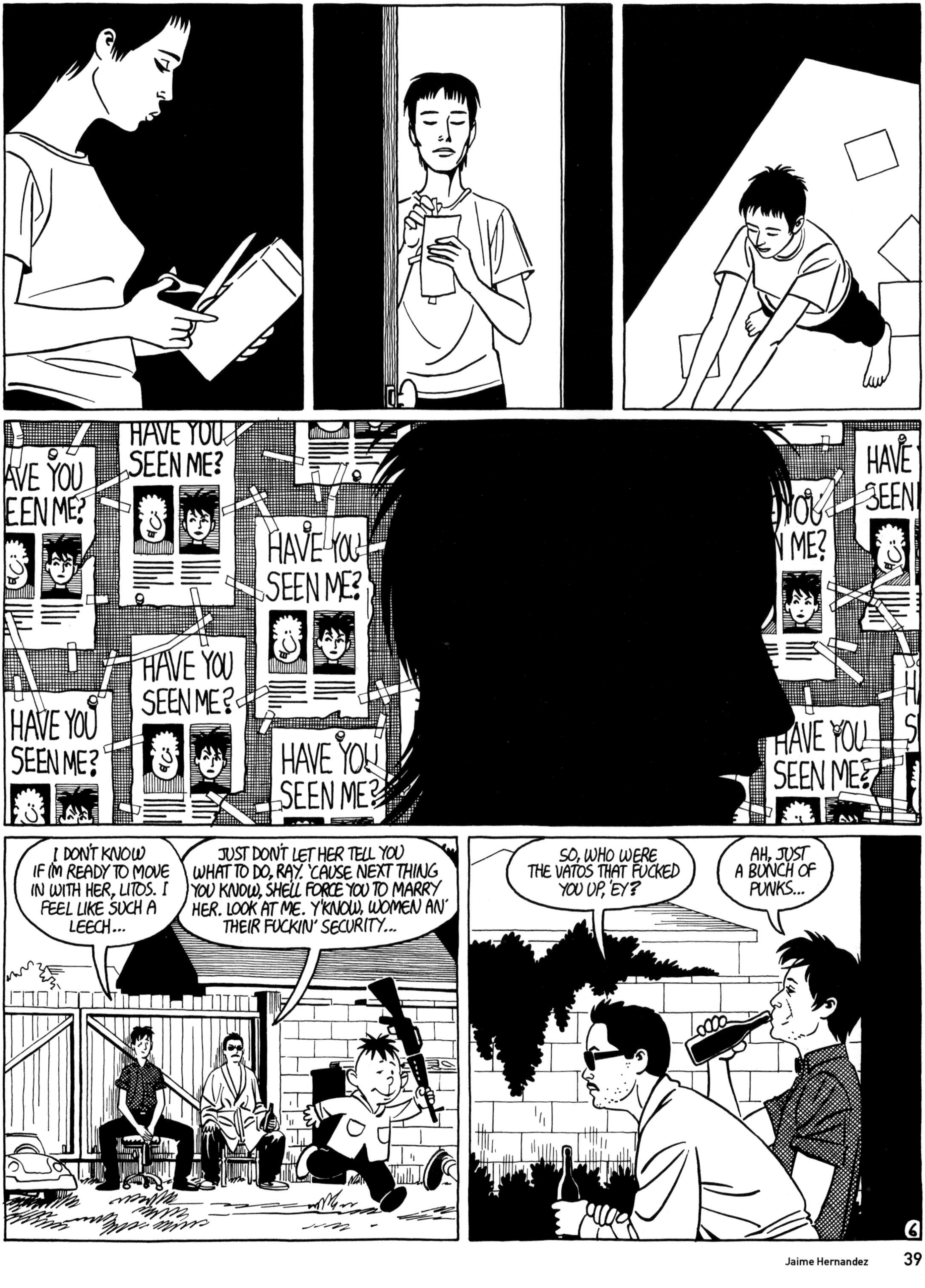
HAVE YOU SEEN ME?
I DON'T KNOW IF I'M READY TO MOVE IN WITH HER, LITOS. I FEEL LIKE SUCH A LEECH...
JUST DON'T LET HER TELL YOU WHAT TO DO, RAY. 'CAUSE NEXT THING YOU KNOW, SHE'LL FORCE YOU TO MARRY HER. LOOK AT ME. Y'KNOW, WOMEN AN' THEIR FUCKIN' SECURITY...
SO, WHO WERE THE VATOS THAT FUCKED YOU UP, 'EY?
AH, JUST A BUNCH OF PUNKS...
6

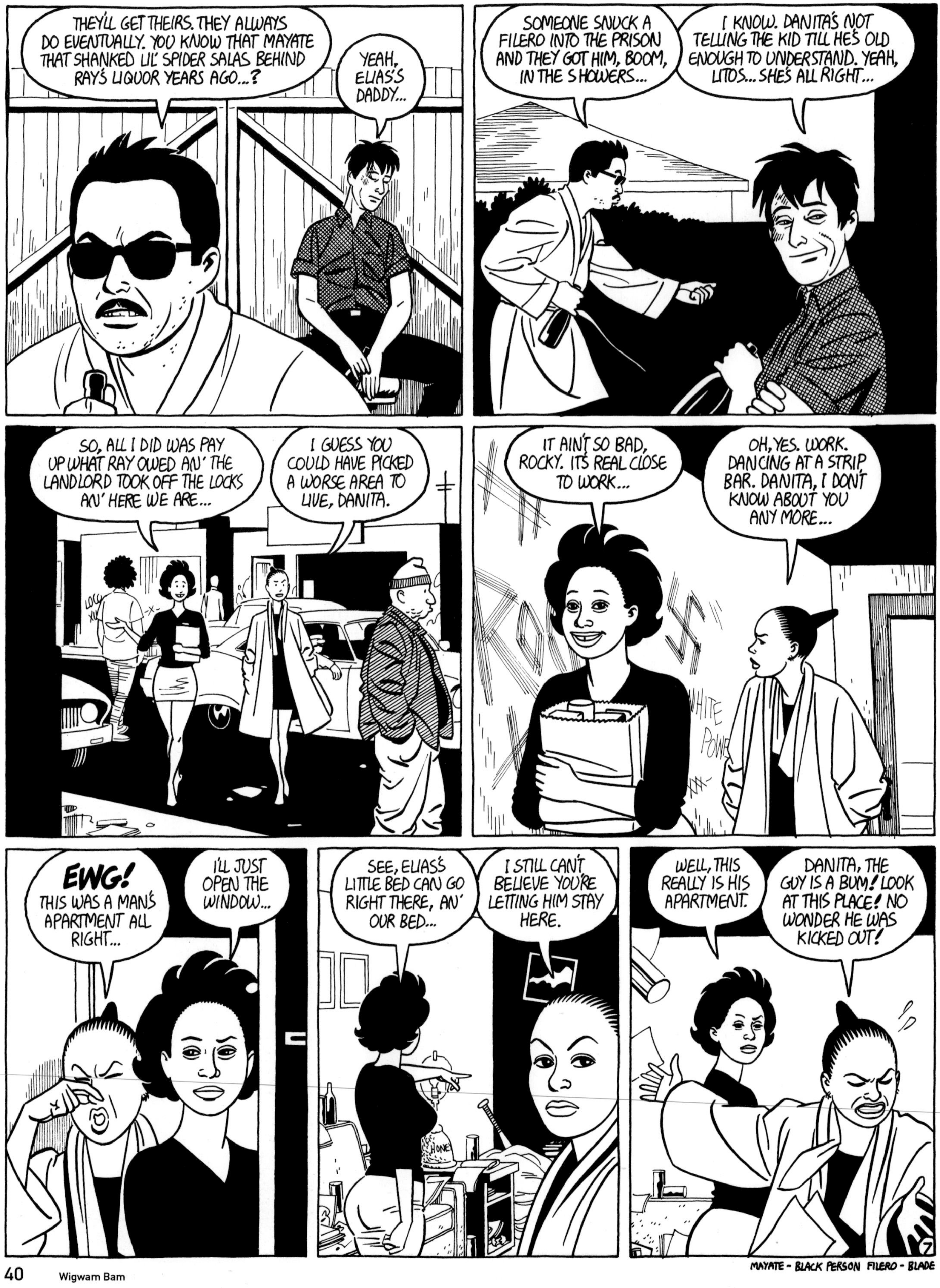
THEY'LL GET THEIRS. THEY ALWAYS DO EVENTUALLY. YOU KNOW THAT MAYATE THAT SHANKED LIL' SPIDER SALAS BEHIND RAY'S LIQUOR YEARS AGO...?
YEAH, ELIAS'S DADDY...
SOMEONE SNUCK A FILERO INTO THE PRISON AND THEY GOT HIM, BOOM, IN THE SHOWERS...
I KNOW. DANITA'S NOT TELLING THE KID TILL HE'S OLD ENOUGH TO UNDERSTAND. YEAH, LITOS... SHE'S ALL RIGHT...
SO, ALL I DID WAS PAY UP WHAT RAY OWED AN' THE LANDLORD TOOK OFF THE LOCKS AN' HERE WE ARE...
I GUESS YOU COULD HAVE PICKED A WORSE AREA TO LIVE, DANITA.
IT AIN'T SO BAD, ROCKY. IT'S REAL CLOSE TO WORK...
OH, YES. WORK. DANCING AT A STRIP BAR. DANITA, I DON'T KNOW ABOUT YOU ANY MORE...
EWG! THIS WAS A MAN'S APARTMENT ALL RIGHT...
I'LL JUST OPEN THE WINDOW...
SEE, ELIAS'S LITTLE BED CAN GO RIGHT THERE, AN' OUR BED...
I STILL CAN'T BELIEVE YOU'RE LETTING HIM STAY HERE.
WELL, THIS REALLY IS HIS APARTMENT.
DANITA, THE GUY IS A BUM! LOOK AT THIS PLACE! NO WONDER HE WAS KICKED OUT!
7

MAYATE - BLACK PERSON FILERO - BLADE

YOU ALWAYS END UP WITH THESE LOSERS! CORNELIUS EDWARDS WAS NEVER MAN ENOUGH TO BE A FATHER TO ELIAS. RONNIE HOWARD WILL ALWAYS BE A CLOWN. AND THIS RAY, I DON'T KNOW WHAT THE HELL HE IS! LOOK AT THIS...

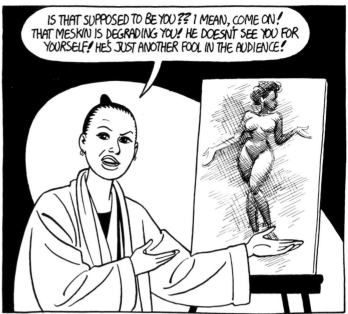

IS THAT SUPPOSED TO BE YOU?? I MEAN, COME ON! THAT MESKIN IS DEGRADING YOU! HE DOESN'T SEE YOU FOR YOURSELF! HE'S JUST ANOTHER FOOL IN THE AUDIENCE!

OH, HI, BABES.

I WAS HOPING YOU WEREN'T HERE YET. THE PLACE IS KINDA BEAT TO SHIT, AS YOU CAN SEE. HEH...

I GOTTA GO BUY SOME MAKE UP FOR WORK TONIGHT. YOU NEED ANYTHING?

NO MORE FOR ME, THANKS. I'M DRIVIN'...

8

Jaime Hernandez 41

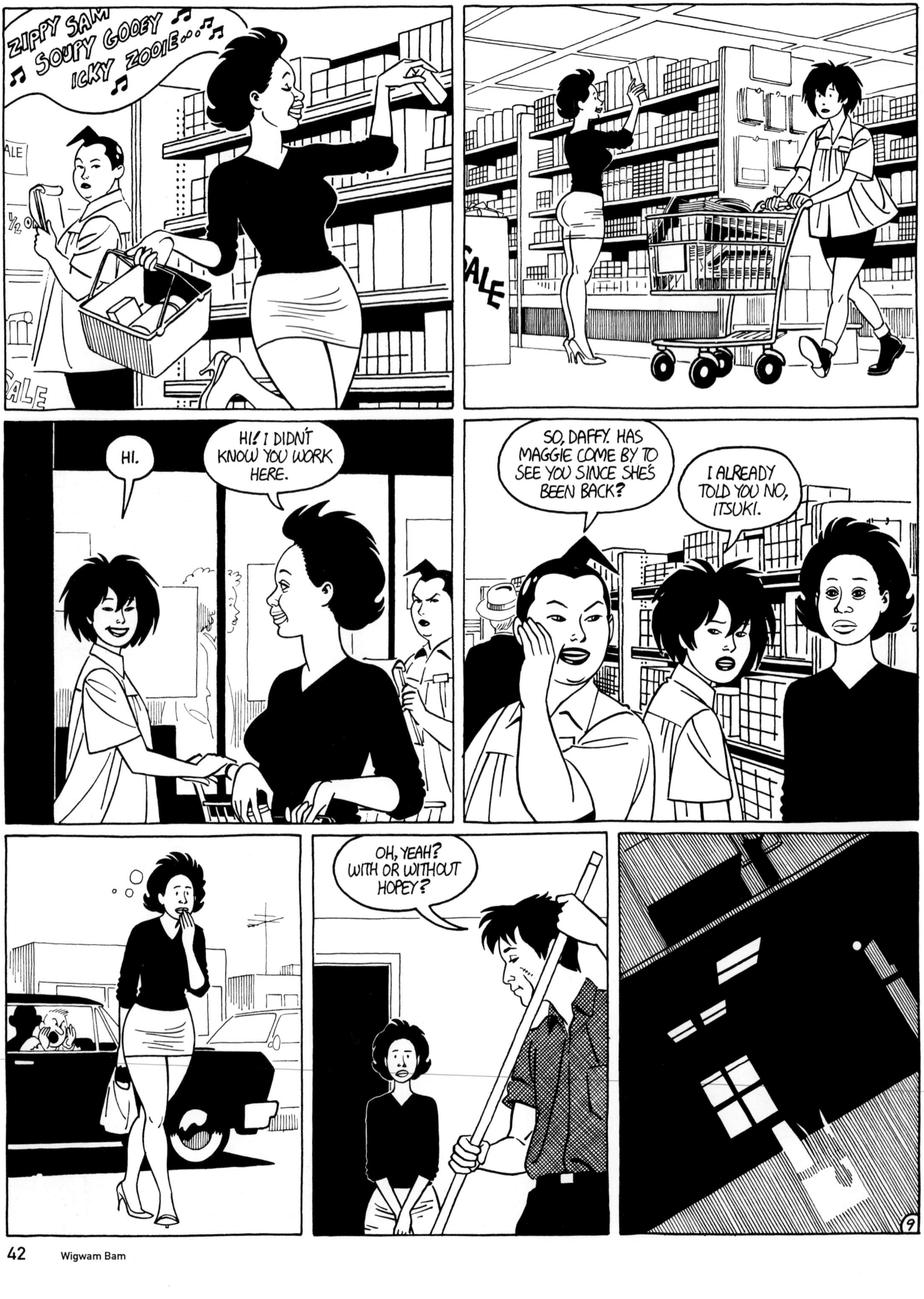
ZIPPY SAM
SOUPY GOOEY
ICKY ZOOIE...
ALE
1/2 O
SALE
SALE
ALE
HI.
HI! I DIDN'T KNOW YOU WORK HERE.
SO, DAFFY. HAS MAGGIE COME BY TO SEE YOU SINCE SHE'S BEEN BACK?
I ALREADY TOLD YOU NO, ITSUKI.
OH, YEAH? WITH OR WITHOUT HOPEY?
9

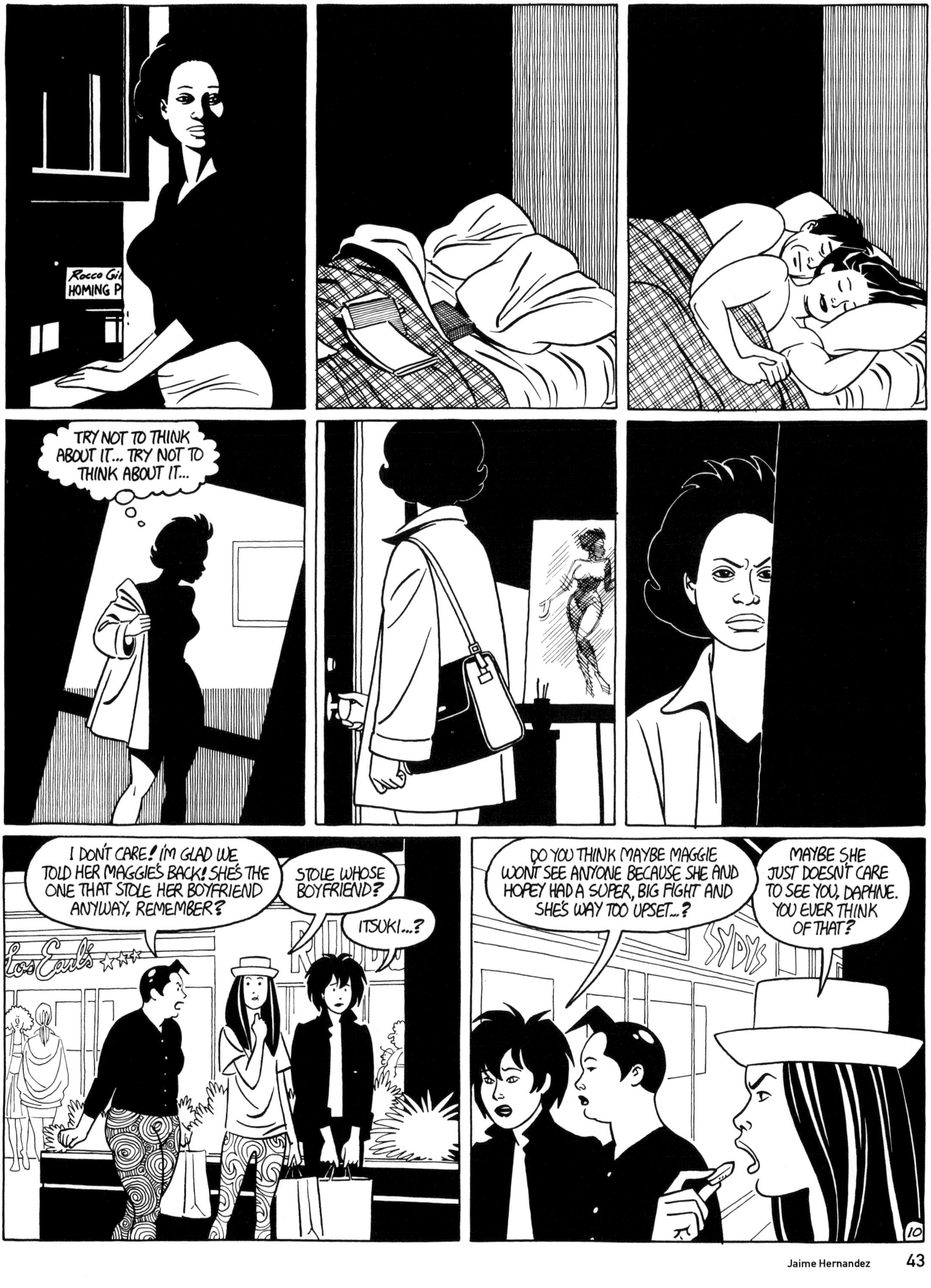
Rocco Gi
HOMING P
TRY NOT TO THINK ABOUT IT... TRY NOT TO THINK ABOUT IT...
I DON'T CARE! I'M GLAD WE TOLD HER MAGGIE'S BACK! SHE'S THE ONE THAT STOLE HER BOYFRIEND ANYWAY, REMEMBER?
STOLE WHOSE BOYFRIEND?
ITSUKI...?
DO YOU THINK MAYBE MAGGIE WON'T SEE ANYONE BECAUSE SHE AND HOPEY HAD A SUPER, BIG FIGHT AND SHE'S WAY TOO UPSET...?
MAYBE SHE JUST DOESN'T CARE TO SEE YOU, DAPHNE. YOU EVER THINK OF THAT?
SYDYS
10

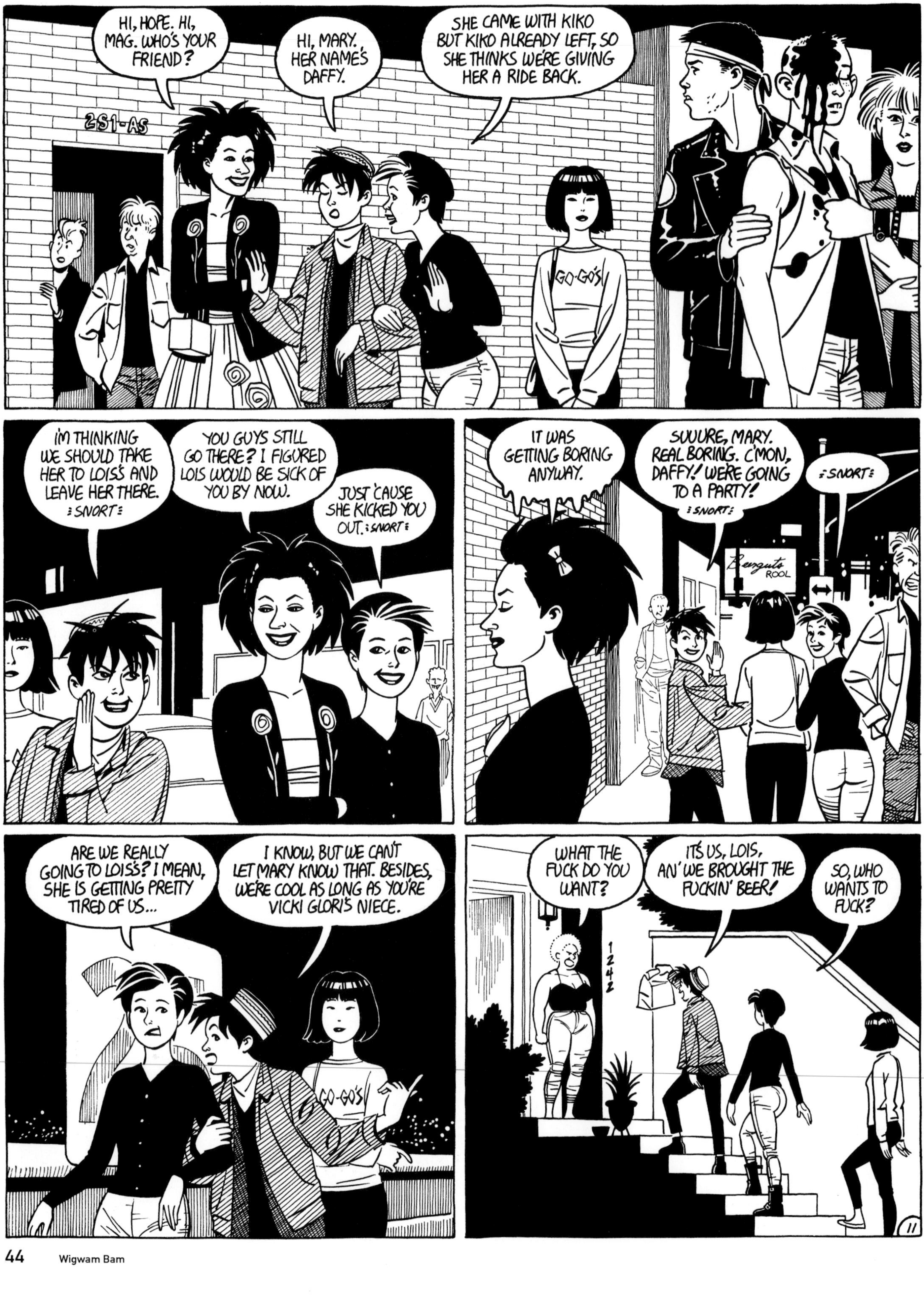
HI, HOPE. HI, MAG. WHO'S YOUR FRIEND?
HI, MARY. HER NAME'S DAFFY.
SHE CAME WITH KIKO BUT KIKO ALREADY LEFT, SO SHE THINKS WE'RE GIVING HER A RIDE BACK.
2S1-AS
GO-GO'S
I'M THINKING WE SHOULD TAKE HER TO LOIS'S AND LEAVE HER THERE. SNORT
YOU GUYS STILL GO THERE? I FIGURED LOIS WOULD BE SICK OF YOU BY NOW.
JUST 'CAUSE SHE KICKED YOU OUT. SNORT
IT WAS GETTING BORING ANYWAY.
SUUURE, MARY. REAL BORING. C'MON, DAFFY! WE'RE GOING TO A PARTY! SNORT
SNORT
ARE WE REALLY GOING TO LOIS'S? I MEAN, SHE IS GETTING PRETTY TIRED OF US...
I KNOW, BUT WE CAN'T LET MARY KNOW THAT. BESIDES, WE'RE COOL AS LONG AS YOU'RE VICKI GLORI'S NIECE.
GO-GO'S
WHAT THE FUCK DO YOU WANT?
IT'S US, LOIS, AN' WE BROUGHT THE FUCKIN' BEER!
SO, WHO WANTS TO FUCK?
1242
11

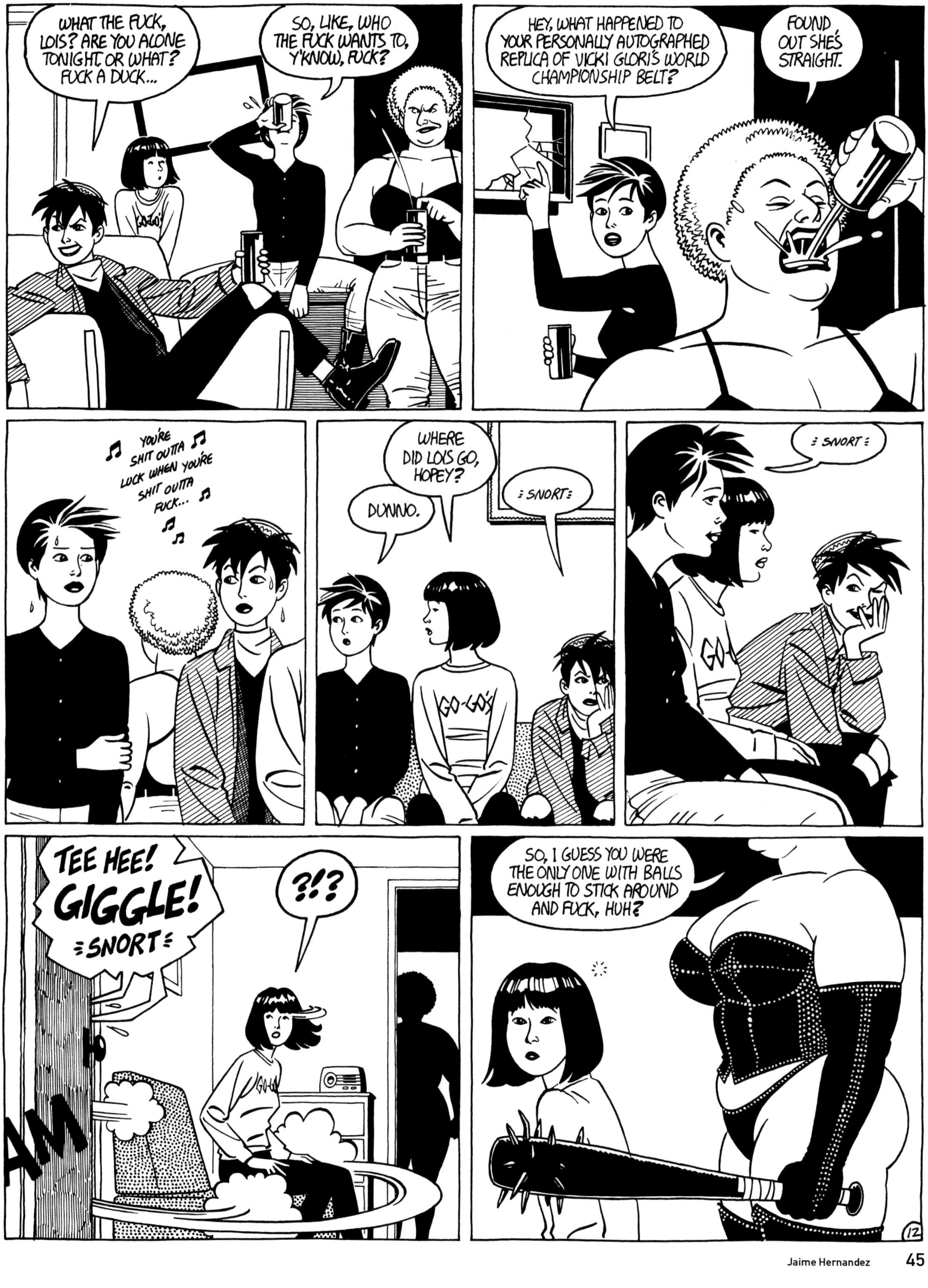
WHAT THE FUCK, LOIS? ARE YOU ALONE TONIGHT, OR WHAT? FUCK A DUCK...
SO, LIKE, WHO THE FUCK WANTS TO, Y'KNOW, FUCK?
HEY, WHAT HAPPENED TO YOUR PERSONALLY AUTOGRAPHED REPLICA OF VICKI GLORI'S WORLD CHAMPIONSHIP BELT?
FOUND OUT SHE'S STRAIGHT.
YOU'RE SHIT OUTTA LUCK WHEN YOU'RE SHIT OUTTA FUCK...
WHERE DID LOIS GO, HOPEY?
DUNNO.
SNORT
GO-GO'S
SNORT
TEE HEE! GIGGLE! SNORT
?!?
SO, I GUESS YOU WERE THE ONLY ONE WITH BALLS ENOUGH TO STICK AROUND AND FUCK, HUH?
12

WHO KNOWS? MAYBE THERE WAS A DEATH IN HER FAMILY AND THAT'S WHY MAGGIE WON'T...

WHY ARE YOU MAKING SUCH A BIG, FAT DEAL ABOUT IT? **WHO CARES?**

DAFFY HAS ONLY BEEN A CLOSE FRIEND TO THESE GIRLS SINCE YOU WERE ABOUT SIX OR SEVEN YEARS OLD!

NO, NAMI'S RIGHT. WHO CARES? I CERTAINLY DON'T ANY MORE.

AW, DON'T TALK LIKE THAT, DAFFY...

THERE SHE IS!

LOOK, DAPHNE! THERE SHE IS! IT'S YOUR FRIEND! LOOK, DAPHNE, LOOK!

WELL, WHAT ARE YOU WAITING FOR? DON'T LET HER GET AWAY!

THAT'S NOT MAGGIE!

IT'S NOT? THEN WHO IS IT?

?!

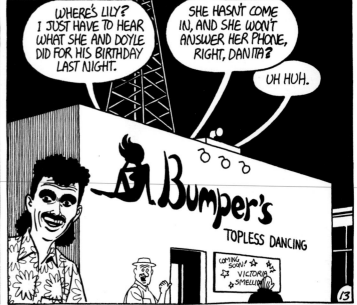

WHERE'S LILY? I JUST HAVE TO HEAR WHAT SHE AND DOYLE DID FOR HIS BIRTHDAY LAST NIGHT.

SHE HASN'T COME IN, AND SHE WON'T ANSWER HER PHONE, RIGHT, DANITA?

UH HUH.

Bumper's
TOPLESS DANCING

COMING SOON! ☆ ☆ VICTORIA ☆ SMELLI...

13

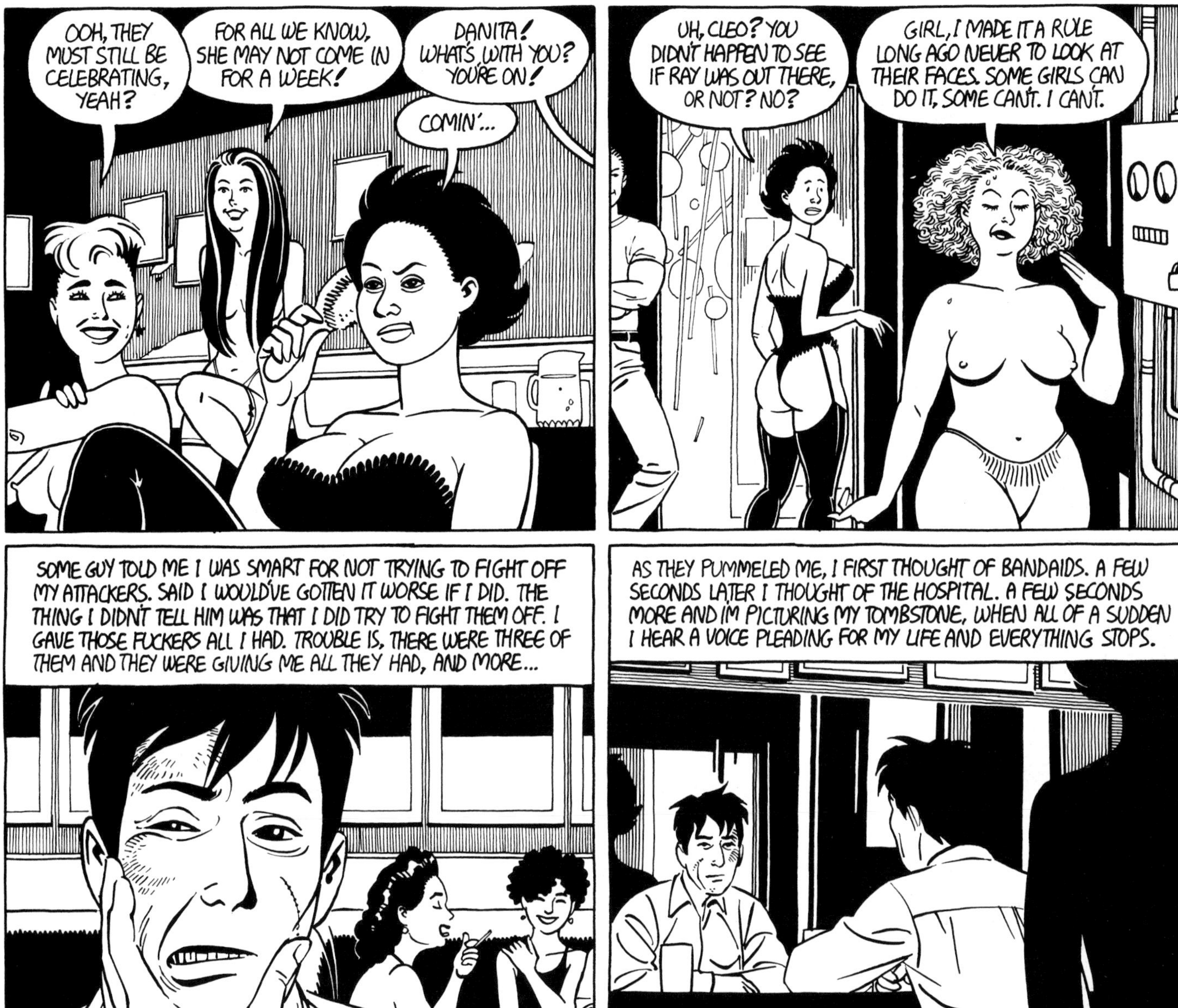
OOH, THEY MUST STILL BE CELEBRATING, YEAH?
FOR ALL WE KNOW, SHE MAY NOT COME IN FOR A WEEK!
DANITA! WHAT'S WITH YOU? YOU'RE ON!
COMIN'...
UH, CLEO? YOU DIDN'T HAPPEN TO SEE IF RAY WAS OUT THERE, OR NOT? NO?
GIRL, I MADE IT A RULE LONG AGO NEVER TO LOOK AT THEIR FACES. SOME GIRLS CAN DO IT, SOME CAN'T. I CAN'T.
SOME GUY TOLD ME I WAS SMART FOR NOT TRYING TO FIGHT OFF MY ATTACKERS. SAID I WOULD'VE GOTTEN IT WORSE IF I DID. THE THING I DIDN'T TELL HIM WAS THAT I DID TRY TO FIGHT THEM OFF. I GAVE THOSE FUCKERS ALL I HAD. TROUBLE IS, THERE WERE THREE OF THEM AND THEY WERE GIVING ME ALL THEY HAD, AND MORE...
AS THEY PUMMELED ME, I FIRST THOUGHT OF BANDAIDS. A FEW SECONDS LATER I THOUGHT OF THE HOSPITAL. A FEW SECONDS MORE AND I'M PICTURING MY TOMBSTONE, WHEN ALL OF A SUDDEN I HEAR A VOICE PLEADING FOR MY LIFE AND EVERYTHING STOPS.
WHEN I LOOK UP WITH MY ONE GOOD EYE TO SEE WHO MY GLORIOUS SAVIOR IS, I FIND IT'S THE SAME GUY WHO THREW THE FIRST PUNCH. IT'S ROBBIE GARCIA.
WHO IS ROBBIE GARCIA, YOU ASK? HE'S ONLY SOME FUCKING KID WHO PLAYS ON THE LITTLE LEAGUE TEAM MY BROTHER COACHES. THESE ASSHOLES WERE NO MORE THAN FIFTEEN FUCKING YEARS OLD...
SO AS I TRY TO PRETEND I DON'T FEEL LIKE I SLEPT WITH A LIVE JACKHAMMER, ROBBIE GOES ON NERVOUSLY APOLOGIZING THAT IT'S ALL A MISTAKE, THEY THOUGHT I WAS SOME-ONE ELSE, BLAH BLAH BLAH... AS IF I'M GONNA KICK HIS ASS. KICK HIS ASS...
14

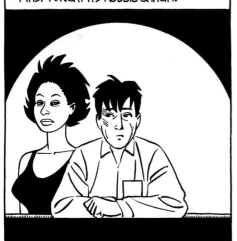

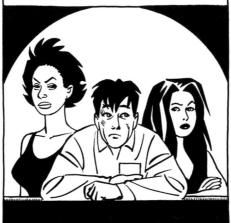

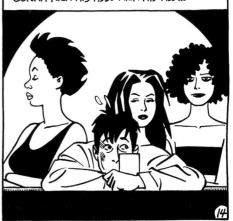

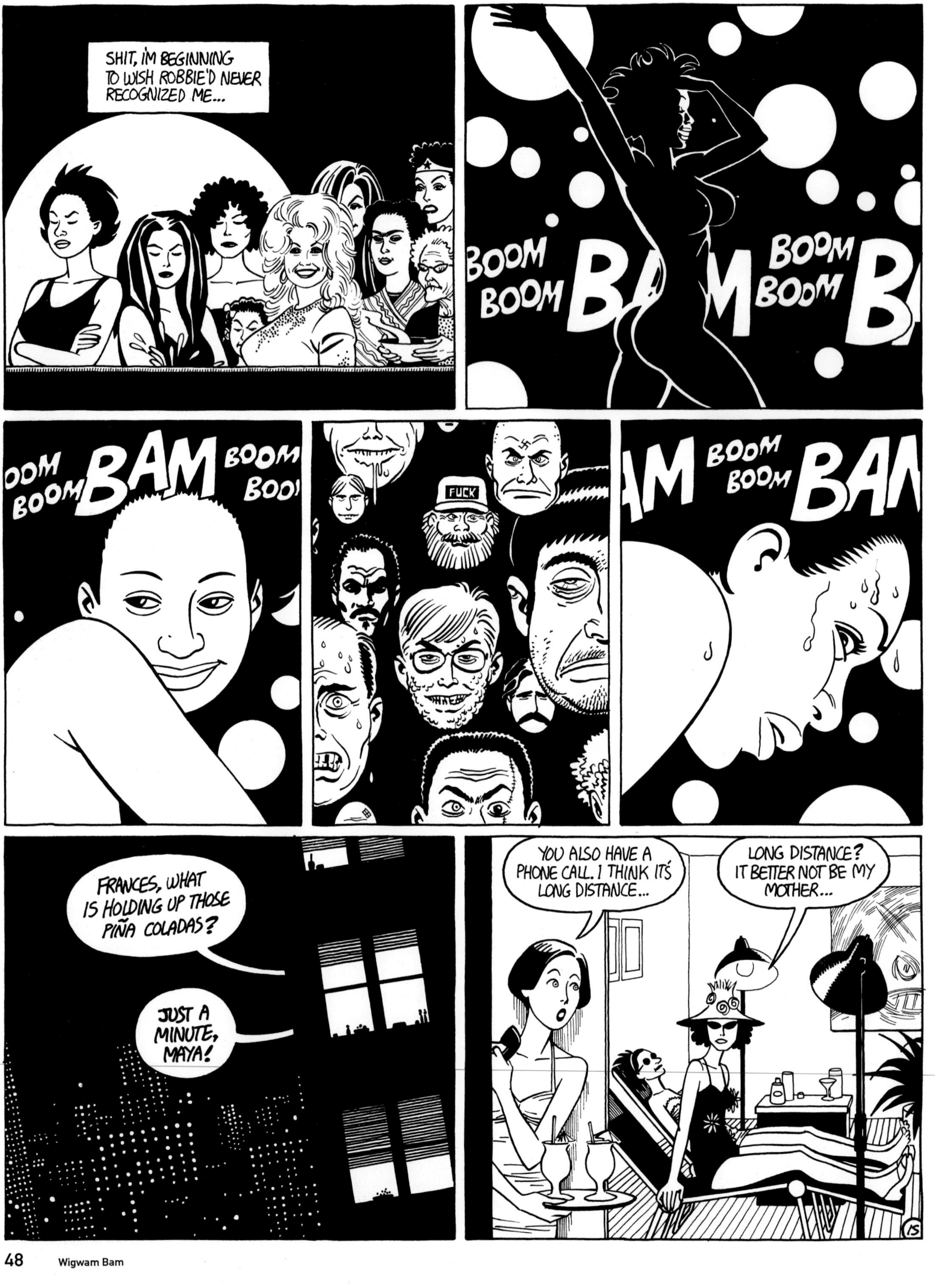
SHIT, I'M BEGINNING TO WISH ROBBIE'D NEVER RECOGNIZED ME...
BOOM BOOM BAM BOOM BOOM
OOM BOOM BAM BOOM BOO
FUCK
AM BOOM BOOM BAM
FRANCES, WHAT IS HOLDING UP THOSE PIÑA COLADAS?
JUST A MINUTE, MAYA!
YOU ALSO HAVE A PHONE CALL. I THINK IT'S LONG DISTANCE...
LONG DISTANCE? IT BETTER NOT BE MY MOTHER...
15

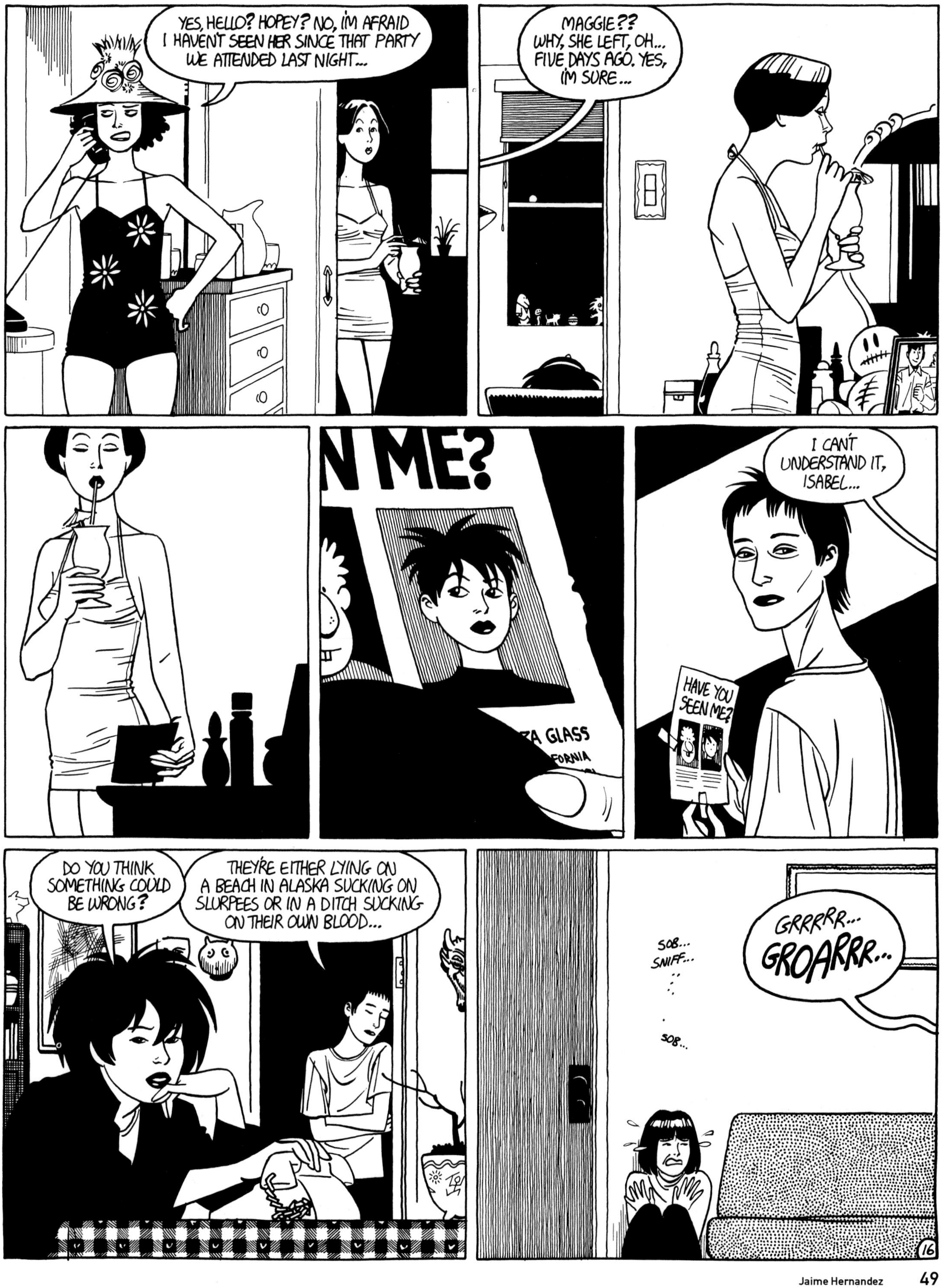

YES, HELLO? HOPEY? NO, I'M AFRAID I HAVEN'T SEEN HER SINCE THAT PARTY WE ATTENDED LAST NIGHT...
MAGGIE?? WHY, SHE LEFT, OH... FIVE DAYS AGO. YES, I'M SURE...
N ME?
ZA GLASS
FORNIA
I CAN'T UNDERSTAND IT, ISABEL...
HAVE YOU SEEN ME?
DO YOU THINK SOMETHING COULD BE WRONG?
THEY'RE EITHER LYING ON A BEACH IN ALASKA SUCKING ON SLURPEES OR IN A DITCH SUCKING ON THEIR OWN BLOOD...
SOB... SNIFF...
SOB...
GRRRRR... GROARRR...
16

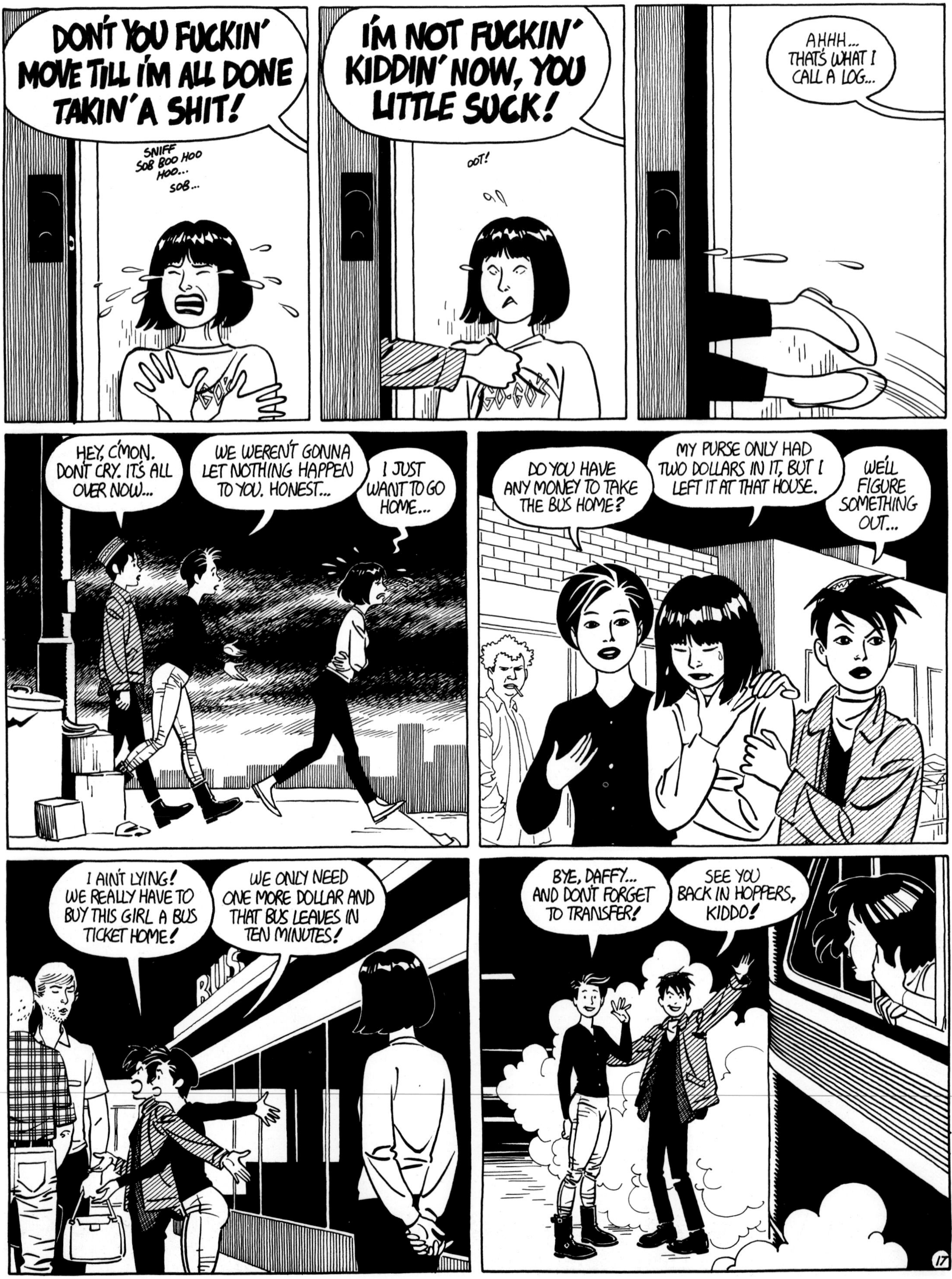
DON'T YOU FUCKIN' MOVE TILL I'M ALL DONE TAKIN' A SHIT!
SNIFF SOB BOO HOO HOO... SOB...
I'M NOT FUCKIN' KIDDIN' NOW, YOU LITTLE SUCK!
OOT!
AHHH... THAT'S WHAT I CALL A LOG...
HEY, C'MON. DON'T CRY. IT'S ALL OVER NOW...
WE WEREN'T GONNA LET NOTHING HAPPEN TO YOU. HONEST...
I JUST WANT TO GO HOME...
DO YOU HAVE ANY MONEY TO TAKE THE BUS HOME?
MY PURSE ONLY HAD TWO DOLLARS IN IT, BUT I LEFT IT AT THAT HOUSE.
WE'LL FIGURE SOMETHING OUT...
I AIN'T LYING! WE REALLY HAVE TO BUY THIS GIRL A BUS TICKET HOME!
WE ONLY NEED ONE MORE DOLLAR AND THAT BUS LEAVES IN TEN MINUTES!
BYE, DAFFY... AND DON'T FORGET TO TRANSFER!
SEE YOU BACK IN HOPPERS, KIDDO!
17

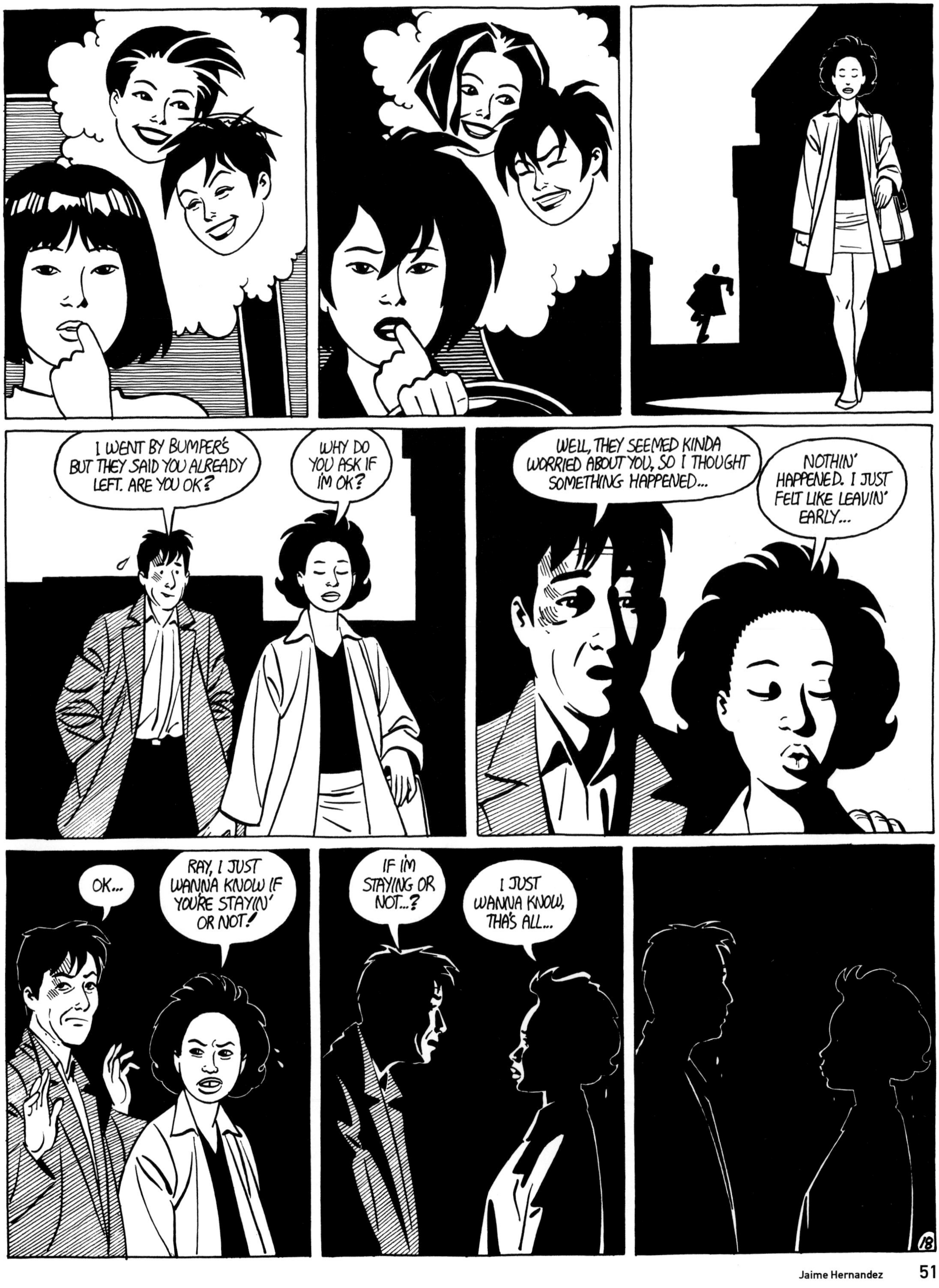
I WENT BY BUMPER'S BUT THEY SAID YOU ALREADY LEFT. ARE YOU OK?
WHY DO YOU ASK IF I'M OK?
WELL, THEY SEEMED KINDA WORRIED ABOUT YOU, SO I THOUGHT SOMETHING HAPPENED...
NOTHIN' HAPPENED. I JUST FELT LIKE LEAVIN' EARLY...
OK...
RAY, I JUST WANNA KNOW IF YOU'RE STAYIN' OR NOT!
IF I'M STAYING OR NOT...?
I JUST WANNA KNOW, THAT'S ALL...
18

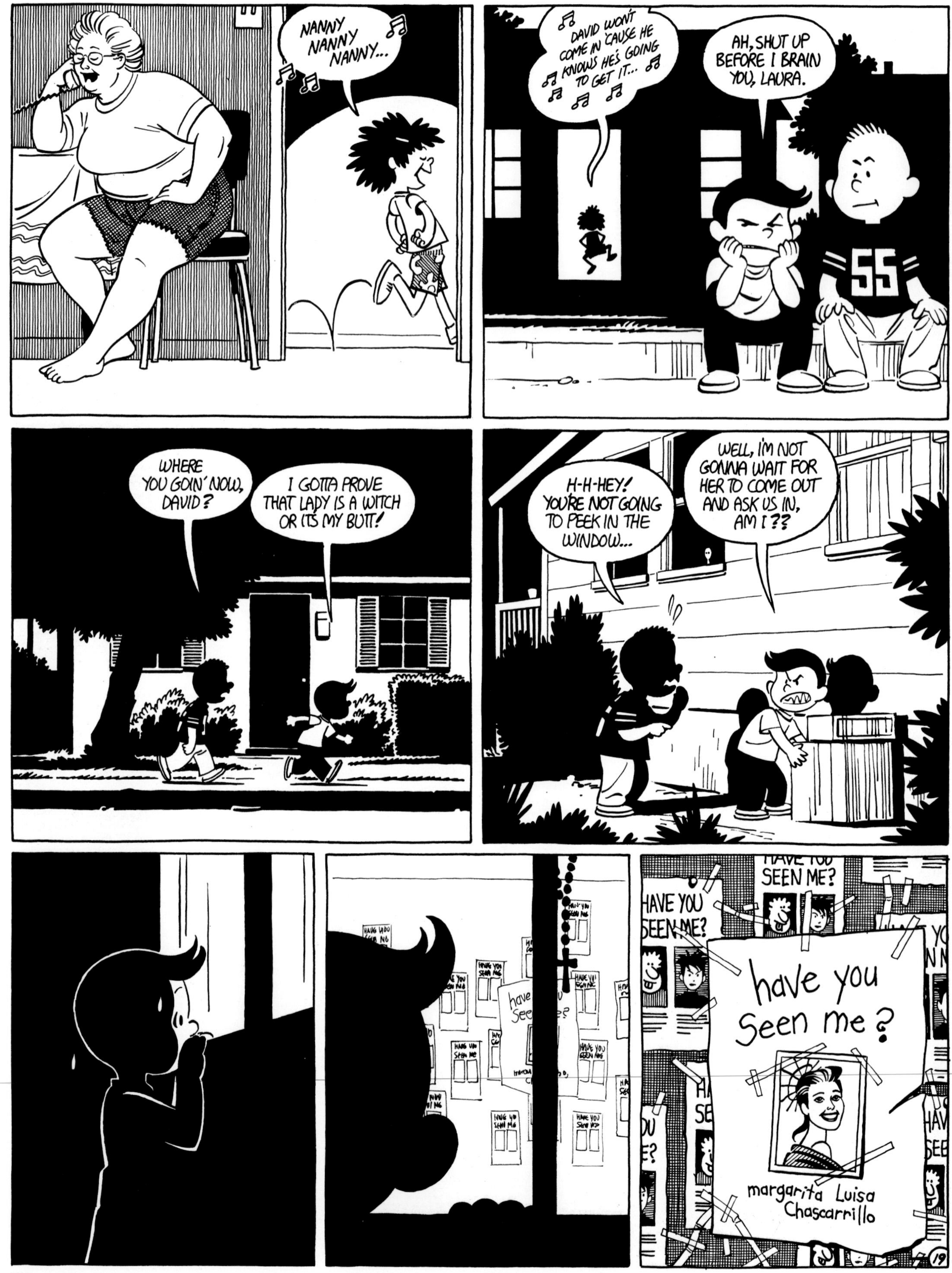
NANNY NANNY NANNY...
DAVID WON'T COME IN 'CAUSE HE KNOWS HE'S GOING TO GET IT...
AH, SHUT UP BEFORE I BRAIN YOU, LAURA.
55
WHERE YOU GOIN' NOW, DAVID?
I GOTTA PROVE THAT LADY IS A WITCH OR ITS MY BUTT!
H-H-HEY! YOU'RE NOT GOING TO PEEK IN THE WINDOW...
WELL, I'M NOT GONNA WAIT FOR HER TO COME OUT AND ASK US IN, AM I??
SEEN ME?
HAVE YOU SEEN ME?
have you Seen me?
margarita Luisa Chascarrillo
19

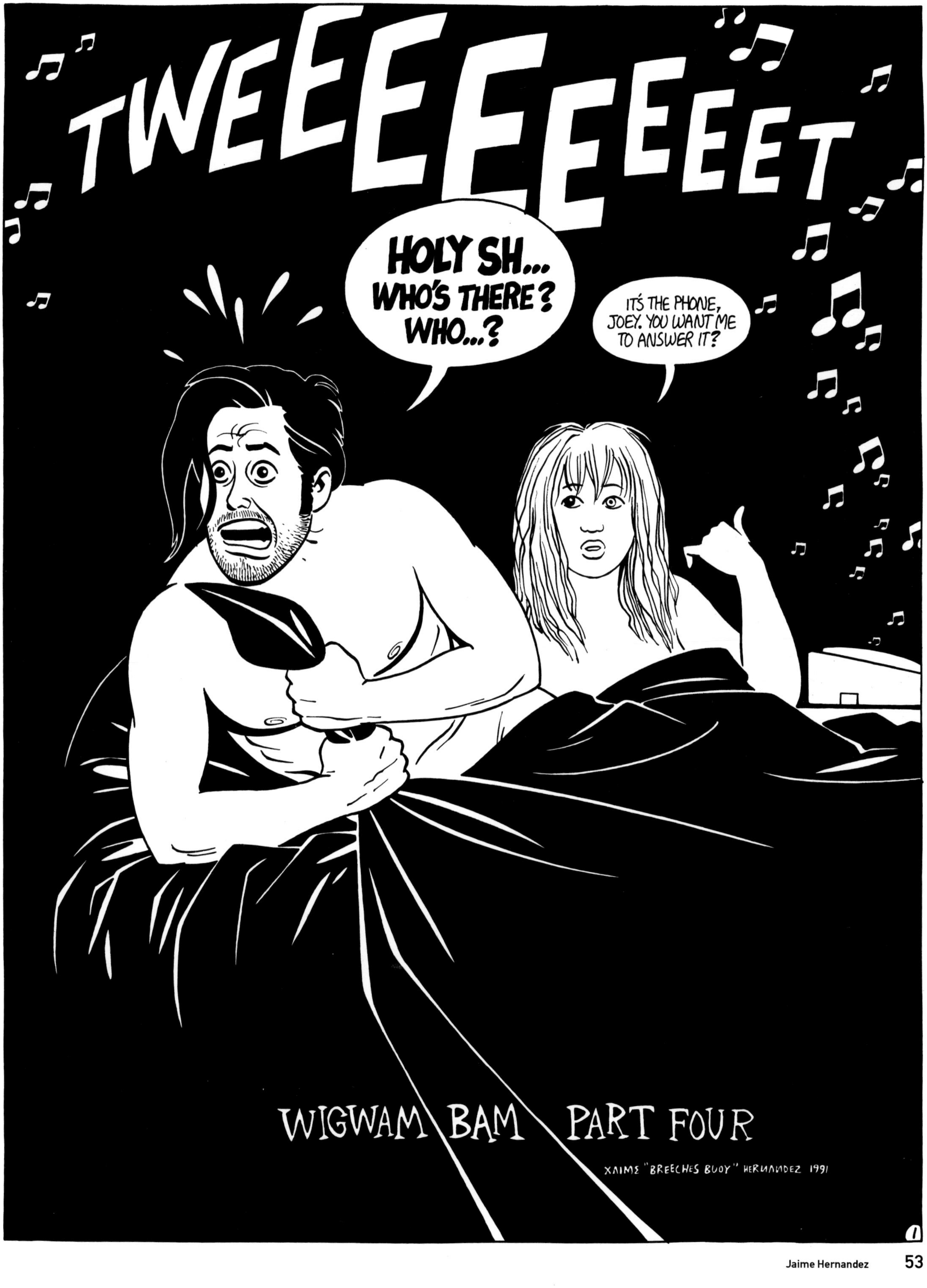
TWEEEEEEEET
HOLY SH... WHO'S THERE? WHO...?
IT'S THE PHONE, JOEY. YOU WANT ME TO ANSWER IT?
WIGWAM BAM PART FOUR
XAIME "BREECHES BUOY" HERNANDEZ 1991
1

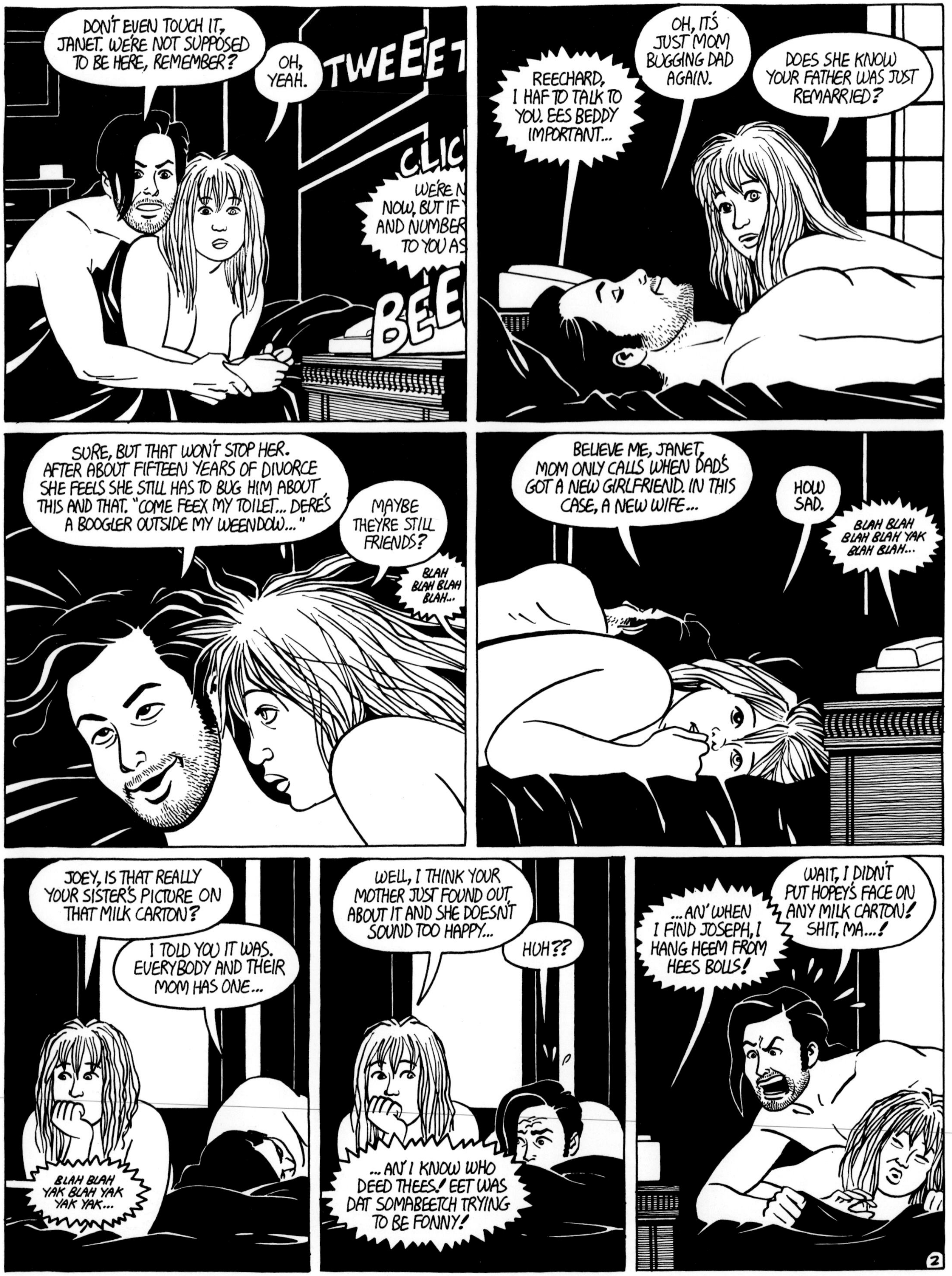
DON'T EVEN TOUCH IT, JANET. WE'RE NOT SUPPOSED TO BE HERE, REMEMBER?
OH, YEAH.
TWEEET
CLIC
WE'RE N NOW, BUT IF AND NUMBER TO YOU AS
BEE
REECHARD, I HAF TO TALK TO YOU. EES BEDDY IMPORTANT...
OH, IT'S JUST MOM BUGGING DAD AGAIN.
DOES SHE KNOW YOUR FATHER WAS JUST REMARRIED?
SURE, BUT THAT WON'T STOP HER. AFTER ABOUT FIFTEEN YEARS OF DIVORCE SHE FEELS SHE STILL HAS TO BUG HIM ABOUT THIS AND THAT. "COME FEEX MY TOILET... DERE'S A BOOGLER OUTSIDE MY WEENDOW..."
MAYBE THEY'RE STILL FRIENDS?
BLAH BLAH BLAH BLAH...
BELIEVE ME, JANET, MOM ONLY CALLS WHEN DAD'S GOT A NEW GIRLFRIEND. IN THIS CASE, A NEW WIFE...
HOW SAD.
BLAH BLAH BLAH BLAH YAK BLAH BLAH...
JOEY, IS THAT REALLY YOUR SISTER'S PICTURE ON THAT MILK CARTON?
I TOLD YOU IT WAS. EVERYBODY AND THEIR MOM HAS ONE...
BLAH BLAH YAK BLAH YAK YAK YAK...
WELL, I THINK YOUR MOTHER JUST FOUND OUT ABOUT IT AND SHE DOESN'T SOUND TOO HAPPY...
HUH??
...AN' I KNOW WHO DEED THEES! EET WAS DAT SOMABEETCH TRYING TO BE FONNY!
...AN' WHEN I FIND JOSEPH, I HANG HEEM FROM HEES BOLLS!
WAIT, I DIDN'T PUT HOPEY'S FACE ON ANY MILK CARTON! SHIT, MA...!
2

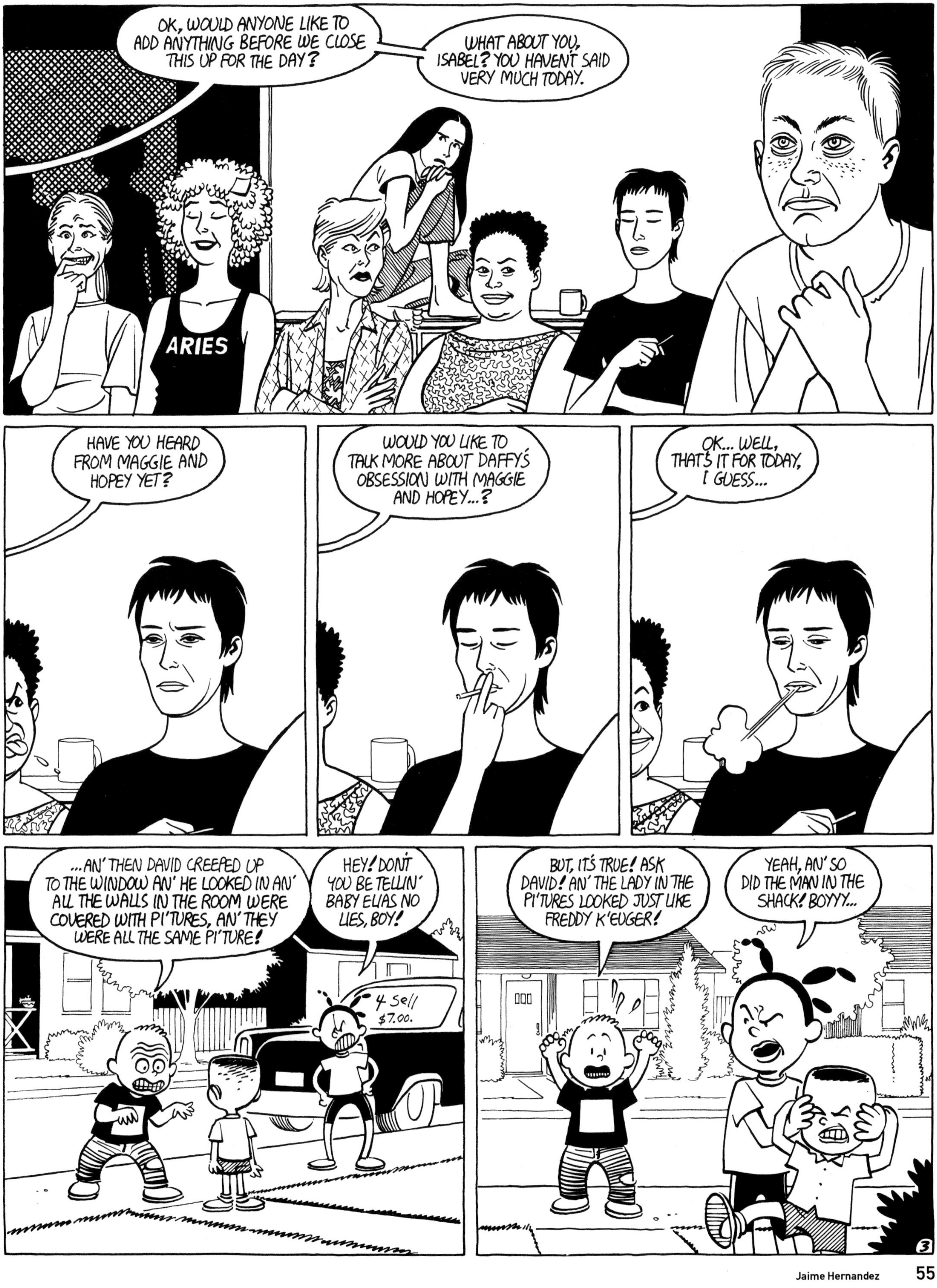
OK, WOULD ANYONE LIKE TO ADD ANYTHING BEFORE WE CLOSE THIS UP FOR THE DAY?
WHAT ABOUT YOU, ISABEL? YOU HAVEN'T SAID VERY MUCH TODAY.
ARIES
HAVE YOU HEARD FROM MAGGIE AND HOPEY YET?
WOULD YOU LIKE TO TALK MORE ABOUT DAFFY'S OBSESSION WITH MAGGIE AND HOPEY...?
OK... WELL, THAT'S IT FOR TODAY, I GUESS...
...AN' THEN DAVID CREEPED UP TO THE WINDOW AN' HE LOOKED IN AN' ALL THE WALLS IN THE ROOM WERE COVERED WITH PI'TURES, AN' THEY WERE ALL THE SAME PI'TURE!
HEY! DON'T YOU BE TELLIN' BABY ELIAS NO LIES, BOY!
4 sell $7.00.
BUT, IT'S TRUE! ASK DAVID! AN' THE LADY IN THE PI'TURES LOOKED JUST LIKE FREDDY K'EUGER!
YEAH, AN' SO DID THE MAN IN THE SHACK! BOYYY...
3

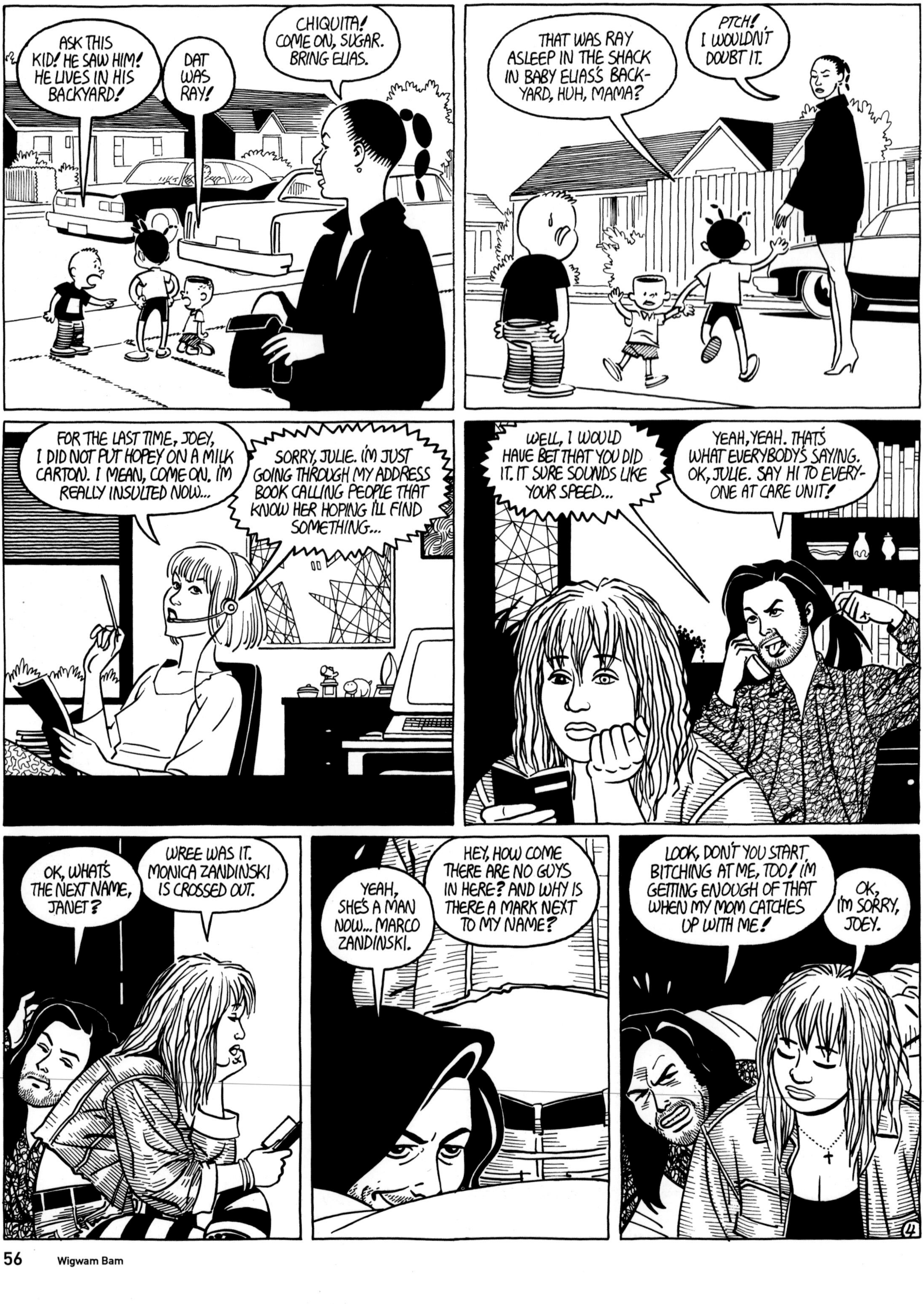
ASK THIS KID! HE SAW HIM! HE LIVES IN HIS BACKYARD!
DAT WAS RAY!
CHIQUITA! COME ON, SUGAR. BRING ELIAS.
THAT WAS RAY ASLEEP IN THE SHACK IN BABY ELIAS'S BACK-YARD, HUH, MAMA?
PTCH! I WOULDN'T DOUBT IT.
FOR THE LAST TIME, JOEY, I DID NOT PUT HOPEY ON A MILK CARTON. I MEAN, COME ON. I'M REALLY INSULTED NOW...
SORRY, JULIE. I'M JUST GOING THROUGH MY ADDRESS BOOK CALLING PEOPLE THAT KNOW HER HOPING I'LL FIND SOMETHING...
WELL, I WOULD HAVE BET THAT YOU DID IT. IT SURE SOUNDS LIKE YOUR SPEED...
YEAH, YEAH. THAT'S WHAT EVERYBODY'S SAYING. OK, JULIE. SAY HI TO EVERY-ONE AT CARE UNIT!
OK, WHAT'S THE NEXT NAME, JANET?
WREE WAS IT. MONICA ZANDINSKI IS CROSSED OUT.
YEAH, SHE'S A MAN NOW... MARCO ZANDINSKI.
HEY, HOW COME THERE ARE NO GUYS IN HERE? AND WHY IS THERE A MARK NEXT TO MY NAME?
LOOK, DON'T YOU START BITCHING AT ME, TOO! I'M GETTING ENOUGH OF THAT WHEN MY MOM CATCHES UP WITH ME!
OK, I'M SORRY, JOEY.
4

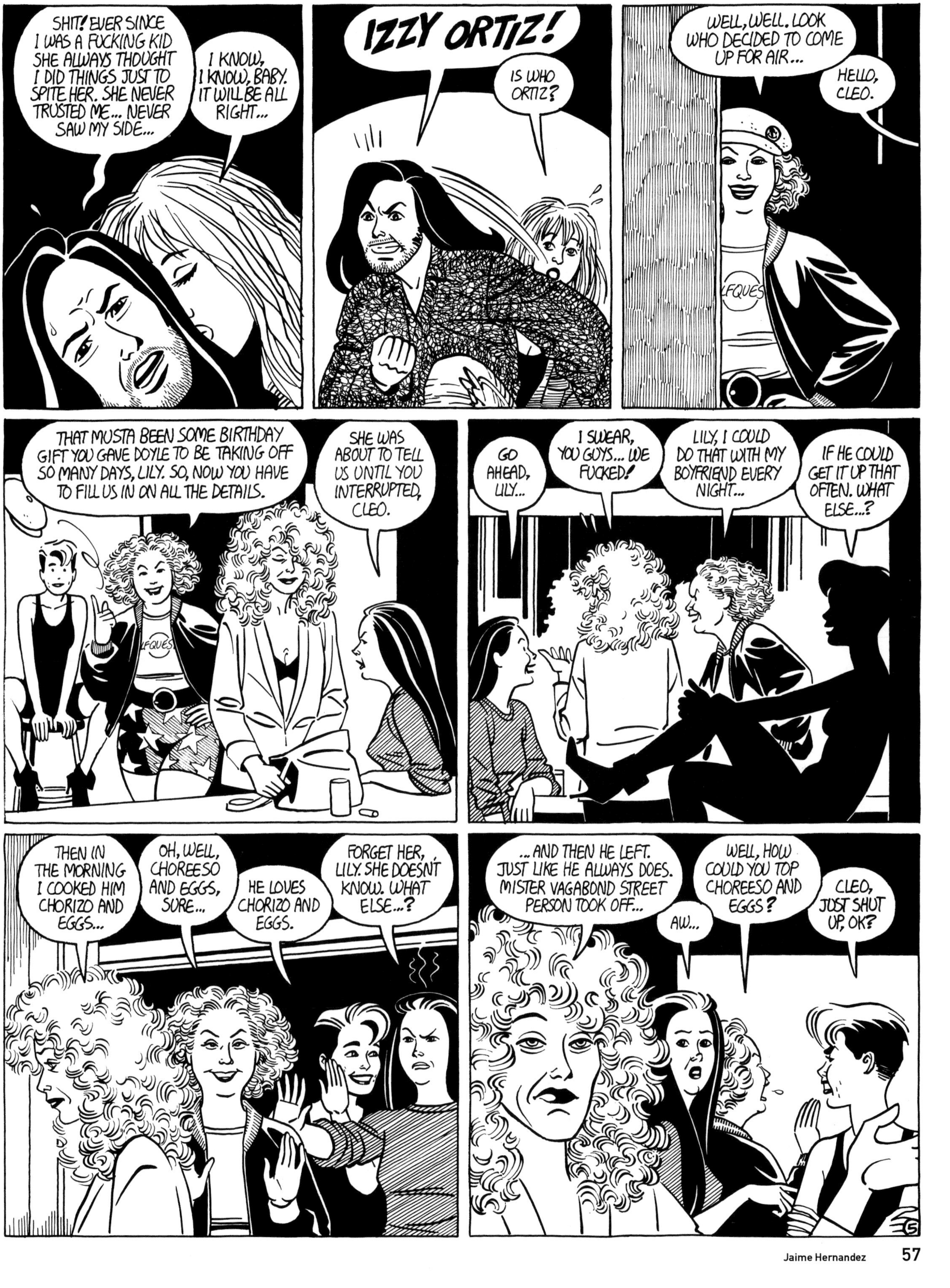
SHIT! EVER SINCE I WAS A FUCKING KID SHE ALWAYS THOUGHT I DID THINGS JUST TO SPITE HER. SHE NEVER TRUSTED ME... NEVER SAW MY SIDE...
I KNOW, I KNOW, BABY. IT WILL BE ALL RIGHT...
IZZY ORTIZ!
IS WHO ORTIZ?
WELL, WELL. LOOK WHO DECIDED TO COME UP FOR AIR...
HELLO, CLEO.
LFQUES
THAT MUSTA BEEN SOME BIRTHDAY GIFT YOU GAVE DOYLE TO BE TAKING OFF SO MANY DAYS, LILY. SO, NOW YOU HAVE TO FILL US IN ON ALL THE DETAILS.
SHE WAS ABOUT TO TELL US UNTIL YOU INTERRUPTED, CLEO.
LFQUES
GO AHEAD, LILY...
I SWEAR, YOU GUYS... WE FUCKED!
LILY, I COULD DO THAT WITH MY BOYFRIEND EVERY NIGHT...
IF HE COULD GET IT UP THAT OFTEN. WHAT ELSE...?
THEN IN THE MORNING I COOKED HIM CHORIZO AND EGGS...
OH, WELL, CHOREESO AND EGGS, SURE...
HE LOVES CHORIZO AND EGGS.
FORGET HER, LILY. SHE DOESN'T KNOW. WHAT ELSE...?
...AND THEN HE LEFT. JUST LIKE HE ALWAYS DOES. MISTER VAGABOND STREET PERSON TOOK OFF...
AW...
WELL, HOW COULD YOU TOP CHOREESO AND EGGS?
CLEO, JUST SHUT UP, OK?
5

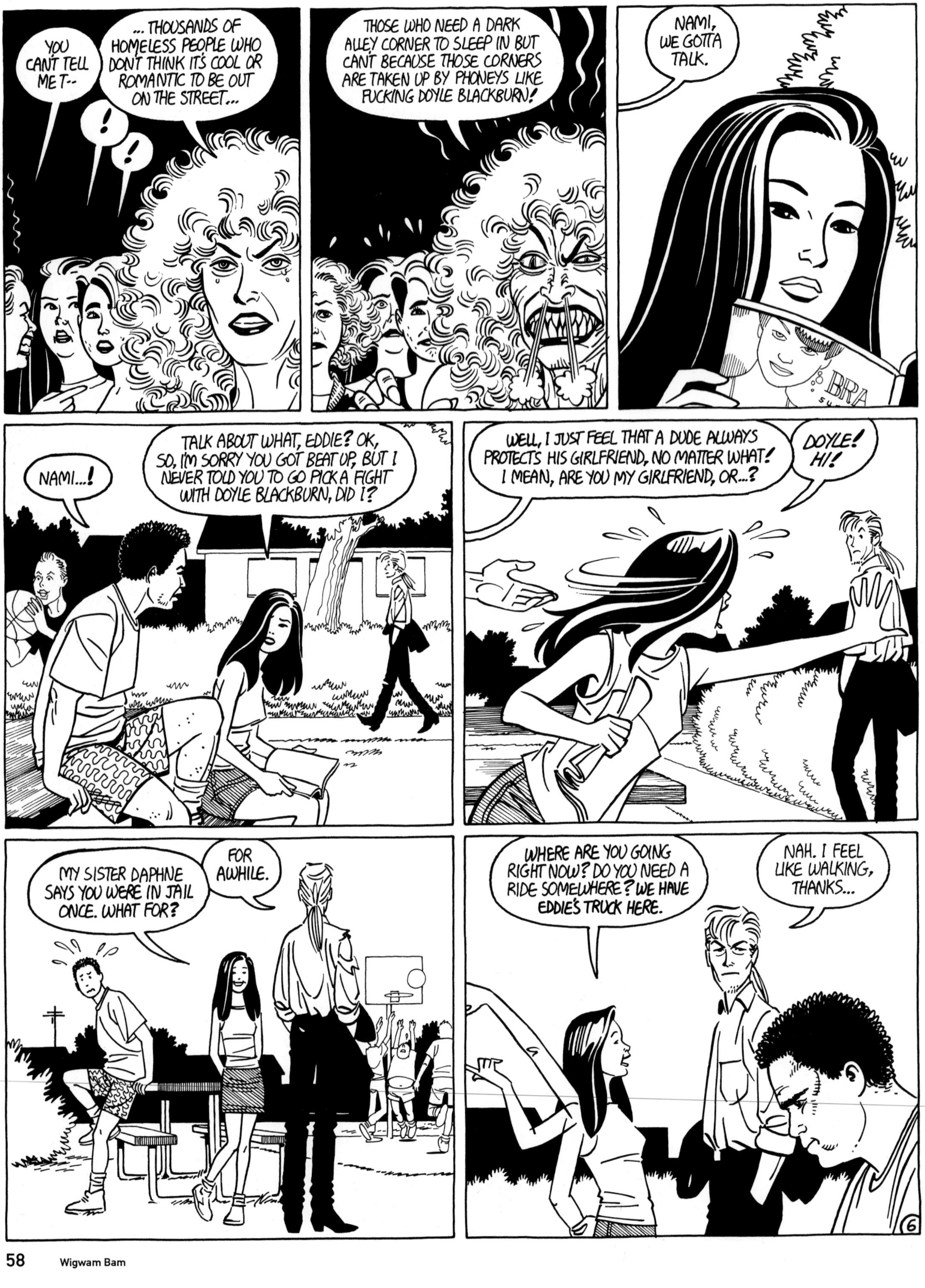
YOU CAN'T TELL ME T--
...THOUSANDS OF HOMELESS PEOPLE WHO DON'T THINK IT'S COOL OR ROMANTIC TO BE OUT ON THE STREET...
!
!
THOSE WHO NEED A DARK ALLEY CORNER TO SLEEP IN BUT CAN'T BECAUSE THOSE CORNERS ARE TAKEN UP BY PHONEYS LIKE FUCKING DOYLE BLACKBURN!
NAMI, WE GOTTA TALK.
BRA
NAMI...!
TALK ABOUT WHAT, EDDIE? OK, SO, I'M SORRY YOU GOT BEAT UP, BUT I NEVER TOLD YOU TO GO PICK A FIGHT WITH DOYLE BLACKBURN, DID I?
WELL, I JUST FEEL THAT A DUDE ALWAYS PROTECTS HIS GIRLFRIEND, NO MATTER WHAT! I MEAN, ARE YOU MY GIRLFRIEND, OR...?
DOYLE! HI!
MY SISTER DAPHNE SAYS YOU WERE IN JAIL ONCE. WHAT FOR?
FOR AWHILE.
WHERE ARE YOU GOING RIGHT NOW? DO YOU NEED A RIDE SOMEWHERE? WE HAVE EDDIE'S TRUCK HERE.
NAH. I FEEL LIKE WALKING, THANKS...
6

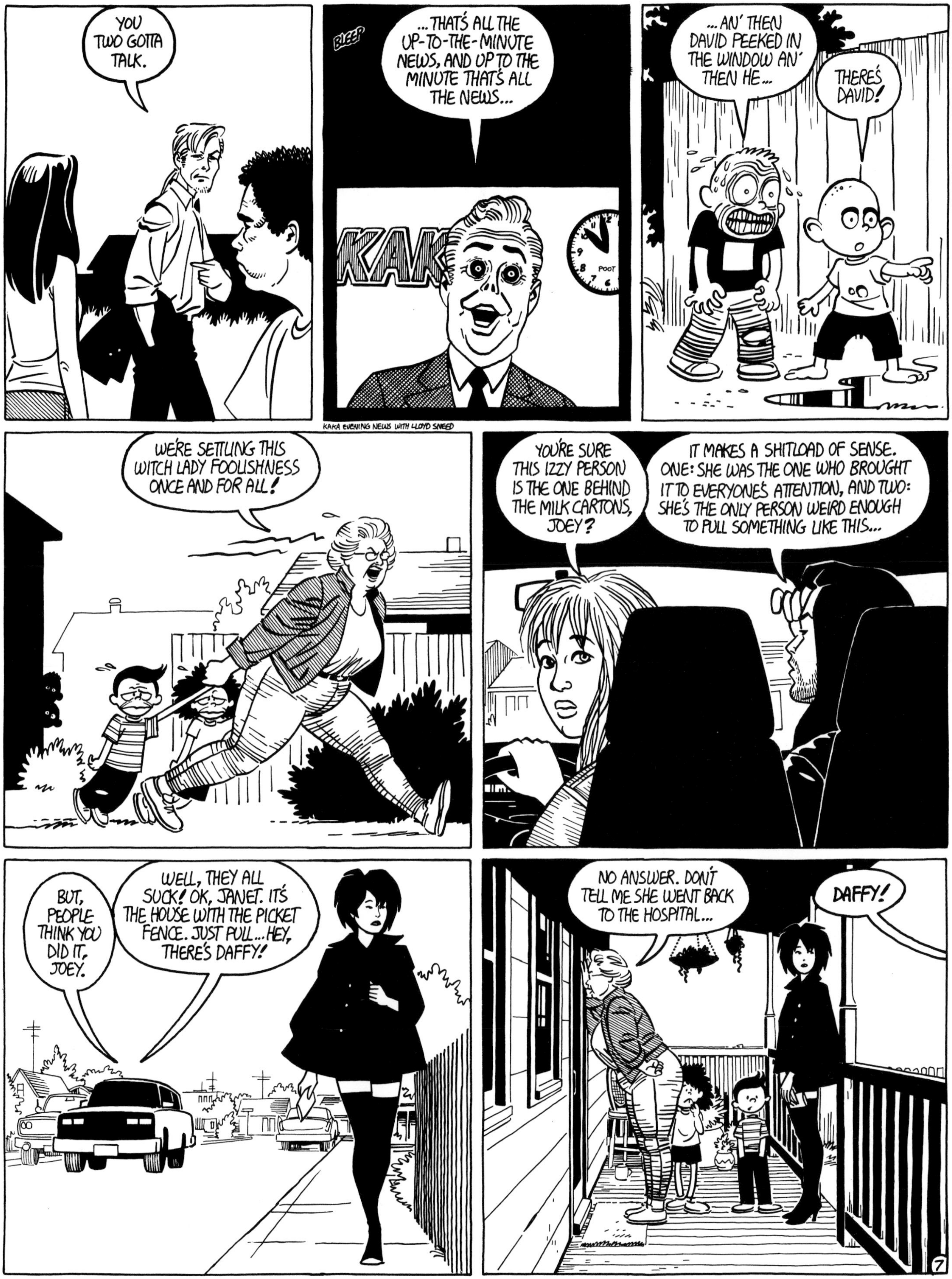
YOU TWO GOTTA TALK.
BLEEP
...THAT'S ALL THE UP-TO-THE-MINUTE NEWS, AND UP TO THE MINUTE THAT'S ALL THE NEWS...
KAK
POOT
KAKA EVENING NEWS WITH LLOYD SNEED
...AN' THEN DAVID PEEKED IN THE WINDOW AN' THEN HE...
THERE'S DAVID!
WE'RE SETTLING THIS WITCH LADY FOOLISHNESS ONCE AND FOR ALL!
YOU'RE SURE THIS IZZY PERSON IS THE ONE BEHIND THE MILK CARTONS, JOEY?
IT MAKES A SHITLOAD OF SENSE. ONE: SHE WAS THE ONE WHO BROUGHT IT TO EVERYONE'S ATTENTION, AND TWO: SHE'S THE ONLY PERSON WEIRD ENOUGH TO PULL SOMETHING LIKE THIS...
BUT, PEOPLE THINK YOU DID IT, JOEY.
WELL, THEY ALL SUCK! OK, JANET. IT'S THE HOUSE WITH THE PICKET FENCE. JUST PULL...HEY, THERE'S DAFFY!
NO ANSWER. DON'T TELL ME SHE WENT BACK TO THE HOSPITAL...
DAFFY!
7

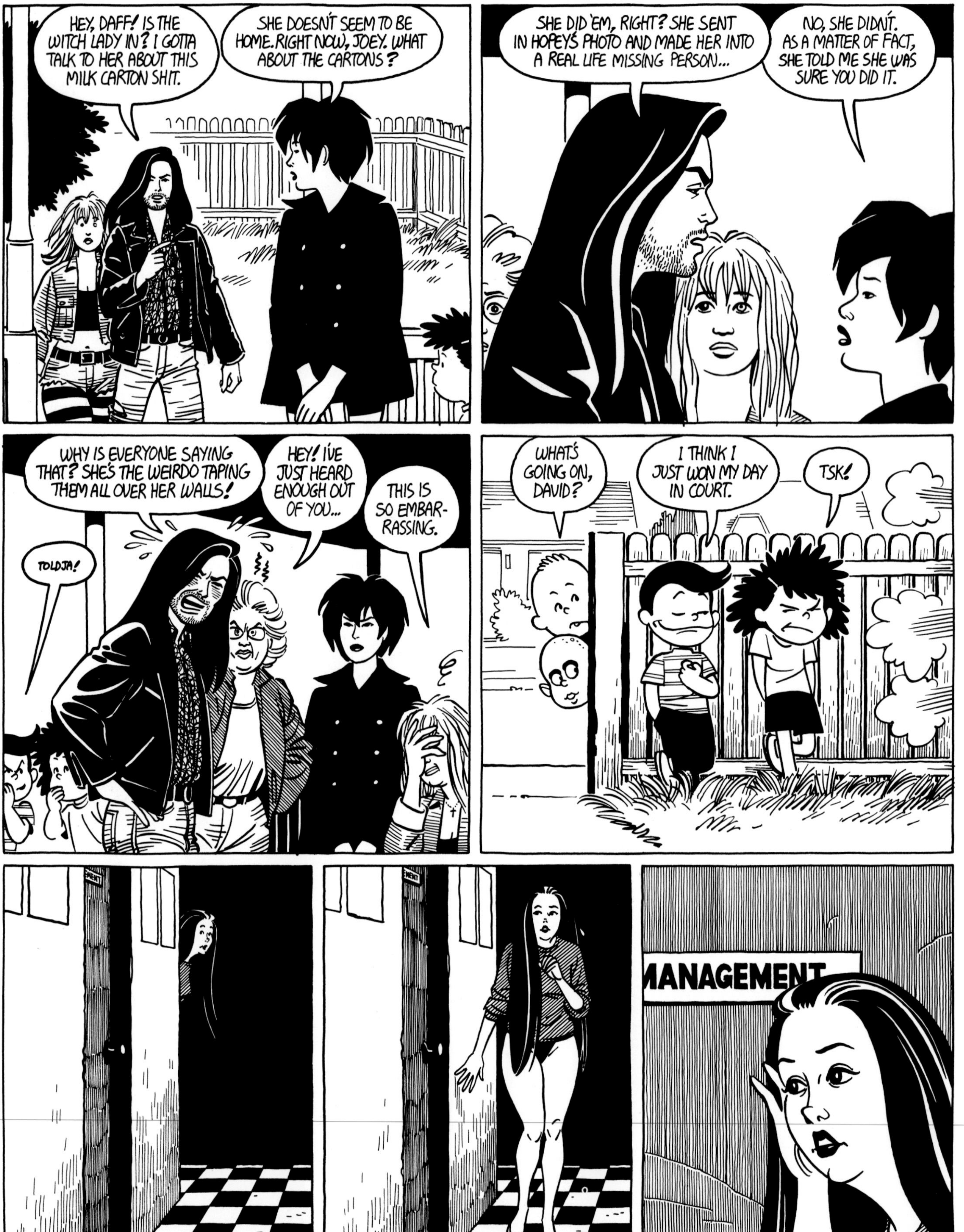
HEY, DAFF! IS THE WITCH LADY IN? I GOTTA TALK TO HER ABOUT THIS MILK CARTON SHIT.
SHE DOESN'T SEEM TO BE HOME. RIGHT NOW, JOEY. WHAT ABOUT THE CARTONS?
SHE DID 'EM, RIGHT? SHE SENT IN HOPEY'S PHOTO AND MADE HER INTO A REAL LIFE MISSING PERSON...
NO, SHE DIDN'T. AS A MATTER OF FACT, SHE TOLD ME SHE WAS SURE YOU DID IT.
WHY IS EVERYONE SAYING THAT? SHE'S THE WEIRDO TAPING THEM ALL OVER HER WALLS!
TOLDJA!
HEY! I'VE JUST HEARD ENOUGH OUT OF YOU...
THIS IS SO EMBARRASSING.
WHAT'S GOING ON, DAVID?
I THINK I JUST WON MY DAY IN COURT.
TSK!
MANAGEMENT
8

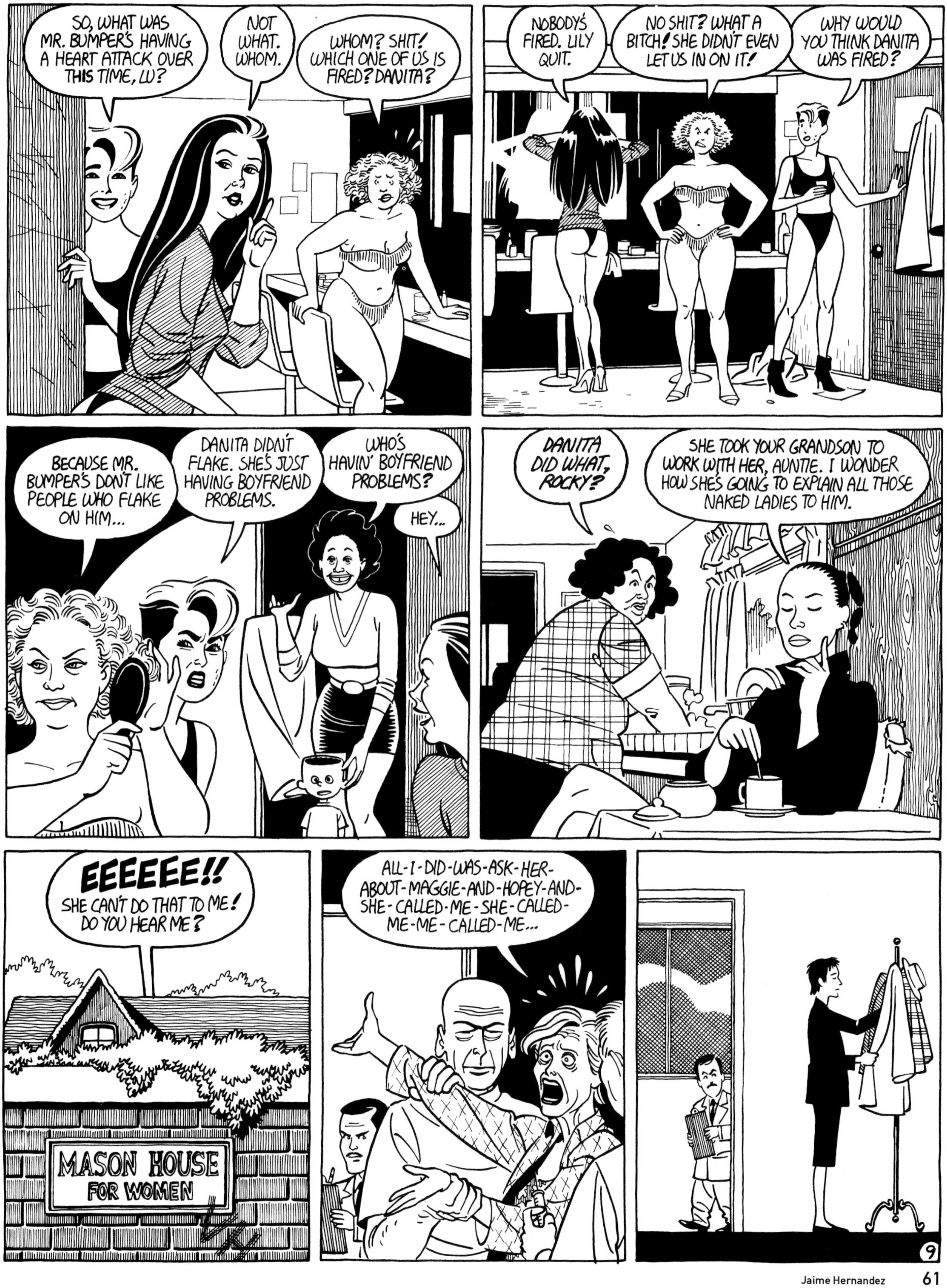

SO, WHAT WAS MR. BUMPER'S HAVING A HEART ATTACK OVER THIS TIME, LU?
NOT WHAT. WHOM.
WHOM? SHIT! WHICH ONE OF US IS FIRED? DANITA?
NOBODY'S FIRED. LILY QUIT.
NO SHIT? WHAT A BITCH! SHE DIDN'T EVEN LET US IN ON IT!
WHY WOULD YOU THINK DANITA WAS FIRED?
BECAUSE MR. BUMPER'S DON'T LIKE PEOPLE WHO FLAKE ON HIM...
DANITA DIDN'T FLAKE. SHE'S JUST HAVING BOYFRIEND PROBLEMS.
WHO'S HAVIN' BOYFRIEND PROBLEMS?
HEY...
DANITA DID WHAT, ROCKY?
SHE TOOK YOUR GRANDSON TO WORK WITH HER, AUNTIE. I WONDER HOW SHE'S GOING TO EXPLAIN ALL THOSE NAKED LADIES TO HIM.
EEEEEE!! SHE CAN'T DO THAT TO ME! DO YOU HEAR ME?
MASON HOUSE FOR WOMEN
ALL-I-DID-WAS-ASK-HER-ABOUT-MAGGIE-AND-HOPEY-AND-SHE-CALLED-ME-SHE-CALLED-ME-ME-CALLED-ME...
9

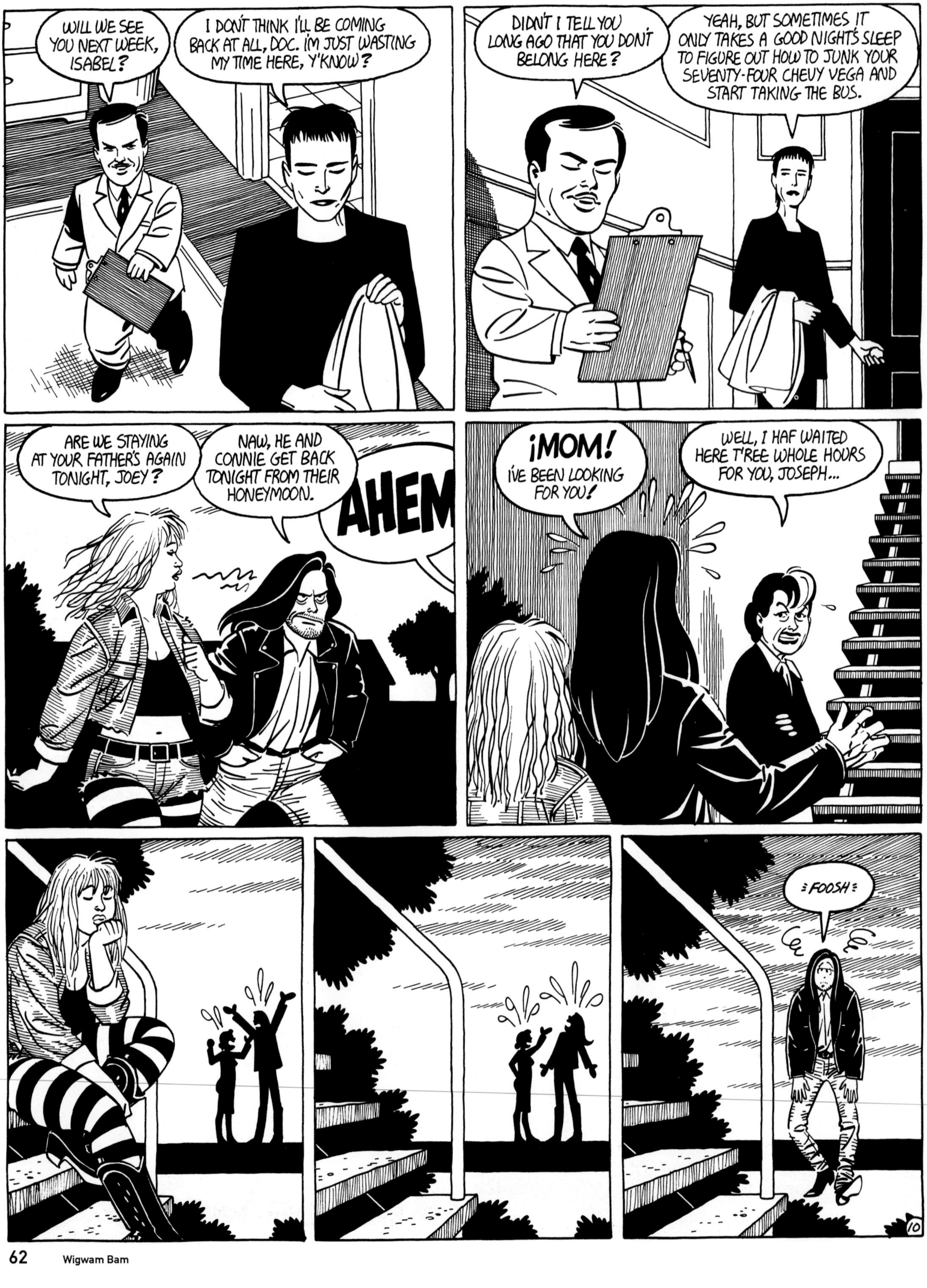
WILL WE SEE YOU NEXT WEEK, ISABEL?
I DON'T THINK I'LL BE COMING BACK AT ALL, DOC. I'M JUST WASTING MY TIME HERE, Y'KNOW?
DIDN'T I TELL YOU LONG AGO THAT YOU DON'T BELONG HERE?
YEAH, BUT SOMETIMES IT ONLY TAKES A GOOD NIGHT'S SLEEP TO FIGURE OUT HOW TO JUNK YOUR SEVENTY-FOUR CHEVY VEGA AND START TAKING THE BUS.
ARE WE STAYING AT YOUR FATHER'S AGAIN TONIGHT, JOEY?
NAW, HE AND CONNIE GET BACK TONIGHT FROM THEIR HONEYMOON.
AHEM
¡MOM! I'VE BEEN LOOKING FOR YOU!
WELL, I HAF WAITED HERE T'REE WHOLE HOURS FOR YOU, JOSEPH...
FOOSH
10

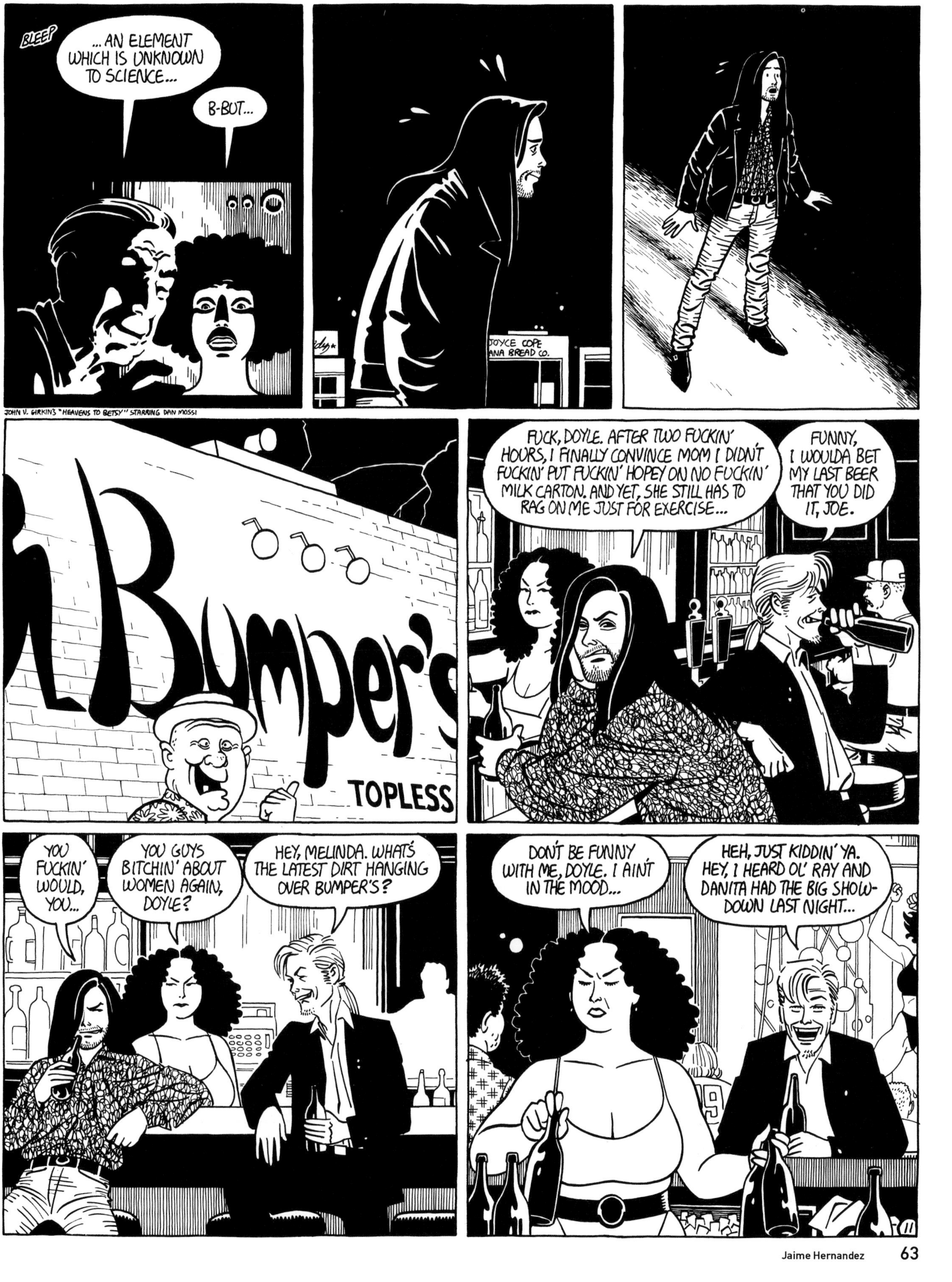

BLEEP
...AN ELEMENT WHICH IS UNKNOWN TO SCIENCE...
B-BUT...
JOYCE COPE
ANA BREAD CO.
JOHN V. GIRKIN'S "HEAVENS TO BETSY" STARRING DAN MOSSI
Bumper's
TOPLESS
FUCK, DOYLE. AFTER TWO FUCKIN' HOURS, I FINALLY CONVINCE MOM I DIDN'T FUCKIN' PUT FUCKIN' HOPEY ON NO FUCKIN' MILK CARTON. AND YET, SHE STILL HAS TO RAG ON ME JUST FOR EXERCISE...
FUNNY, I WOULDA BET MY LAST BEER THAT YOU DID IT, JOE.
YOU FUCKIN' WOULD, YOU...
YOU GUYS BITCHIN' ABOUT WOMEN AGAIN, DOYLE?
HEY, MELINDA. WHAT'S THE LATEST DIRT HANGING OVER BUMPER'S?
DON'T BE FUNNY WITH ME, DOYLE. I AIN'T IN THE MOOD...
HEH, JUST KIDDIN' YA. HEY, I HEARD OL' RAY AND DANITA HAD THE BIG SHOW-DOWN LAST NIGHT...
11

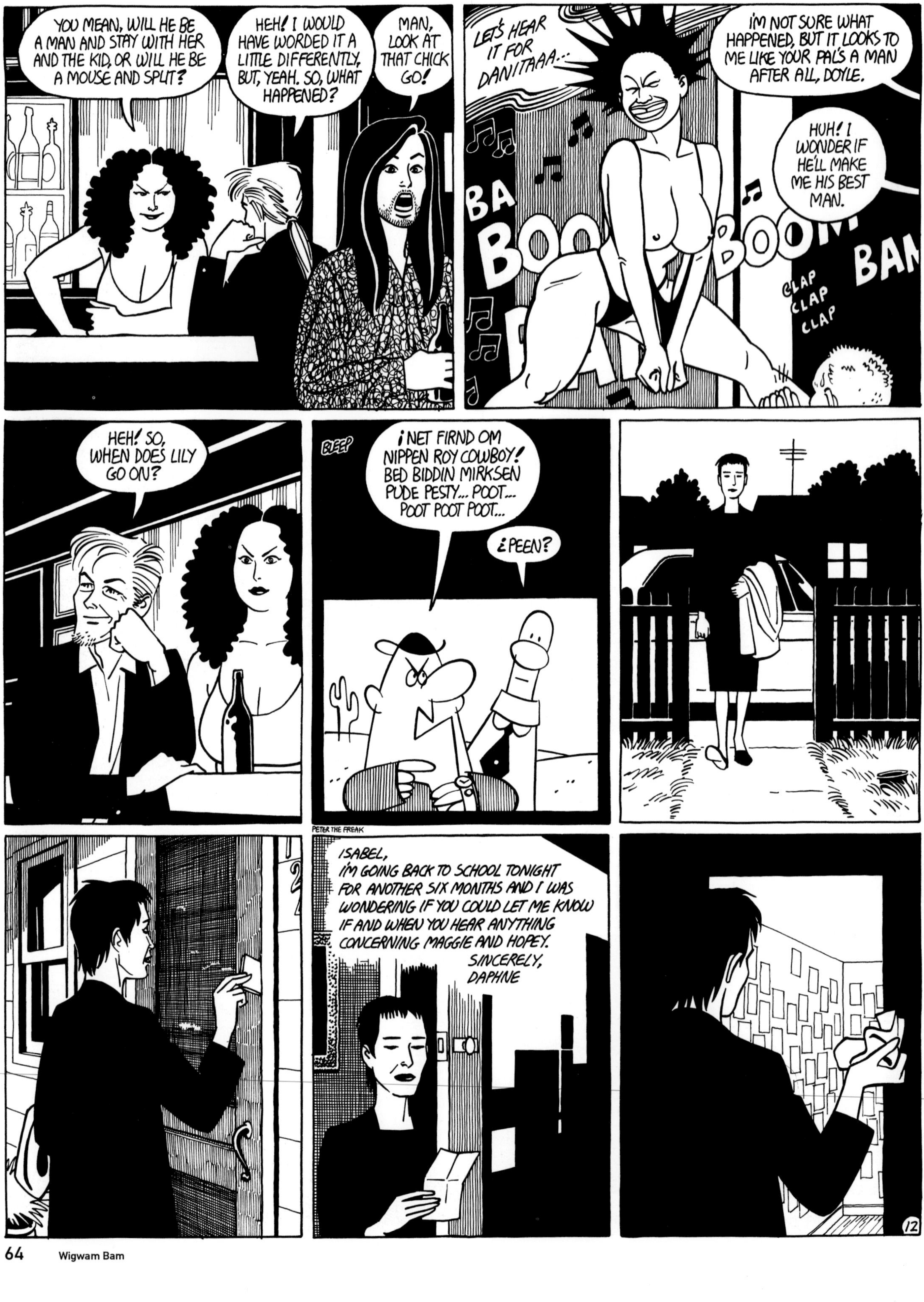

YOU MEAN, WILL HE BE A MAN AND STAY WITH HER AND THE KID, OR WILL HE BE A MOUSE AND SPLIT?
HEH! I WOULD HAVE WORDED IT A LITTLE DIFFERENTLY, BUT, YEAH. SO, WHAT HAPPENED?
MAN, LOOK AT THAT CHICK GO!
LET'S HEAR IT FOR DANITAAA...
I'M NOT SURE WHAT HAPPENED, BUT IT LOOKS TO ME LIKE YOUR PAL'S A MAN AFTER ALL, DOYLE.
HUH! I WONDER IF HE'LL MAKE ME HIS BEST MAN.
BA BOOM BOOM BAM
CLAP CLAP CLAP
HEH! SO, WHEN DOES LILY GO ON?
BLEEP
¡NET FIRND OM NIPPEN ROY COWBOY! BED BIDDIN MIRKSEN PUDE PESTY... POOT... POOT POOT POOT...
¿PEEN?
PETER THE FREAK
ISABEL,
I'M GOING BACK TO SCHOOL TONIGHT FOR ANOTHER SIX MONTHS AND I WAS WONDERING IF YOU COULD LET ME KNOW IF AND WHEN YOU HEAR ANYTHING CONCERNING MAGGIE AND HOPEY.
SINCERELY,
DAPHNE
12

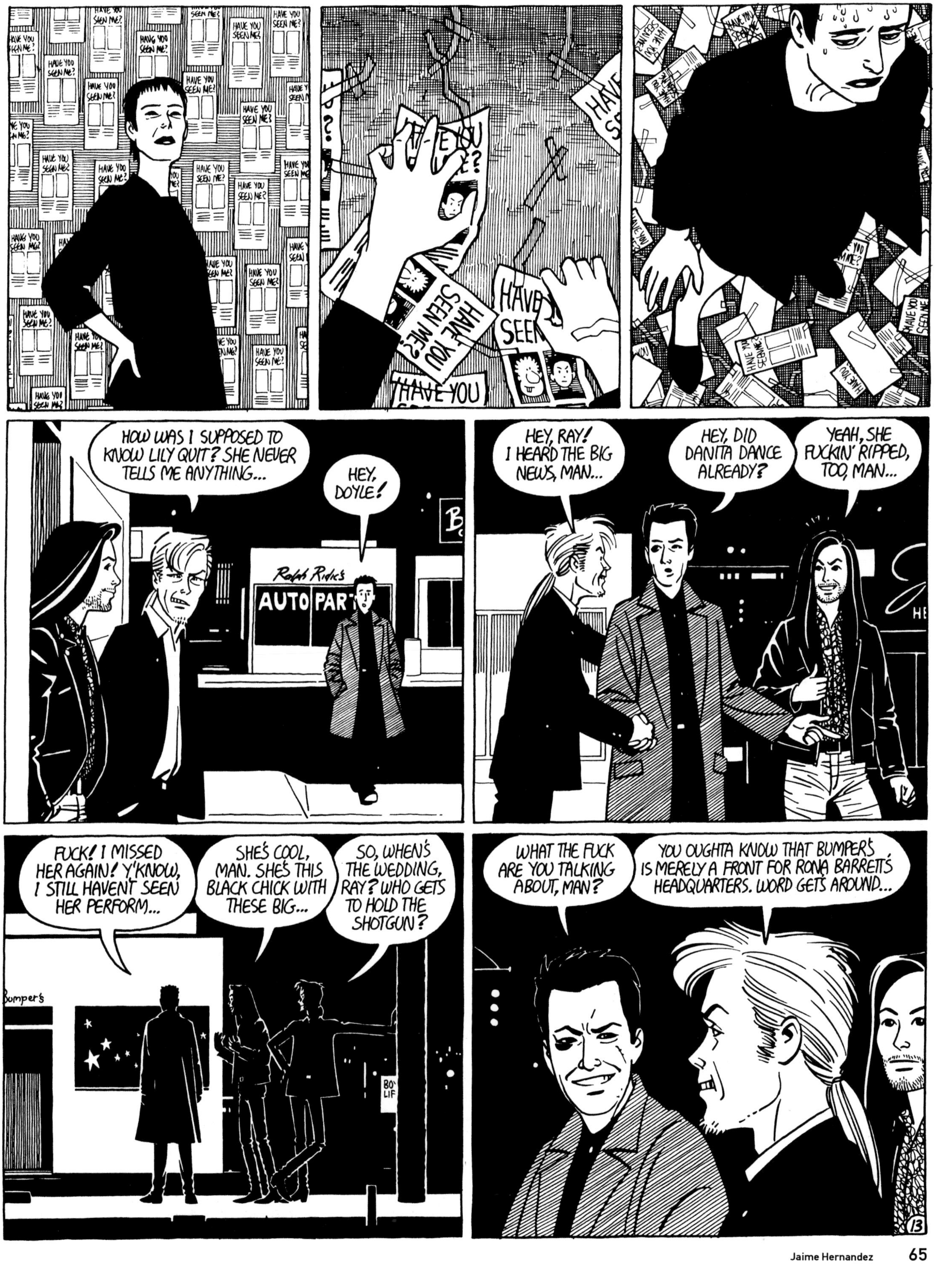
HOW WAS I SUPPOSED TO KNOW LILY QUIT? SHE NEVER TELLS ME ANYTHING...
HEY, DOYLE!
HEY, RAY! I HEARD THE BIG NEWS, MAN...
HEY, DID DANITA DANCE ALREADY?
YEAH, SHE FUCKIN' RIPPED, TOO, MAN...
FUCK! I MISSED HER AGAIN! Y'KNOW, I STILL HAVEN'T SEEN HER PERFORM...
SHE'S COOL, MAN. SHE'S THIS BLACK CHICK WITH THESE BIG...
SO, WHEN'S THE WEDDING, RAY? WHO GETS TO HOLD THE SHOTGUN?
Bumper's
WHAT THE FUCK ARE YOU TALKING ABOUT, MAN?
YOU OUGHTA KNOW THAT BUMPER'S IS MERELY A FRONT FOR RONA BARRETT'S HEADQUARTERS. WORD GETS AROUND...
13

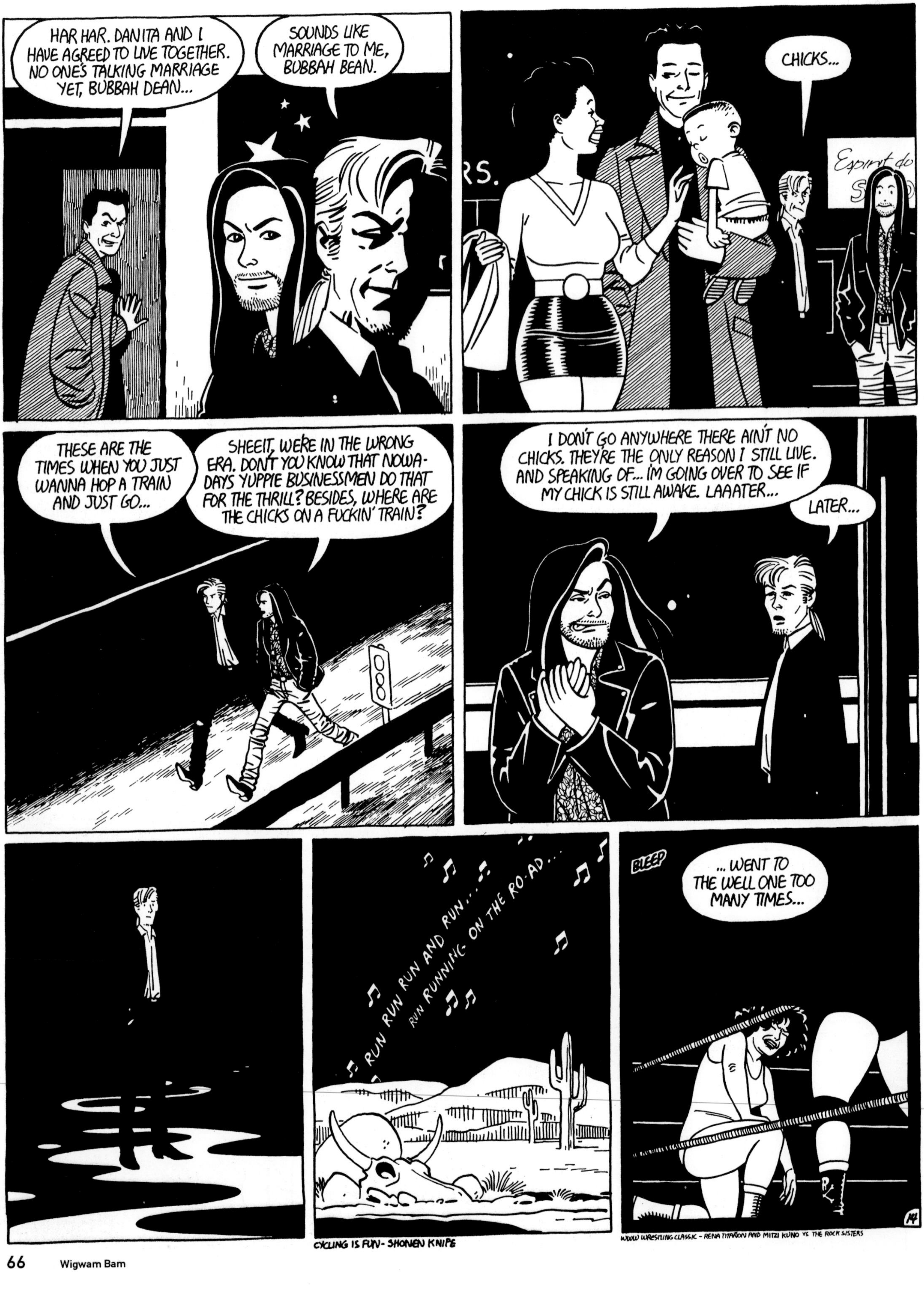
HAR HAR. DANITA AND I HAVE AGREED TO LIVE TOGETHER. NO ONE'S TALKING MARRIAGE YET, BUBBAH DEAN...
SOUNDS LIKE MARRIAGE TO ME, BUBBAH BEAN.
CHICKS...
THESE ARE THE TIMES WHEN YOU JUST WANNA HOP A TRAIN AND JUST GO...
SHEEIT, WE'RE IN THE WRONG ERA. DON'T YOU KNOW THAT NOWADAYS YUPPIE BUSINESSMEN DO THAT FOR THE THRILL? BESIDES, WHERE ARE THE CHICKS ON A FUCKIN' TRAIN?
I DON'T GO ANYWHERE THERE AIN'T NO CHICKS. THEY'RE THE ONLY REASON I STILL LIVE. AND SPEAKING OF... I'M GOING OVER TO SEE IF MY CHICK IS STILL AWAKE. LAAATER...
LATER...
RUN RUN RUN AND RUN...
RUN RUNNING ON THE RO-AD...
BLEEP
... WENT TO THE WELL ONE TOO MANY TIMES...
CYCLING IS FUN- SHONEN KNIFE
WWW WRESTLING CLASSIC - RENA TITAÑON AND MITZI KUNO VS THE ROCK SISTERS

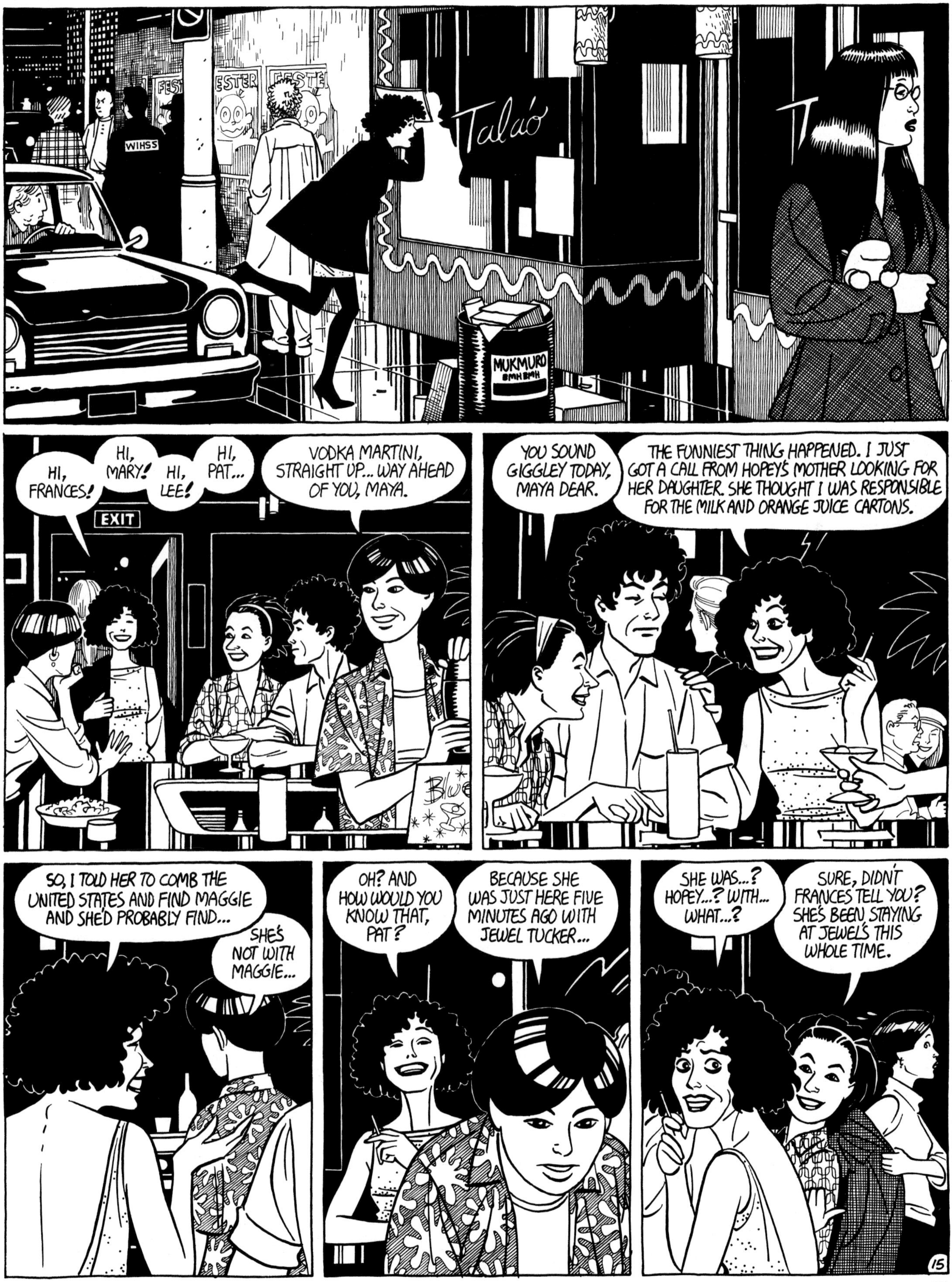

WIHSS
FESTER
Talaó
MUKMURO
BMH BMH
HI, FRANCES!
HI, MARY!
HI, LEE!
HI, PAT...
VODKA MARTINI, STRAIGHT UP... WAY AHEAD OF YOU, MAYA.
EXIT
YOU SOUND GIGGLEY TODAY, MAYA DEAR.
THE FUNNIEST THING HAPPENED. I JUST GOT A CALL FROM HOPEY'S MOTHER LOOKING FOR HER DAUGHTER. SHE THOUGHT I WAS RESPONSIBLE FOR THE MILK AND ORANGE JUICE CARTONS.
SO, I TOLD HER TO COMB THE UNITED STATES AND FIND MAGGIE AND SHE'D PROBABLY FIND...
SHE'S NOT WITH MAGGIE...
OH? AND HOW WOULD YOU KNOW THAT, PAT?
BECAUSE SHE WAS JUST HERE FIVE MINUTES AGO WITH JEWEL TUCKER...
SHE WAS...? HOPEY...? WITH... WHAT...?
SURE, DIDN'T FRANCES TELL YOU? SHE'S BEEN STAYING AT JEWEL'S THIS WHOLE TIME.
15

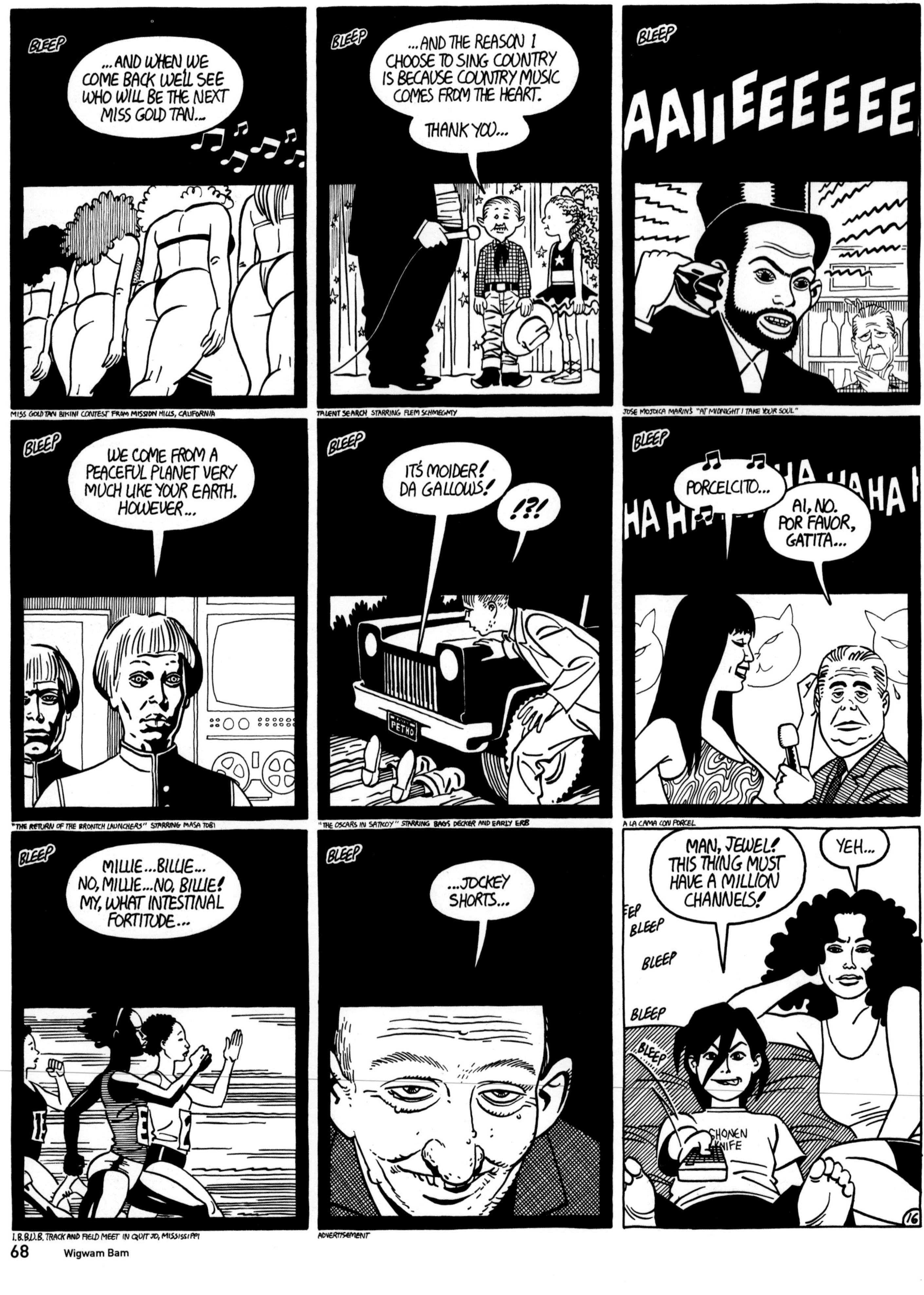
BLEEP
...AND WHEN WE COME BACK WE'LL SEE WHO WILL BE THE NEXT MISS GOLD TAN...
MISS GOLD TAN BIKINI CONTEST FROM MISSION HILLS, CALIFORNIA
BLEEP
...AND THE REASON I CHOOSE TO SING COUNTRY IS BECAUSE COUNTRY MUSIC COMES FROM THE HEART.
THANK YOU...
TALENT SEARCH STARRING FLEM SCHMEGMY
BLEEP
AAIIEEEEEEE
JOSE MOJICA MARIN'S "AT MIDNIGHT I TAKE YOUR SOUL"
BLEEP
WE COME FROM A PEACEFUL PLANET VERY MUCH LIKE YOUR EARTH. HOWEVER...
"THE RETURN OF THE BRONTCH LAUNCHERS" STARRING MASA TOBI
BLEEP
IT'S MOIDER! DA GALLOWS!
!?!
PETHO
"THE OSCARS IN SATKOY" STARRING BAGS DECKER AND EARLY ERB
BLEEP
HA HA HAHA HA
PORCELCITO...
AI, NO. POR FAVOR, GATITA...
A LA CAMA CON PORCEL
BLEEP
MILLIE...BILLIE... NO, MILLIE...NO, BILLIE! MY, WHAT INTESTINAL FORTITUDE...
I.B.B.U.B. TRACK AND FIELD MEET IN QUIT JO, MISSISSIPPI
BLEEP
...JOCKEY SHORTS...
ADVERTISEMENT
MAN, JEWEL! THIS THING MUST HAVE A MILLION CHANNELS!
YEH...
EEP
BLEEP
BLEEP
BLEEP
BLEEP
SHONEN KNIFE
16

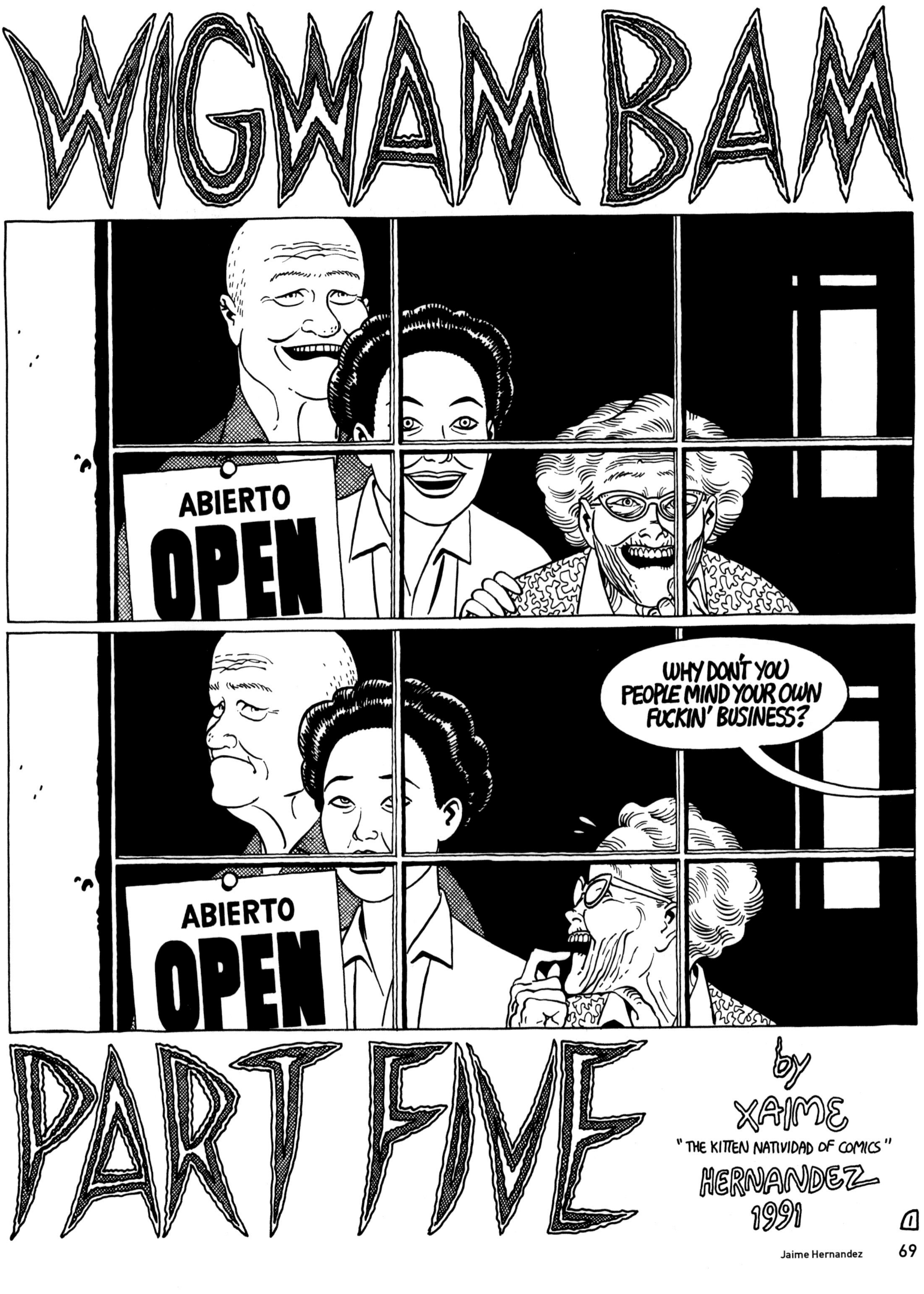
WIGWAM BAM
ABIERTO
OPEN
ABIERTO
OPEN
WHY DON'T YOU PEOPLE MIND YOUR OWN FUCKIN' BUSINESS?
PART FIVE
by
XAIME
"THE KITTEN NATIVIDAD OF COMICS"
HERNANDEZ
1991
1

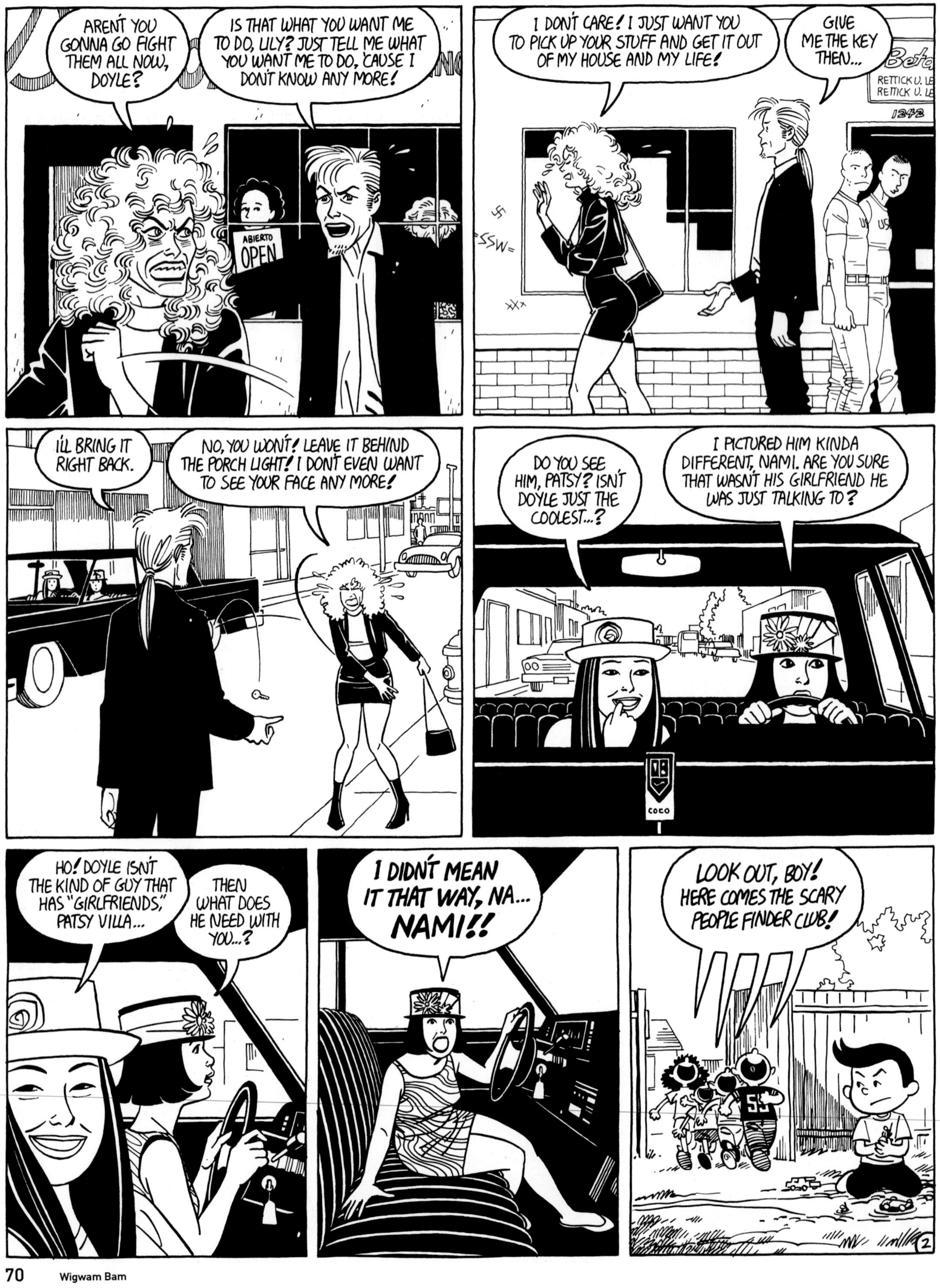
AREN'T YOU GONNA GO FIGHT THEM ALL NOW, DOYLE?
IS THAT WHAT YOU WANT ME TO DO, LILY? JUST TELL ME WHAT YOU WANT ME TO DO, 'CAUSE I DON'T KNOW ANY MORE!
ABIERTO
OPEN
I DON'T CARE! I JUST WANT YOU TO PICK UP YOUR STUFF AND GET IT OUT OF MY HOUSE AND MY LIFE!
GIVE ME THE KEY THEN...
RETTICK U. LE
RETTICK U. LE
1242
I'LL BRING IT RIGHT BACK.
NO, YOU WON'T! LEAVE IT BEHIND THE PORCH LIGHT! I DON'T EVEN WANT TO SEE YOUR FACE ANY MORE!
DO YOU SEE HIM, PATSY? ISN'T DOYLE JUST THE COOLEST...?
I PICTURED HIM KINDA DIFFERENT, NAMI. ARE YOU SURE THAT WASN'T HIS GIRLFRIEND HE WAS JUST TALKING TO?
COCO
HO! DOYLE ISN'T THE KIND OF GUY THAT HAS "GIRLFRIENDS," PATSY VILLA...
THEN WHAT DOES HE NEED WITH YOU...?
I DIDN'T MEAN IT THAT WAY, NA... NAMI!!
LOOK OUT, BOY! HERE COMES THE SCARY PEOPLE FINDER CLUB!
2

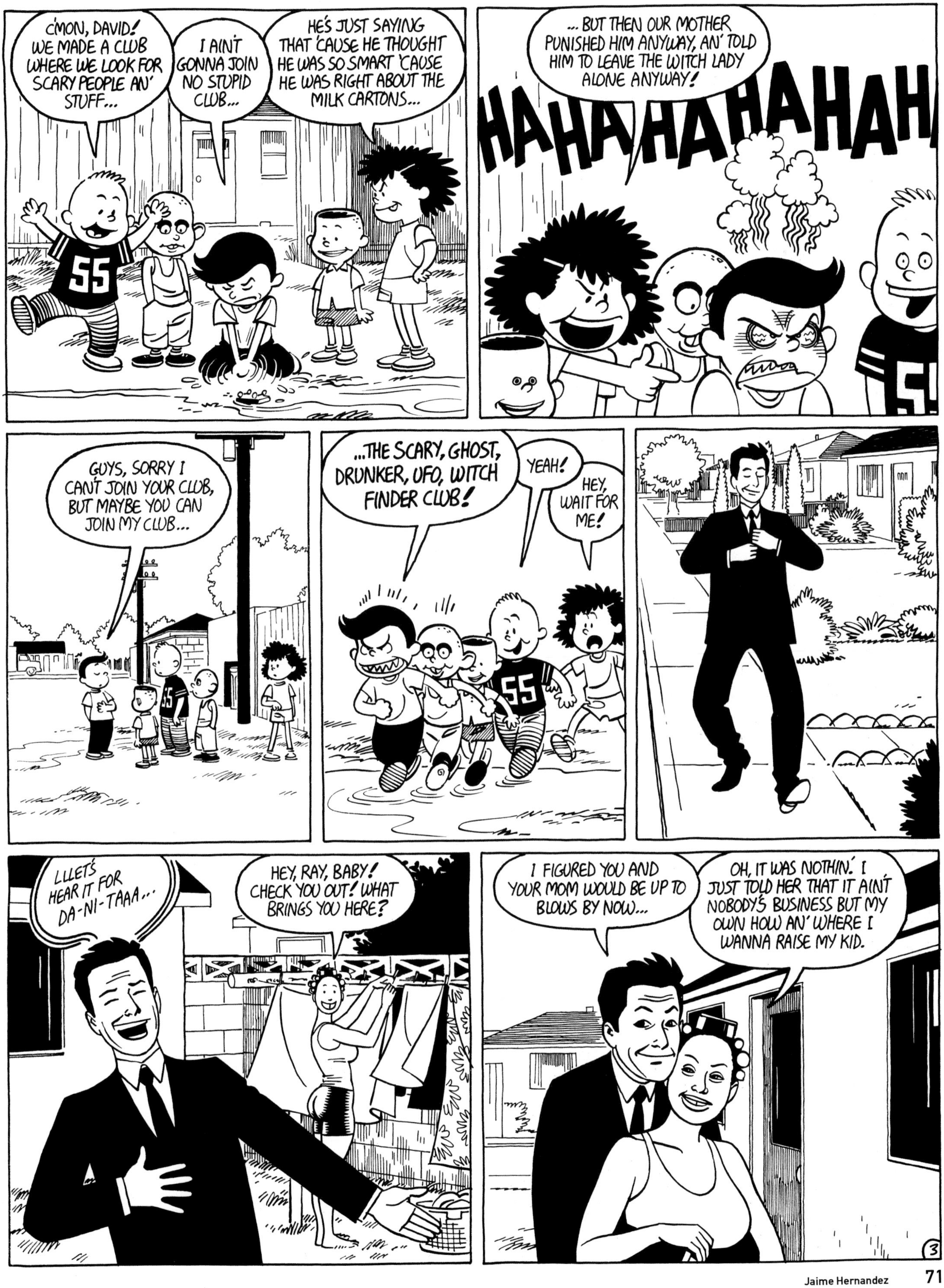
C'MON, DAVID! WE MADE A CLUB WHERE WE LOOK FOR SCARY PEOPLE AN' STUFF...
I AIN'T GONNA JOIN NO STUPID CLUB...
HE'S JUST SAYING THAT 'CAUSE HE THOUGHT HE WAS SO SMART 'CAUSE HE WAS RIGHT ABOUT THE MILK CARTONS...
... BUT THEN OUR MOTHER PUNISHED HIM ANYWAY, AN' TOLD HIM TO LEAVE THE WITCH LADY ALONE ANYWAY!
HAHAHAHAHAHAH
GUYS, SORRY I CAN'T JOIN YOUR CLUB, BUT MAYBE YOU CAN JOIN MY CLUB...
...THE SCARY, GHOST, DRUNKER, UFO, WITCH FINDER CLUB!
YEAH!
HEY, WAIT FOR ME!
LLLET'S HEAR IT FOR DA-NI-TAAA...
HEY, RAY, BABY! CHECK YOU OUT! WHAT BRINGS YOU HERE?
I FIGURED YOU AND YOUR MOM WOULD BE UP TO BLOWS BY NOW...
OH, IT WAS NOTHIN'. I JUST TOLD HER THAT IT AIN'T NOBODY'S BUSINESS BUT MY OWN HOW AN' WHERE I WANNA RAISE MY KID.
3

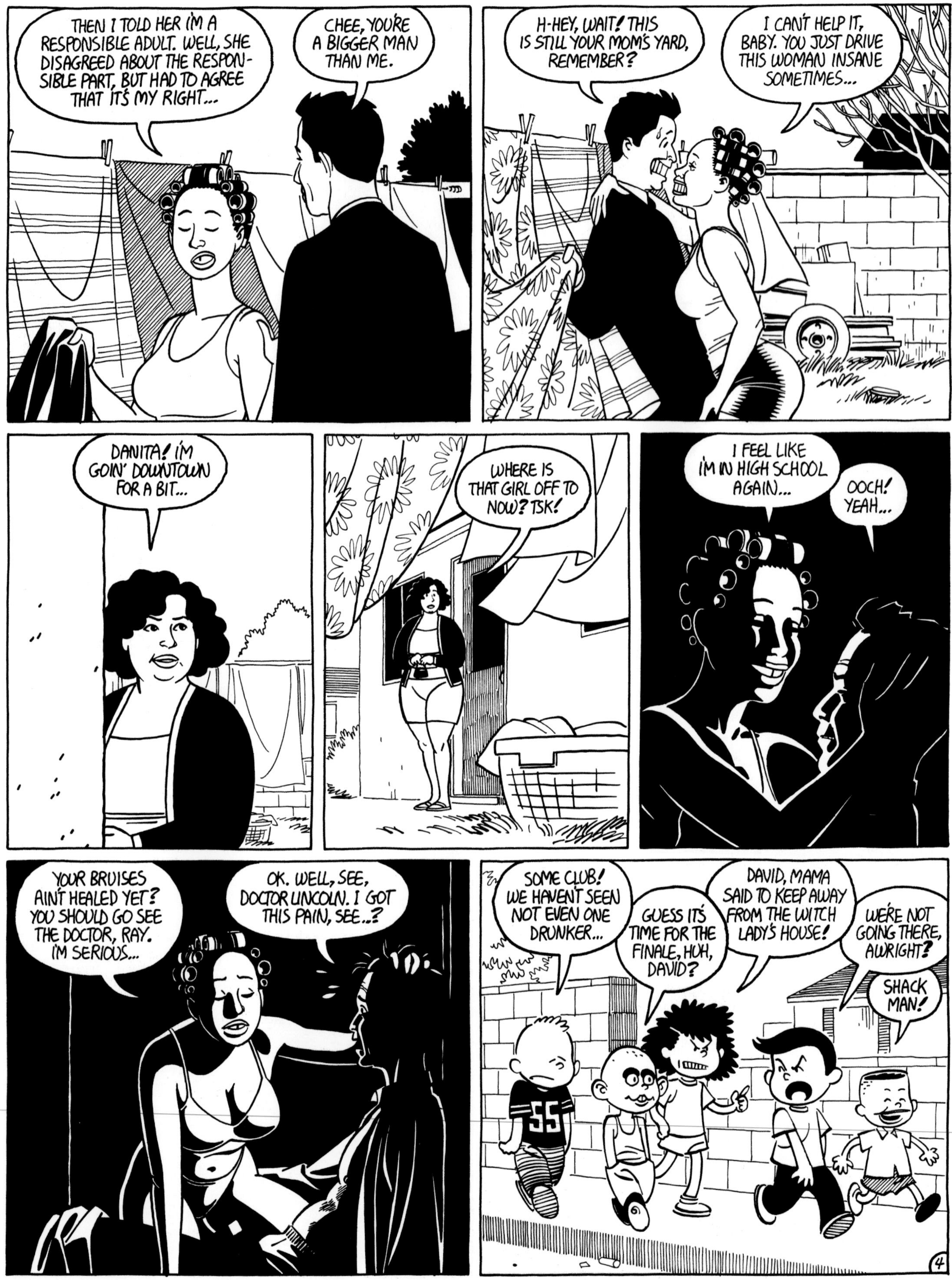
THEN I TOLD HER I'M A RESPONSIBLE ADULT. WELL, SHE DISAGREED ABOUT THE RESPONSIBLE PART, BUT HAD TO AGREE THAT IT'S MY RIGHT...
CHEE, YOU'RE A BIGGER MAN THAN ME.
H-HEY, WAIT! THIS IS STILL YOUR MOM'S YARD, REMEMBER?
I CAN'T HELP IT, BABY. YOU JUST DRIVE THIS WOMAN INSANE SOMETIMES...
DANITA! I'M GOIN' DOWNTOWN FOR A BIT...
WHERE IS THAT GIRL OFF TO NOW? TSK!
I FEEL LIKE I'M IN HIGH SCHOOL AGAIN...
OOCH! YEAH...
YOUR BRUISES AIN'T HEALED YET? YOU SHOULD GO SEE THE DOCTOR, RAY. I'M SERIOUS...
OK. WELL, SEE, DOCTOR LINCOLN. I GOT THIS PAIN, SEE..?
SOME CLUB! WE HAVEN'T SEEN NOT EVEN ONE DRUNKER...
GUESS IT'S TIME FOR THE FINALE, HUH, DAVID?
DAVID, MAMA SAID TO KEEP AWAY FROM THE WITCH LADY'S HOUSE!
WE'RE NOT GOING THERE, AWRIGHT?
SHACK MAN!
55
4

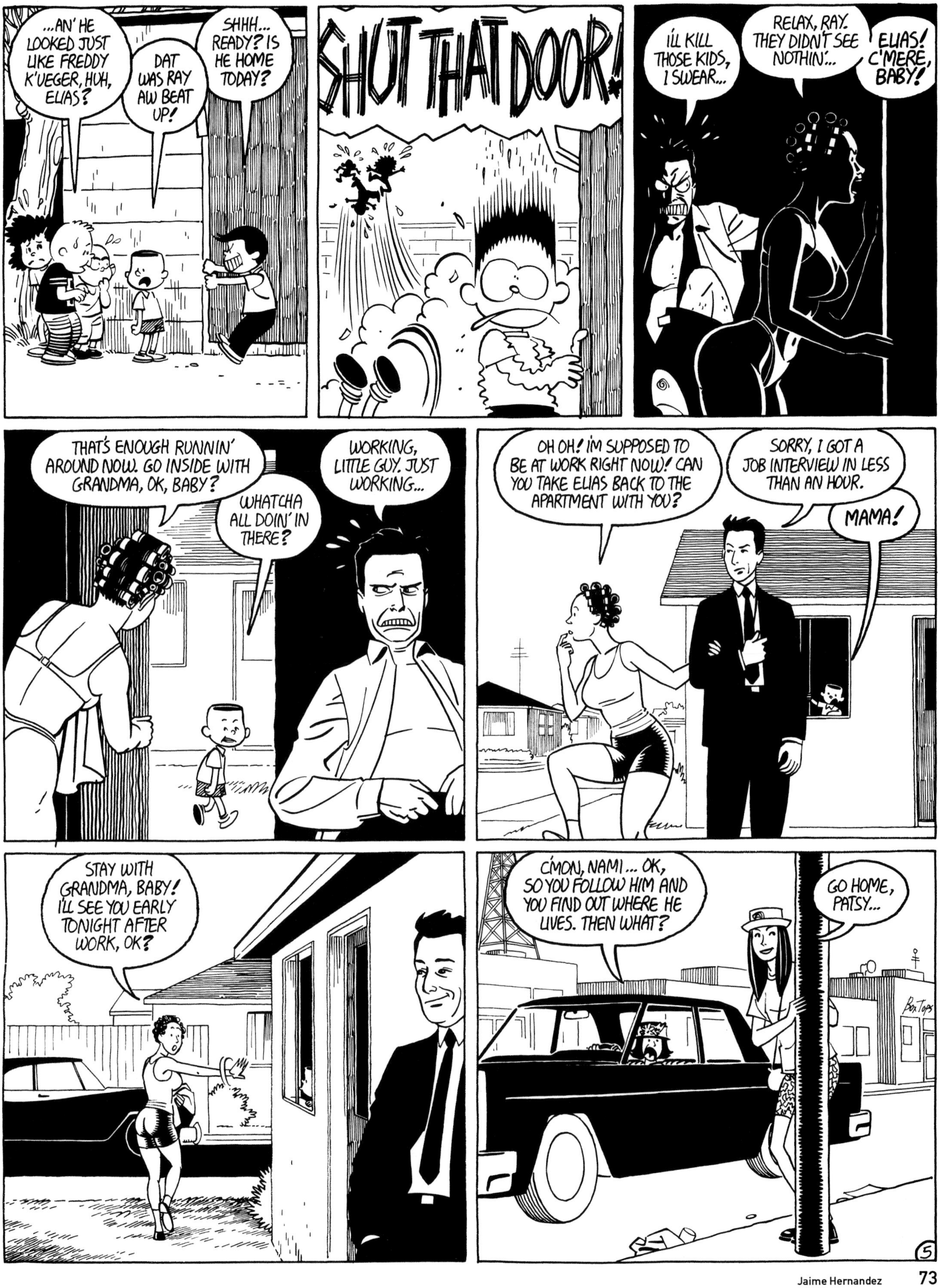
...AN' HE LOOKED JUST LIKE FREDDY K'UEGER, HUH, ELIAS?
DAT WAS RAY AW BEAT UP!
SHHH... READY? IS HE HOME TODAY?
SHUT THAT DOOR!
I'LL KILL THOSE KIDS, I SWEAR...
RELAX, RAY. THEY DIDN'T SEE NOTHIN'...
ELIAS! C'MERE, BABY!
THAT'S ENOUGH RUNNIN' AROUND NOW. GO INSIDE WITH GRANDMA, OK, BABY?
WHATCHA ALL DOIN' IN THERE?
WORKING, LITTLE GUY. JUST WORKING...
OH OH! I'M SUPPOSED TO BE AT WORK RIGHT NOW! CAN YOU TAKE ELIAS BACK TO THE APARTMENT WITH YOU?
SORRY, I GOT A JOB INTERVIEW IN LESS THAN AN HOUR.
MAMA!
STAY WITH GRANDMA, BABY! I'LL SEE YOU EARLY TONIGHT AFTER WORK, OK?
C'MON, NAMI... OK, SO YOU FOLLOW HIM AND YOU FIND OUT WHERE HE LIVES. THEN WHAT?
GO HOME, PATSY...
Box Tops
5

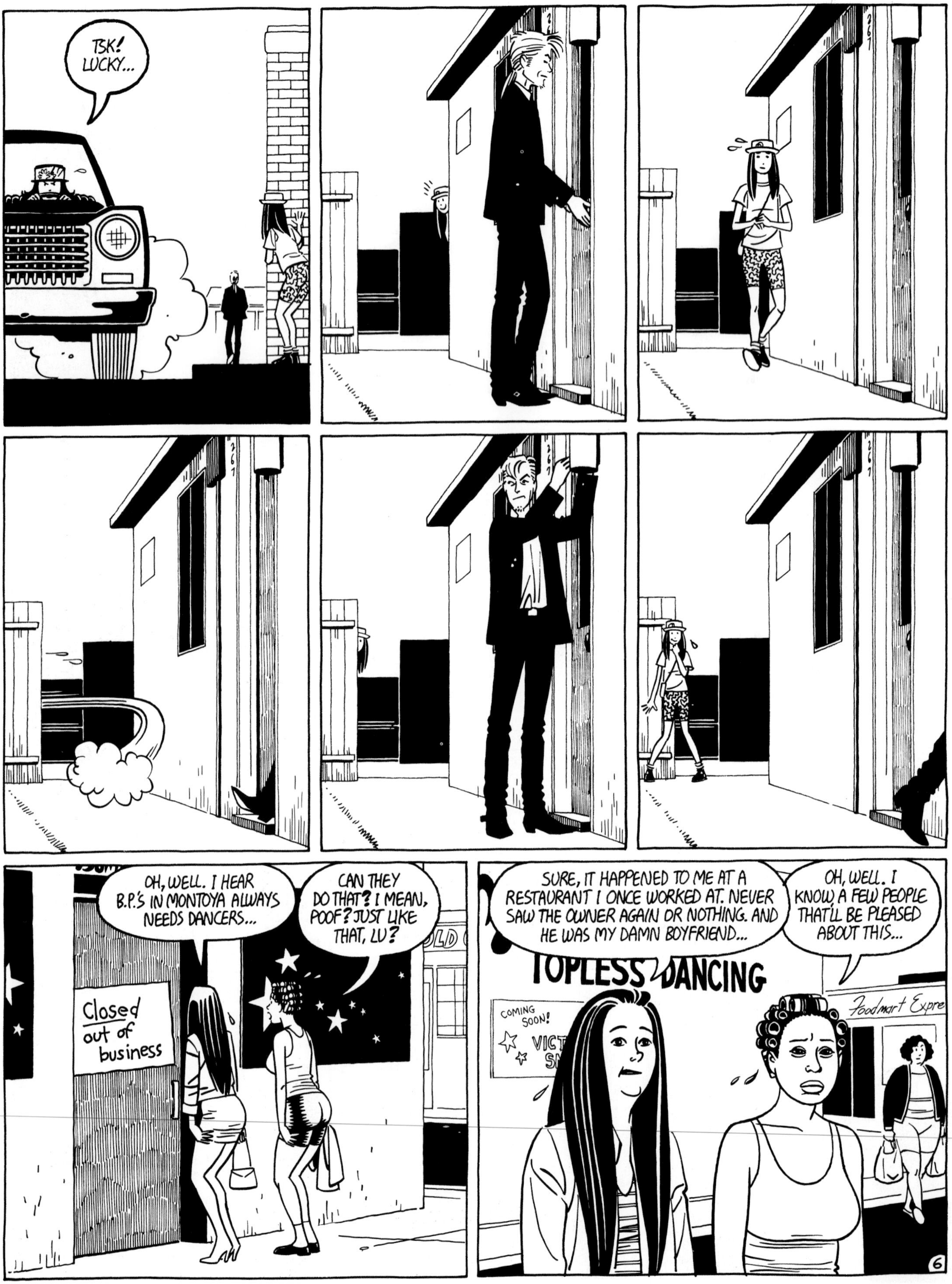
TSK! LUCKY...
OH, WELL. I HEAR B.P.'S IN MONTOYA ALWAYS NEEDS DANCERS...
CAN THEY DO THAT? I MEAN, POOF? JUST LIKE THAT, LU?
Closed out of business
SURE, IT HAPPENED TO ME AT A RESTAURANT I ONCE WORKED AT. NEVER SAW THE OWNER AGAIN OR NOTHING. AND HE WAS MY DAMN BOYFRIEND...
OH, WELL. I KNOW A FEW PEOPLE THAT'LL BE PLEASED ABOUT THIS...
TOPLESS DANCING
COMING SOON!
6

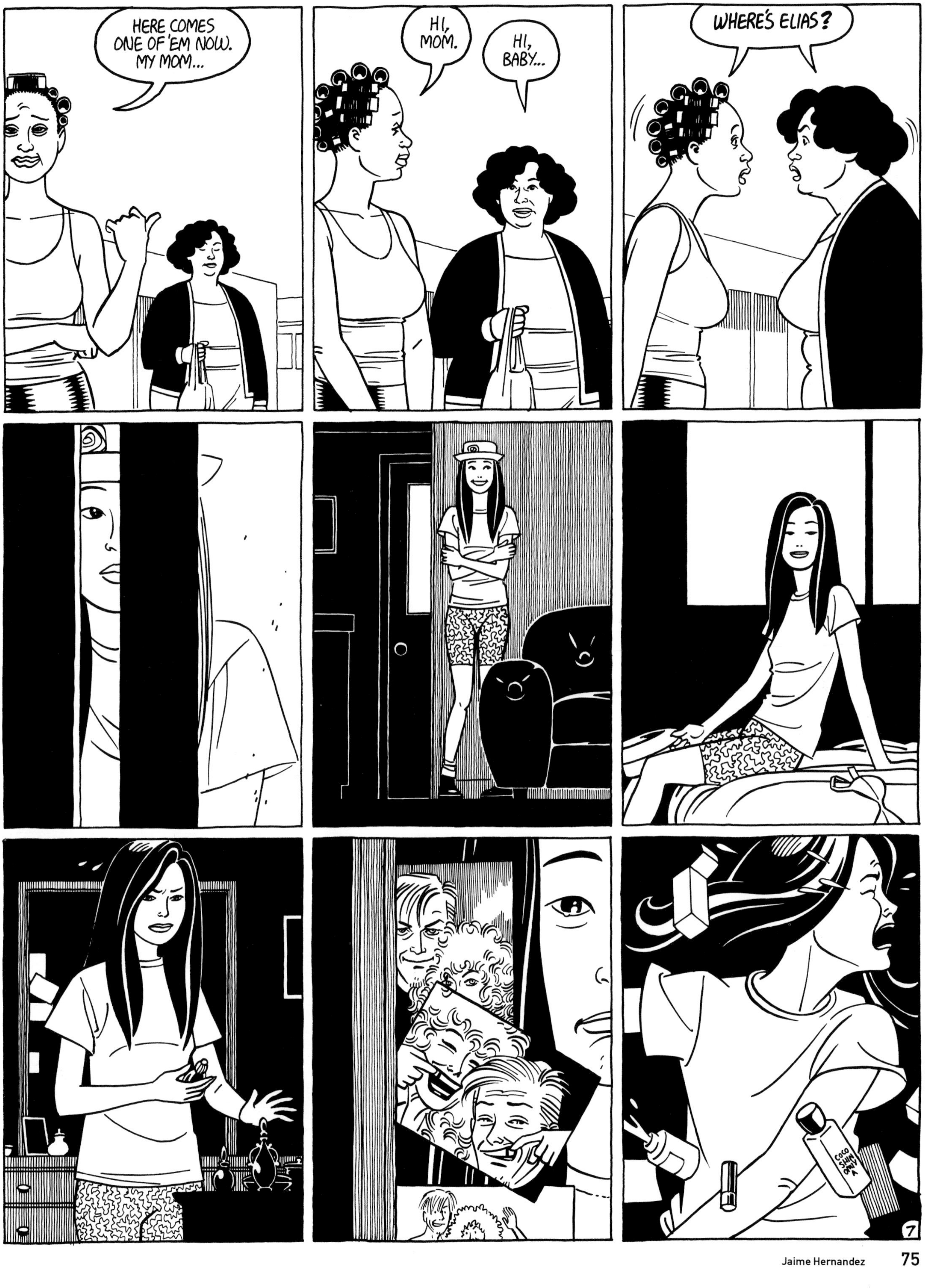
HERE COMES ONE OF 'EM NOW. MY MOM...
HI, MOM.
HI, BABY...
WHERE'S ELIAS?
COCO SHIN OPIA
7

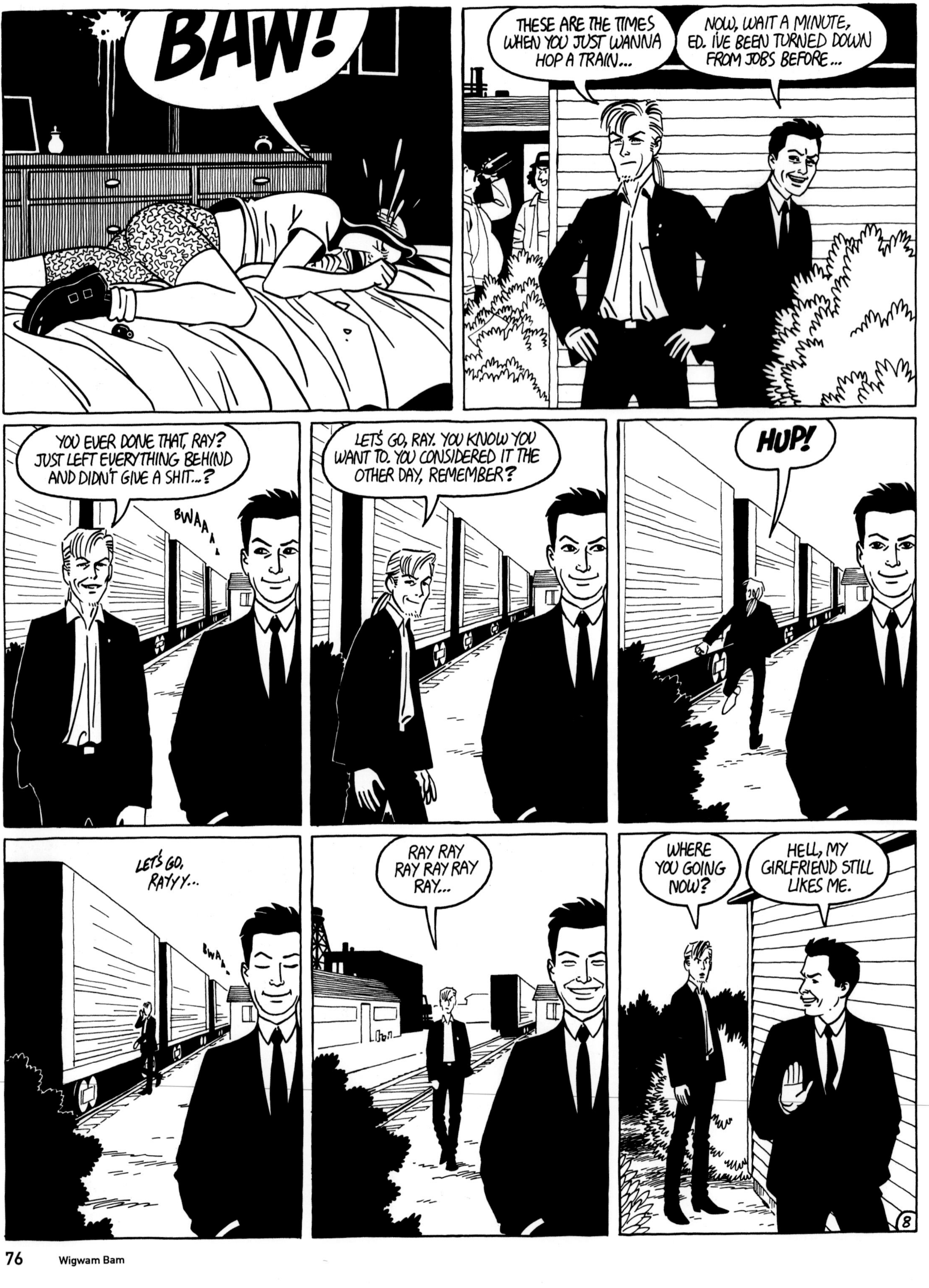
BAW!
THESE ARE THE TIMES WHEN YOU JUST WANNA HOP A TRAIN...
NOW, WAIT A MINUTE, ED. I'VE BEEN TURNED DOWN FROM JOBS BEFORE...
YOU EVER DONE THAT, RAY? JUST LEFT EVERYTHING BEHIND AND DIDN'T GIVE A SHIT...?
BWAAAA
LET'S GO, RAY. YOU KNOW YOU WANT TO. YOU CONSIDERED IT THE OTHER DAY, REMEMBER?
HUP!
LET'S GO, RAYYY...
BWAAA
RAY RAY RAY RAY RAY RAY...
WHERE YOU GOING NOW?
HELL, MY GIRLFRIEND STILL LIKES ME.
8

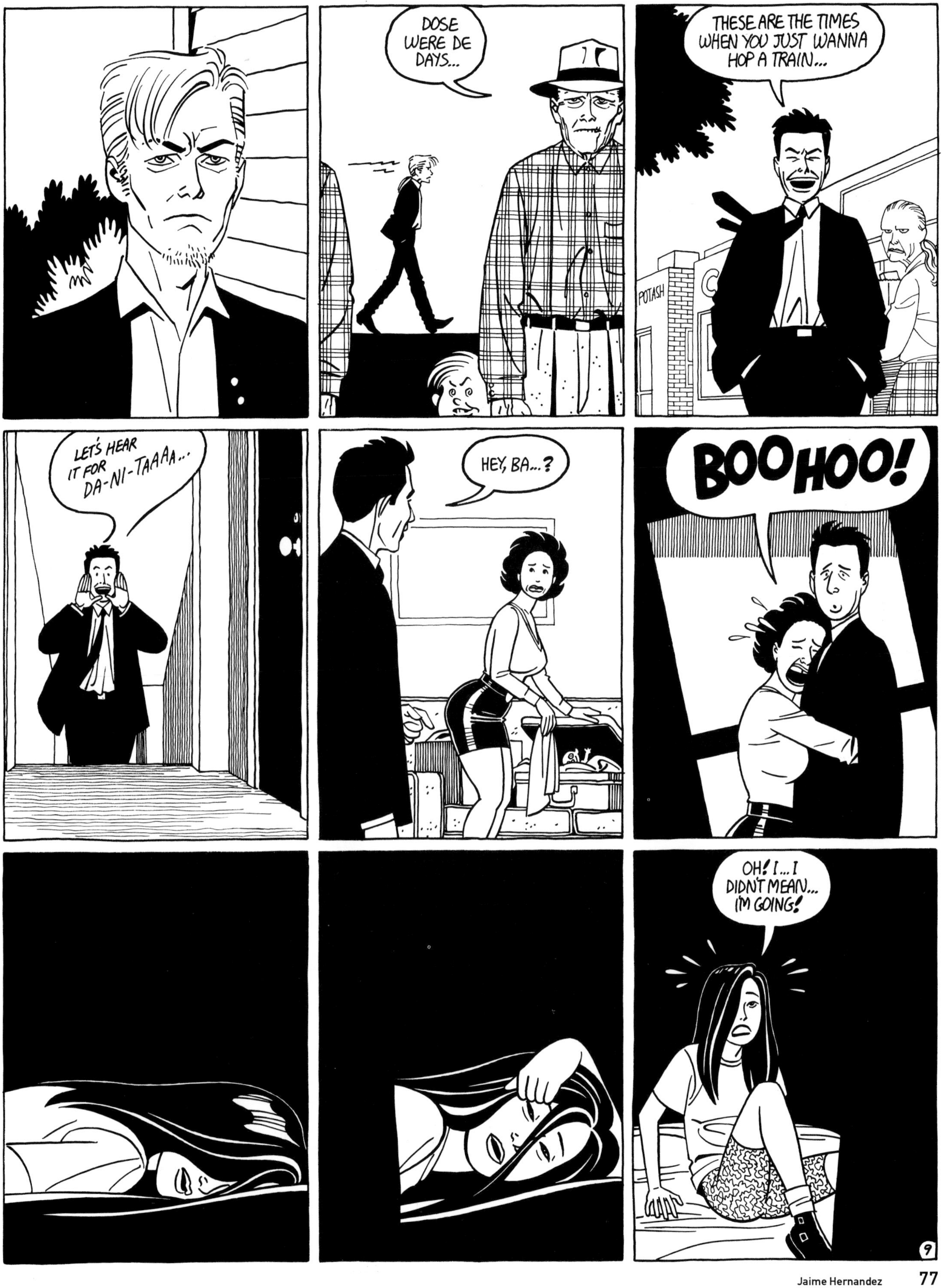
DOSE WERE DE DAYS...
THESE ARE THE TIMES WHEN YOU JUST WANNA HOP A TRAIN...
POTASH
LET'S HEAR IT FOR DA-NI-TAAAAA...
HEY, BA...?
BOO HOO!
OH! I... I DIDN'T MEAN... I'M GOING!
9

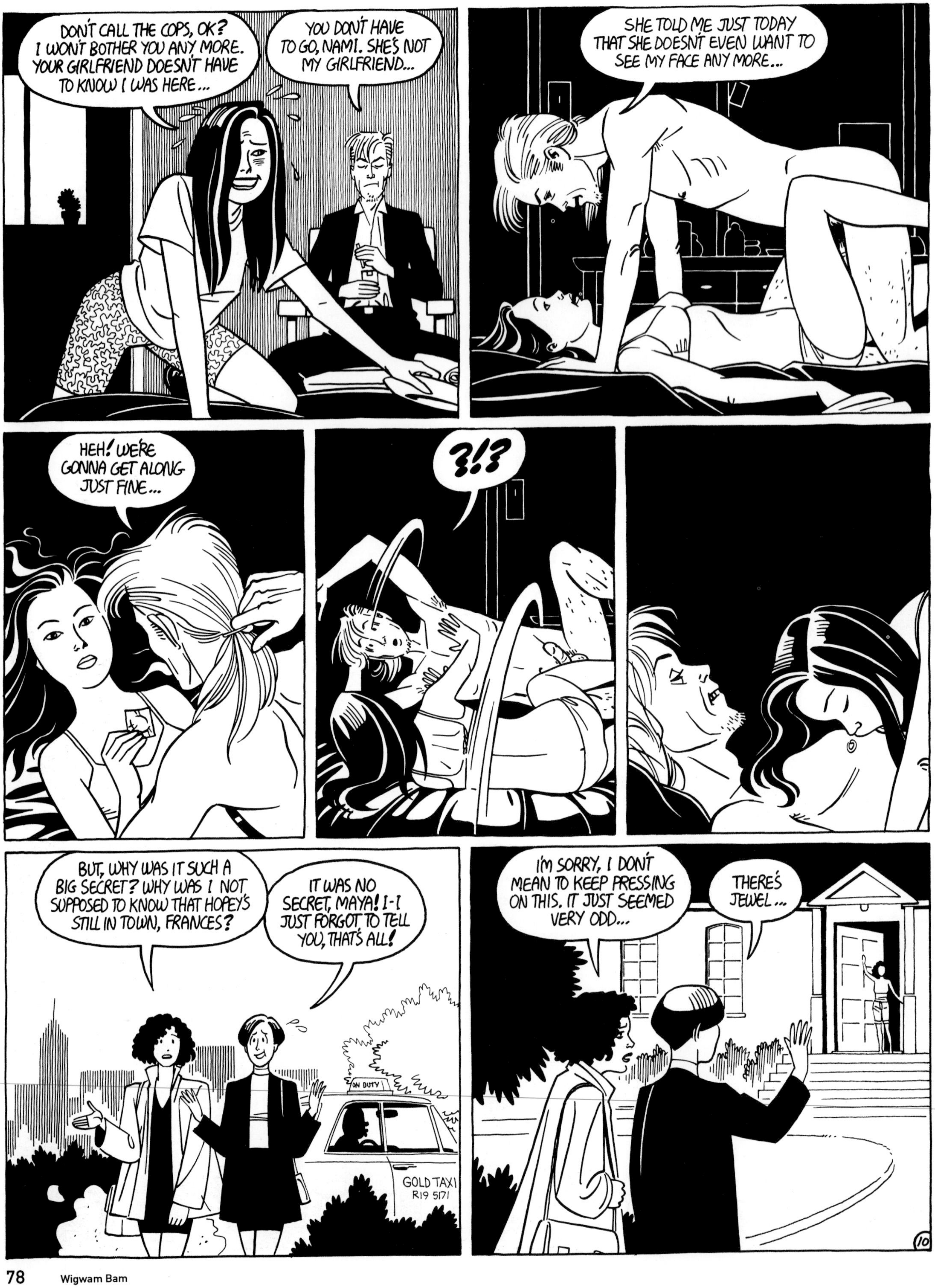
DON'T CALL THE COPS, OK? I WON'T BOTHER YOU ANY MORE. YOUR GIRLFRIEND DOESN'T HAVE TO KNOW I WAS HERE...
YOU DON'T HAVE TO GO, NAMI. SHE'S NOT MY GIRLFRIEND...
SHE TOLD ME JUST TODAY THAT SHE DOESN'T EVEN WANT TO SEE MY FACE ANY MORE...
HEH! WE'RE GONNA GET ALONG JUST FINE...
?!?
BUT, WHY WAS IT SUCH A BIG SECRET? WHY WAS I NOT SUPPOSED TO KNOW THAT HOPEY'S STILL IN TOWN, FRANCES?
IT WAS NO SECRET, MAYA! I-I JUST FORGOT TO TELL YOU, THAT'S ALL!
ON DUTY
GOLD TAXI
R19 5171
I'M SORRY, I DON'T MEAN TO KEEP PRESSING ON THIS. IT JUST SEEMED VERY ODD...
THERE'S JEWEL...
10

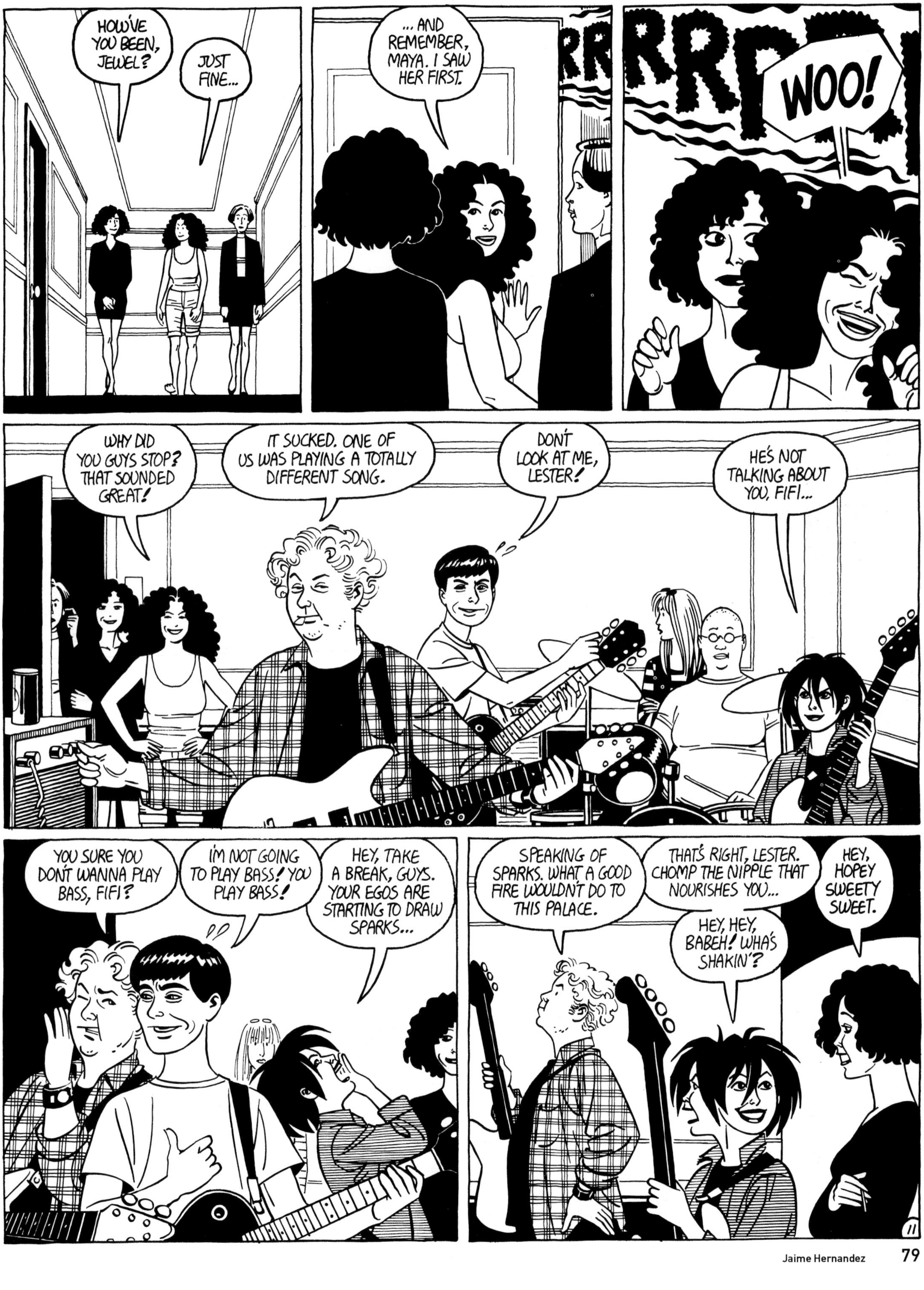

HOW'VE YOU BEEN, JEWEL?
JUST FINE...
... AND REMEMBER, MAYA. I SAW HER FIRST.
RRRRR
WOO!
WHY DID YOU GUYS STOP? THAT SOUNDED GREAT!
IT SUCKED. ONE OF US WAS PLAYING A TOTALLY DIFFERENT SONG.
DON'T LOOK AT ME, LESTER!
HE'S NOT TALKING ABOUT YOU, FIFI...
YOU SURE YOU DON'T WANNA PLAY BASS, FIFI?
I'M NOT GOING TO PLAY BASS! YOU PLAY BASS!
HEY, TAKE A BREAK, GUYS. YOUR EGOS ARE STARTING TO DRAW SPARKS...
SPEAKING OF SPARKS. WHAT A GOOD FIRE WOULDN'T DO TO THIS PALACE.
THAT'S RIGHT, LESTER. CHOMP THE NIPPLE THAT NOURISHES YOU...
HEY, HEY, BABEH! WHA'S SHAKIN'?
HEY, HOPEY SWEETY SWEET.
11

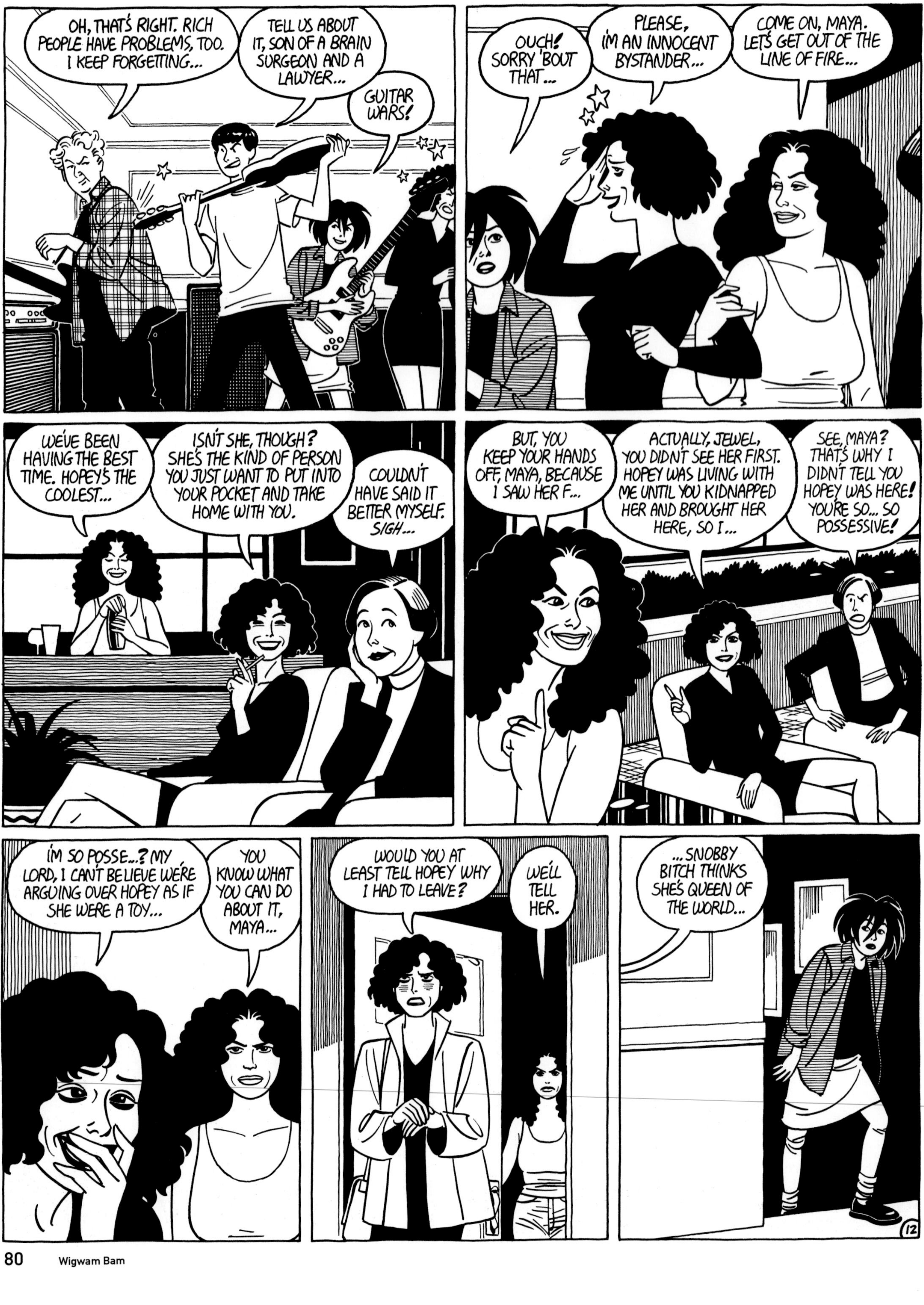
OH, THAT'S RIGHT. RICH PEOPLE HAVE PROBLEMS, TOO. I KEEP FORGETTING...
TELL US ABOUT IT, SON OF A BRAIN SURGEON AND A LAWYER...
GUITAR WARS!
OUCH! SORRY 'BOUT THAT...
PLEASE, I'M AN INNOCENT BYSTANDER...
COME ON, MAYA. LET'S GET OUT OF THE LINE OF FIRE...
WE'VE BEEN HAVING THE BEST TIME. HOPEY'S THE COOLEST...
ISN'T SHE, THOUGH? SHE'S THE KIND OF PERSON YOU JUST WANT TO PUT INTO YOUR POCKET AND TAKE HOME WITH YOU.
COULDN'T HAVE SAID IT BETTER MYSELF. SIGH...
BUT, YOU KEEP YOUR HANDS OFF, MAYA, BECAUSE I SAW HER F...
ACTUALLY, JEWEL, YOU DIDN'T SEE HER FIRST. HOPEY WAS LIVING WITH ME UNTIL YOU KIDNAPPED HER AND BROUGHT HER HERE, SO I...
SEE, MAYA? THAT'S WHY I DIDN'T TELL YOU HOPEY WAS HERE! YOU'RE SO... SO POSSESSIVE!
I'M SO POSSE...? MY LORD, I CAN'T BELIEVE WE'RE ARGUING OVER HOPEY AS IF SHE WERE A TOY...
YOU KNOW WHAT YOU CAN DO ABOUT IT, MAYA...
WOULD YOU AT LEAST TELL HOPEY WHY I HAD TO LEAVE?
WE'LL TELL HER.
...SNOBBY BITCH THINKS SHE'S QUEEN OF THE WORLD...
12

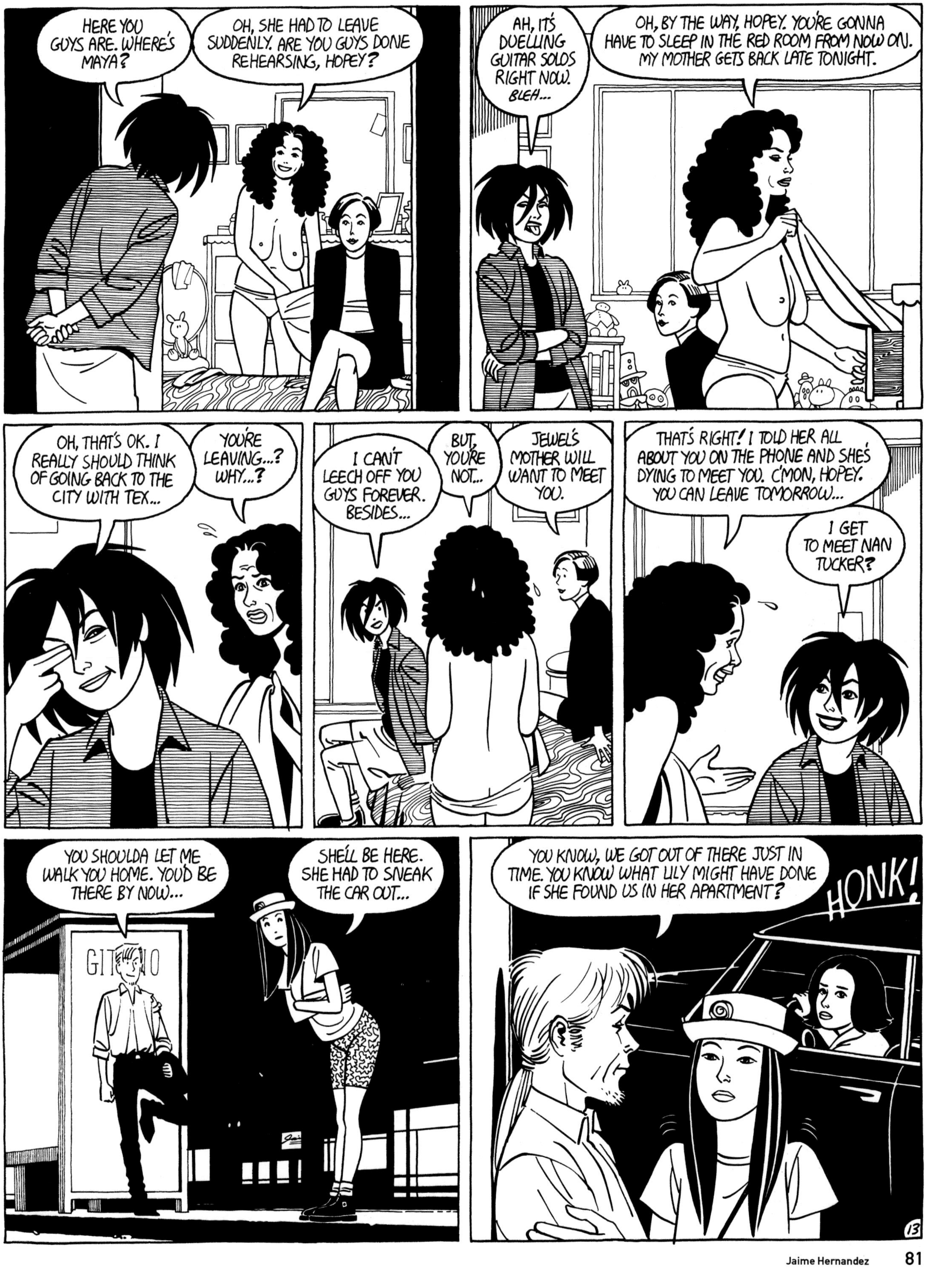
HERE YOU GUYS ARE. WHERE'S MAYA?
OH, SHE HAD TO LEAVE SUDDENLY. ARE YOU GUYS DONE REHEARSING, HOPEY?
AH, IT'S DUELLING GUITAR SOLOS RIGHT NOW. BLEH...
OH, BY THE WAY, HOPEY. YOU'RE GONNA HAVE TO SLEEP IN THE RED ROOM FROM NOW ON. MY MOTHER GETS BACK LATE TONIGHT.
OH, THAT'S OK. I REALLY SHOULD THINK OF GOING BACK TO THE CITY WITH TEX...
YOU'RE LEAVING...? WHY...?
I CAN'T LEECH OFF YOU GUYS FOREVER. BESIDES...
BUT, YOU'RE NOT...
JEWEL'S MOTHER WILL WANT TO MEET YOU.
THAT'S RIGHT! I TOLD HER ALL ABOUT YOU ON THE PHONE AND SHE'S DYING TO MEET YOU. C'MON, HOPEY. YOU CAN LEAVE TOMORROW...
I GET TO MEET NAN TUCKER?
YOU SHOULDA LET ME WALK YOU HOME. YOU'D BE THERE BY NOW...
SHE'LL BE HERE. SHE HAD TO SNEAK THE CAR OUT...
YOU KNOW, WE GOT OUT OF THERE JUST IN TIME. YOU KNOW WHAT LILY MIGHT HAVE DONE IF SHE FOUND US IN HER APARTMENT?
HONK!
13

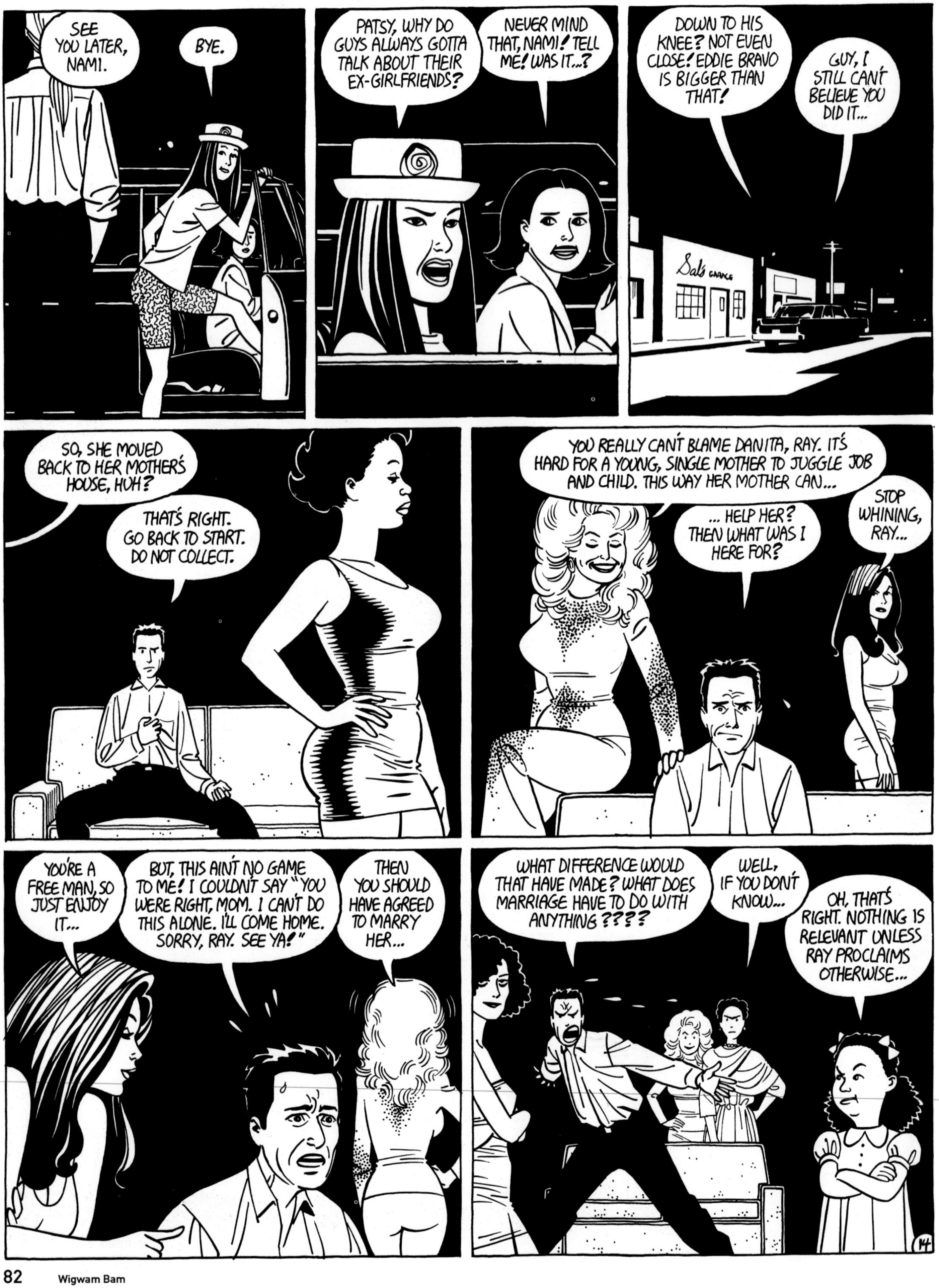
SEE YOU LATER, NAMI.
BYE.
PATSY, WHY DO GUYS ALWAYS GOTTA TALK ABOUT THEIR EX-GIRLFRIENDS?
NEVER MIND THAT, NAMI! TELL ME! WAS IT...?
DOWN TO HIS KNEE? NOT EVEN CLOSE! EDDIE BRAVO IS BIGGER THAN THAT!
GUY, I STILL CAN'T BELIEVE YOU DID IT...
Sal's GARAGE
SO, SHE MOVED BACK TO HER MOTHER'S HOUSE, HUH?
THAT'S RIGHT. GO BACK TO START. DO NOT COLLECT.
YOU REALLY CAN'T BLAME DANITA, RAY. IT'S HARD FOR A YOUNG, SINGLE MOTHER TO JUGGLE JOB AND CHILD. THIS WAY HER MOTHER CAN...
... HELP HER? THEN WHAT WAS I HERE FOR?
STOP WHINING, RAY...
YOU'RE A FREE MAN, SO JUST ENJOY IT...
BUT, THIS AIN'T NO GAME TO ME! I COULDN'T SAY "YOU WERE RIGHT, MOM. I CAN'T DO THIS ALONE. I'LL COME HOME. SORRY, RAY. SEE YA!"
THEN YOU SHOULD HAVE AGREED TO MARRY HER...
WHAT DIFFERENCE WOULD THAT HAVE MADE? WHAT DOES MARRIAGE HAVE TO DO WITH ANYTHING????
WELL, IF YOU DON'T KNOW...
OH, THAT'S RIGHT. NOTHING IS RELEVANT UNLESS RAY PROCLAIMS OTHERWISE...
14

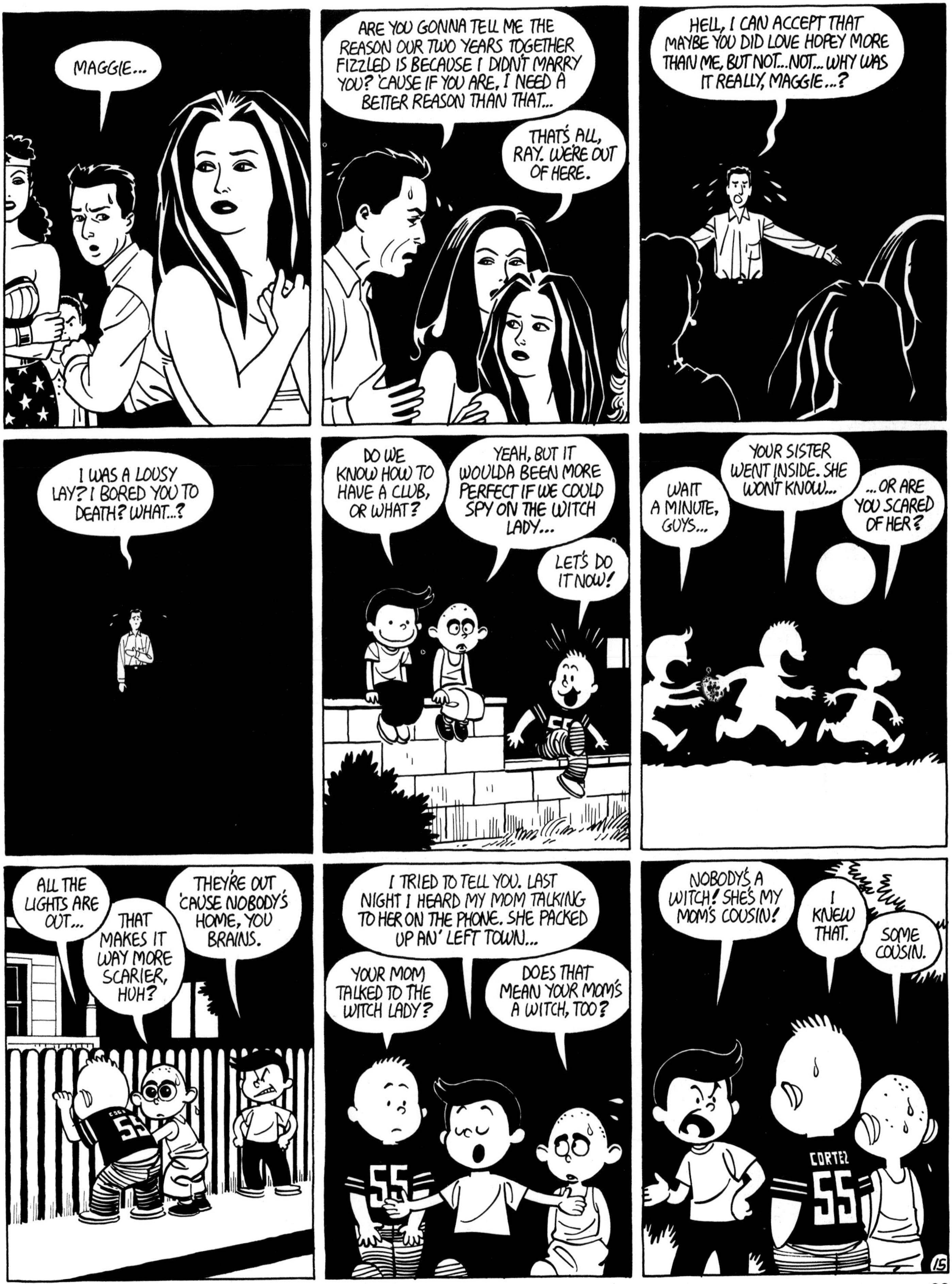

MAGGIE...
ARE YOU GONNA TELL ME THE REASON OUR TWO YEARS TOGETHER FIZZLED IS BECAUSE I DIDN'T MARRY YOU? 'CAUSE IF YOU ARE, I NEED A BETTER REASON THAN THAT...
THAT'S ALL, RAY. WE'RE OUT OF HERE.
HELL, I CAN ACCEPT THAT MAYBE YOU DID LOVE HOPEY MORE THAN ME, BUT NOT...NOT... WHY WAS IT REALLY, MAGGIE...?
I WAS A LOUSY LAY? I BORED YOU TO DEATH? WHAT...?
DO WE KNOW HOW TO HAVE A CLUB, OR WHAT?
YEAH, BUT IT WOULDA BEEN MORE PERFECT IF WE COULD SPY ON THE WITCH LADY...
LET'S DO IT NOW!
WAIT A MINUTE, GUYS...
YOUR SISTER WENT INSIDE. SHE WON'T KNOW...
...OR ARE YOU SCARED OF HER?
ALL THE LIGHTS ARE OUT...
THAT MAKES IT WAY MORE SCARIER, HUH?
THEY'RE OUT 'CAUSE NOBODY'S HOME, YOU BRAINS.
I TRIED TO TELL YOU. LAST NIGHT I HEARD MY MOM TALKING TO HER ON THE PHONE. SHE PACKED UP AN' LEFT TOWN...
YOUR MOM TALKED TO THE WITCH LADY?
DOES THAT MEAN YOUR MOM'S A WITCH, TOO?
NOBODY'S A WITCH! SHE'S MY MOM'S COUSIN!
I KNEW THAT.
SOME COUSIN.
CORTEZ
55
15

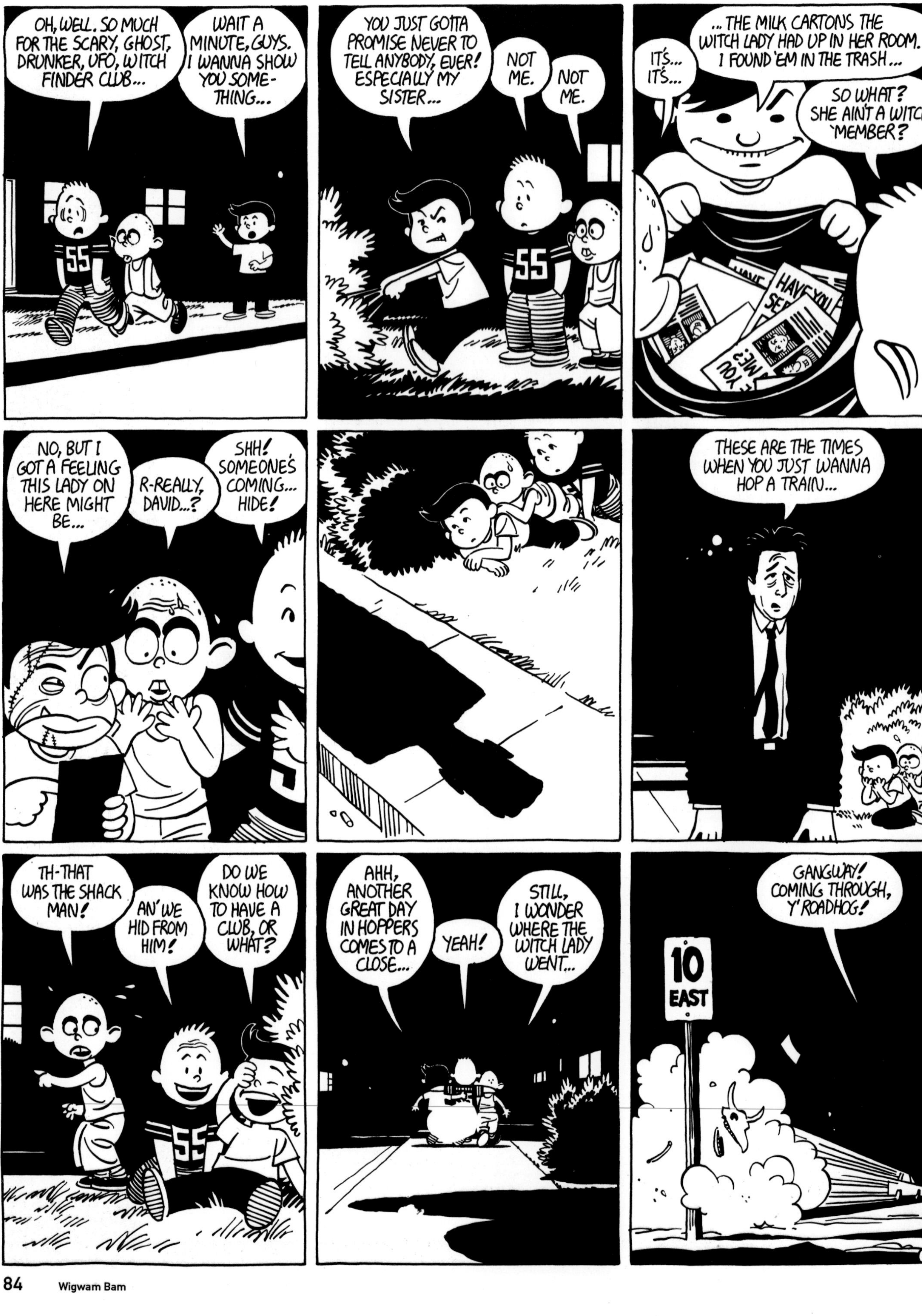
OH, WELL. SO MUCH FOR THE SCARY, GHOST, DRUNKER, UFO, WITCH FINDER CLUB...
WAIT A MINUTE, GUYS. I WANNA SHOW YOU SOME-THING...
YOU JUST GOTTA PROMISE NEVER TO TELL ANYBODY, EVER! ESPECIALLY MY SISTER...
NOT ME.
NOT ME.
IT'S... IT'S...
...THE MILK CARTONS THE WITCH LADY HAD UP IN HER ROOM. I FOUND 'EM IN THE TRASH...
SO WHAT? SHE AIN'T A WITCH, 'MEMBER?
NO, BUT I GOT A FEELING THIS LADY ON HERE MIGHT BE...
R-REALLY, DAVID...?
SHH! SOMEONE'S COMING... HIDE!
THESE ARE THE TIMES WHEN YOU JUST WANNA HOP A TRAIN...
TH-THAT WAS THE SHACK MAN!
AN' WE HID FROM HIM!
DO WE KNOW HOW TO HAVE A CLUB, OR WHAT?
AHH, ANOTHER GREAT DAY IN HOPPERS COMES TO A CLOSE...
YEAH!
STILL, I WONDER WHERE THE WITCH LADY WENT...
10 EAST
GANGWAY! COMING THROUGH, Y' ROADHOG!
16

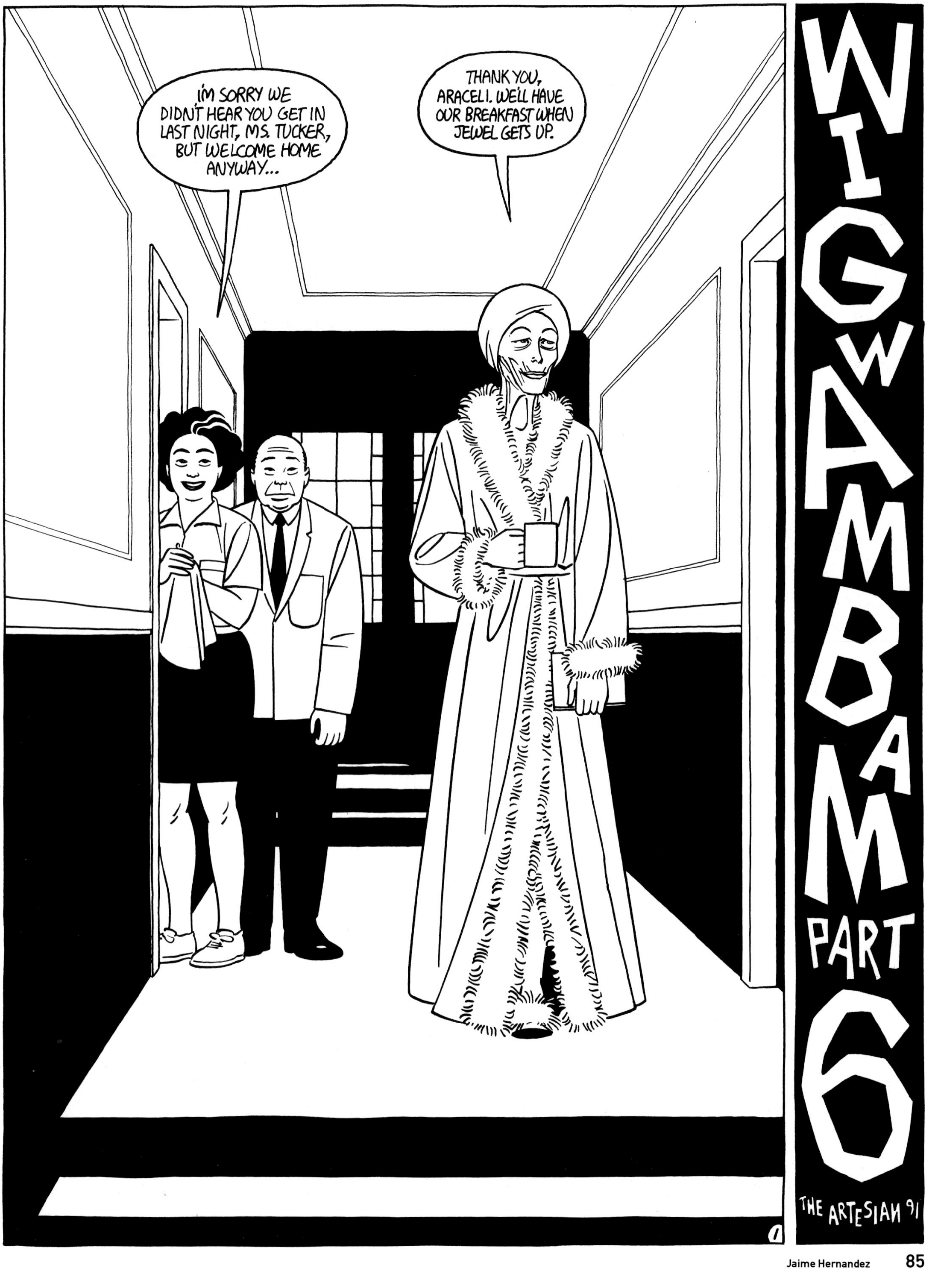
I'M SORRY WE DIDN'T HEAR YOU GET IN LAST NIGHT, MS. TUCKER, BUT WELCOME HOME ANYWAY...
THANK YOU, ARACELI. WE'LL HAVE OUR BREAKFAST WHEN JEWEL GETS UP.
WIGWAMBAM PART 6
THE ARTESIAN 91
1

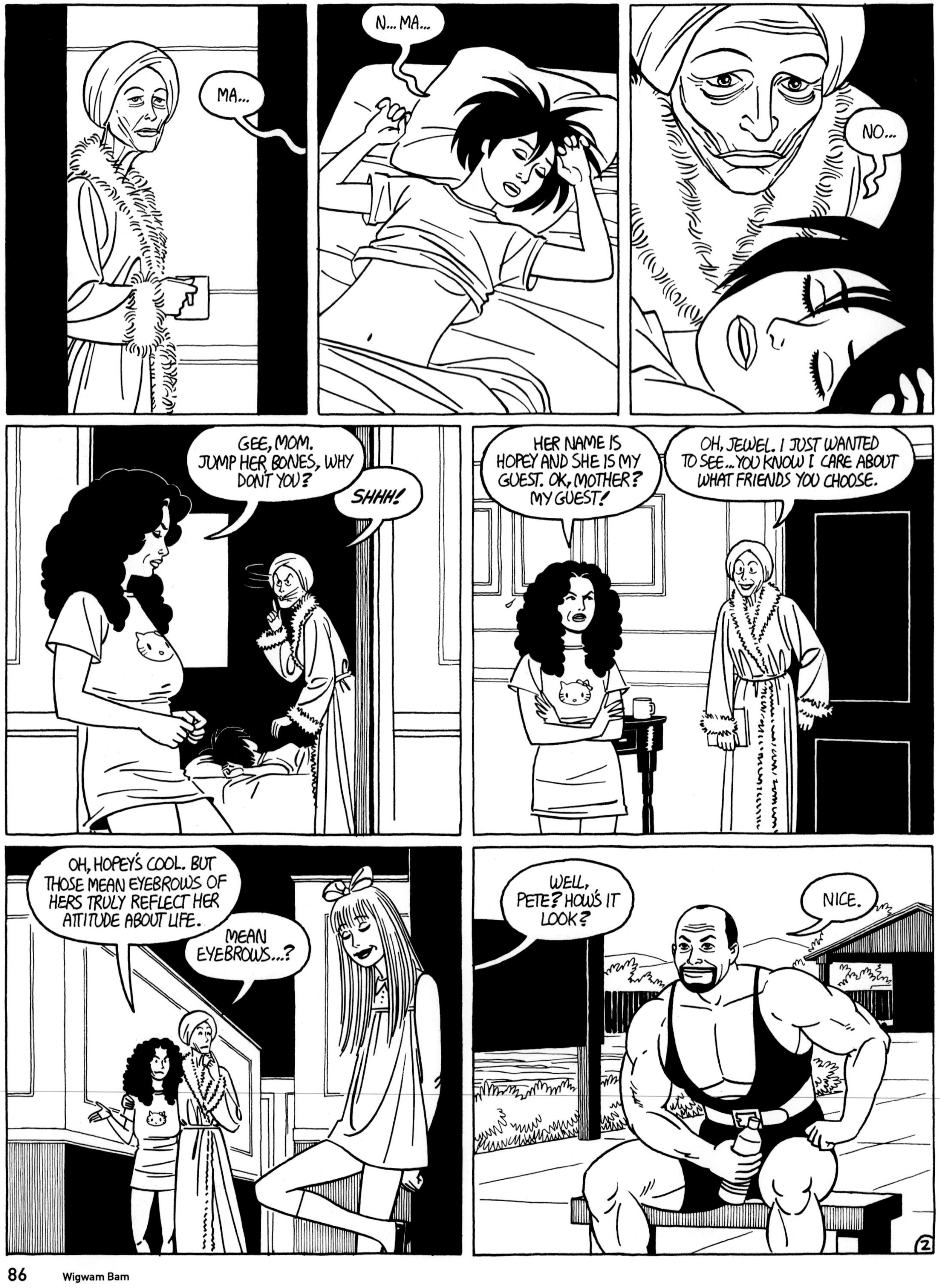
MA...
N... MA...
NO...
GEE, MOM. JUMP HER BONES, WHY DON'T YOU?
SHHH!
HER NAME IS HOPEY AND SHE IS MY GUEST. OK, MOTHER? MY GUEST!
OH, JEWEL. I JUST WANTED TO SEE... YOU KNOW I CARE ABOUT WHAT FRIENDS YOU CHOOSE.
OH, HOPEY'S COOL. BUT THOSE MEAN EYEBROWS OF HERS TRULY REFLECT HER ATTITUDE ABOUT LIFE.
MEAN EYEBROWS...?
WELL, PETE? HOW'S IT LOOK?
NICE.
2

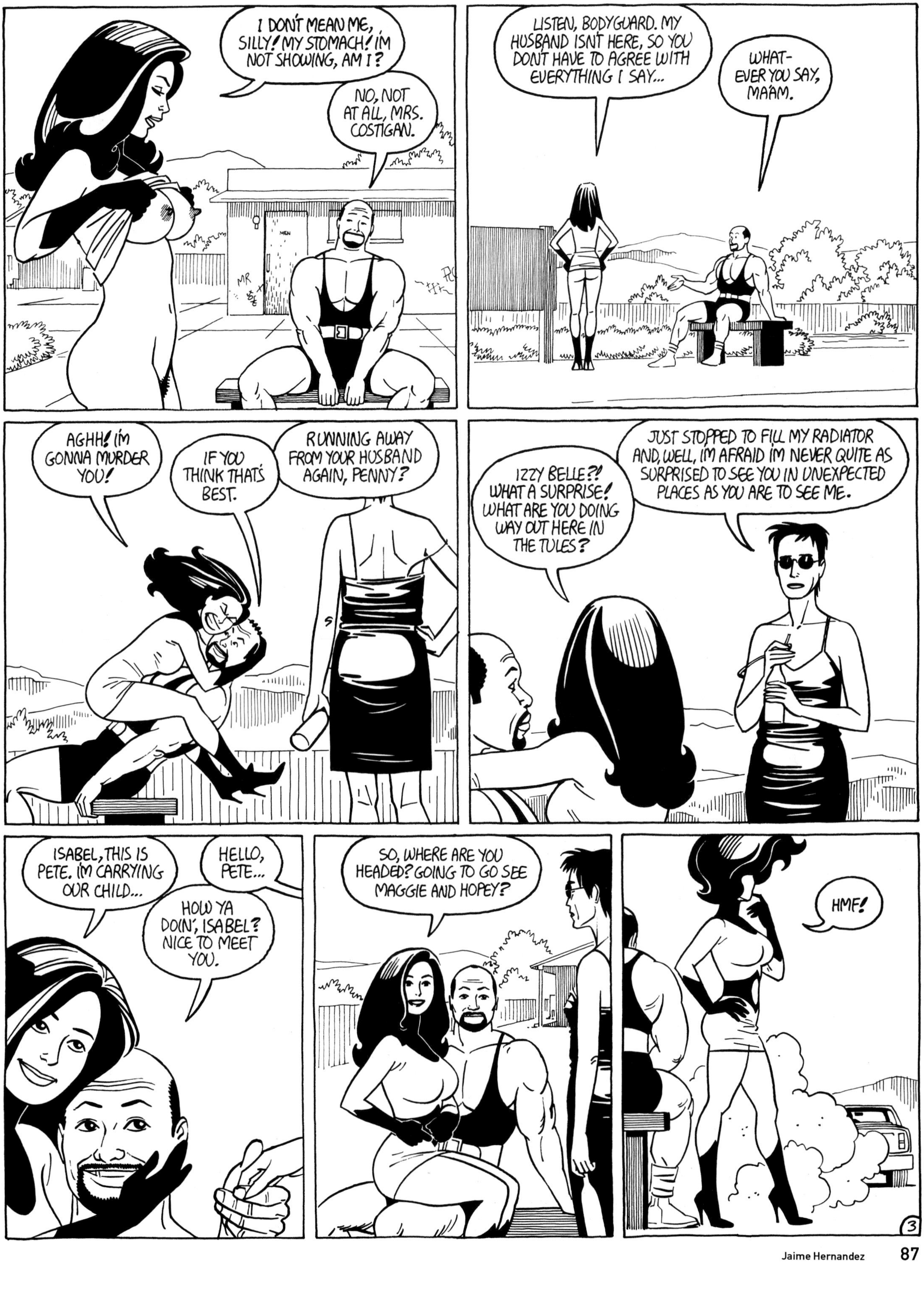
I DON'T MEAN ME, SILLY! MY STOMACH! I'M NOT SHOWING, AM I?
NO, NOT AT ALL, MRS. COSTIGAN.
MEN
LISTEN, BODYGUARD. MY HUSBAND ISN'T HERE, SO YOU DON'T HAVE TO AGREE WITH EVERYTHING I SAY...
WHAT-EVER YOU SAY, MA'AM.
AGHH! I'M GONNA MURDER YOU!
IF YOU THINK THAT'S BEST.
RUNNING AWAY FROM YOUR HUSBAND AGAIN, PENNY?
IZZY BELLE?! WHAT A SURPRISE! WHAT ARE YOU DOING WAY OUT HERE IN THE TULES?
JUST STOPPED TO FILL MY RADIATOR AND, WELL, I'M AFRAID I'M NEVER QUITE AS SURPRISED TO SEE YOU IN UNEXPECTED PLACES AS YOU ARE TO SEE ME.
ISABEL, THIS IS PETE. I'M CARRYING OUR CHILD...
HELLO, PETE...
HOW YA DOIN', ISABEL? NICE TO MEET YOU.
SO, WHERE ARE YOU HEADED? GOING TO GO SEE MAGGIE AND HOPEY?
HMF!
3

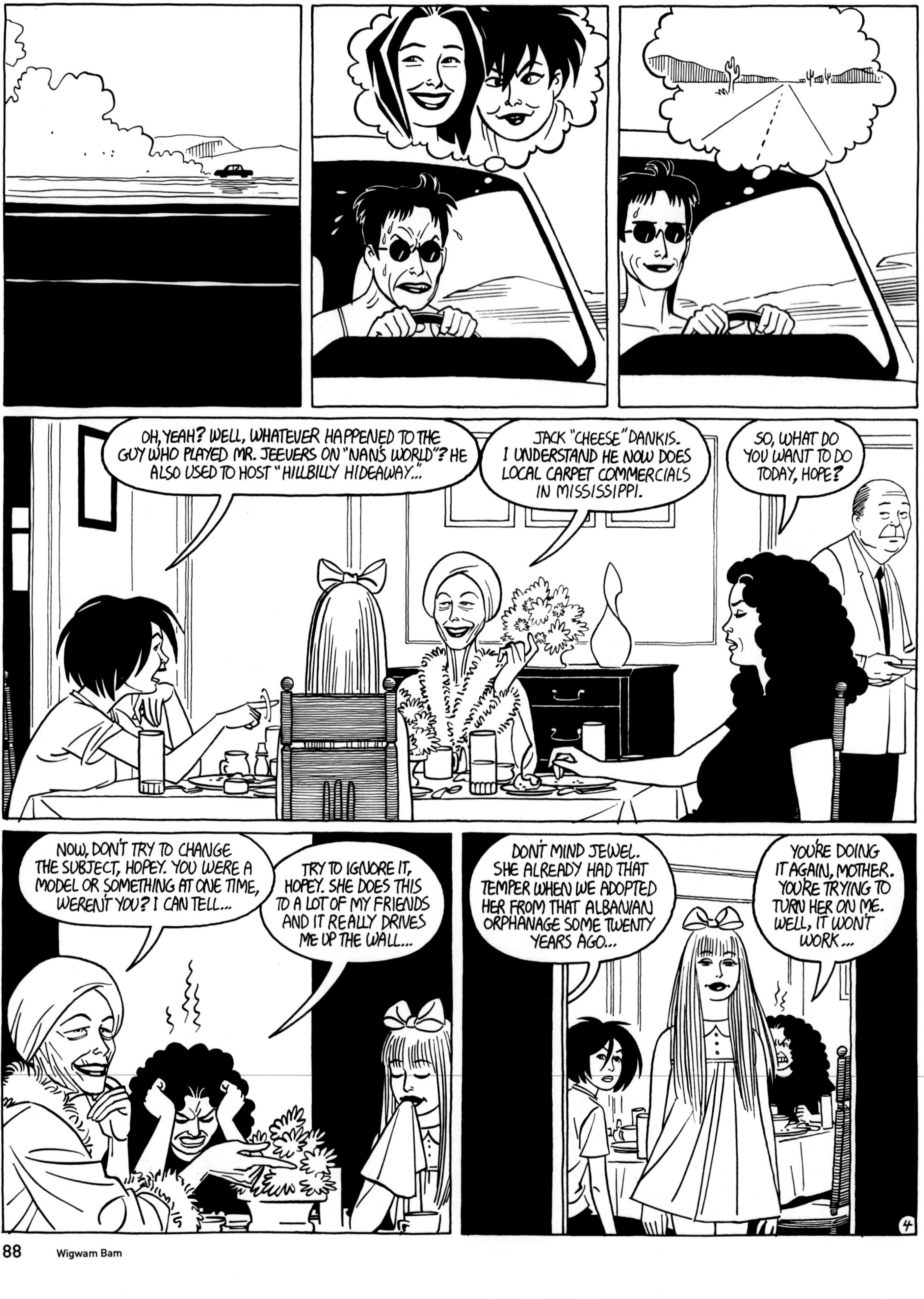
OH, YEAH? WELL, WHATEVER HAPPENED TO THE GUY WHO PLAYED MR. JEEVERS ON "NAN'S WORLD"? HE ALSO USED TO HOST "HILLBILLY HIDEAWAY"...
JACK "CHEESE" DANKIS. I UNDERSTAND HE NOW DOES LOCAL CARPET COMMERCIALS IN MISSISSIPPI.
SO, WHAT DO YOU WANT TO DO TODAY, HOPE?
NOW, DON'T TRY TO CHANGE THE SUBJECT, HOPEY. YOU WERE A MODEL OR SOMETHING AT ONE TIME, WEREN'T YOU? I CAN TELL...
TRY TO IGNORE IT, HOPEY. SHE DOES THIS TO A LOT OF MY FRIENDS AND IT REALLY DRIVES ME UP THE WALL...
DON'T MIND JEWEL. SHE ALREADY HAD THAT TEMPER WHEN WE ADOPTED HER FROM THAT ALBANIAN ORPHANAGE SOME TWENTY YEARS AGO...
YOU'RE DOING IT AGAIN, MOTHER. YOU'RE TRYING TO TURN HER ON ME. WELL, IT WON'T WORK...
4

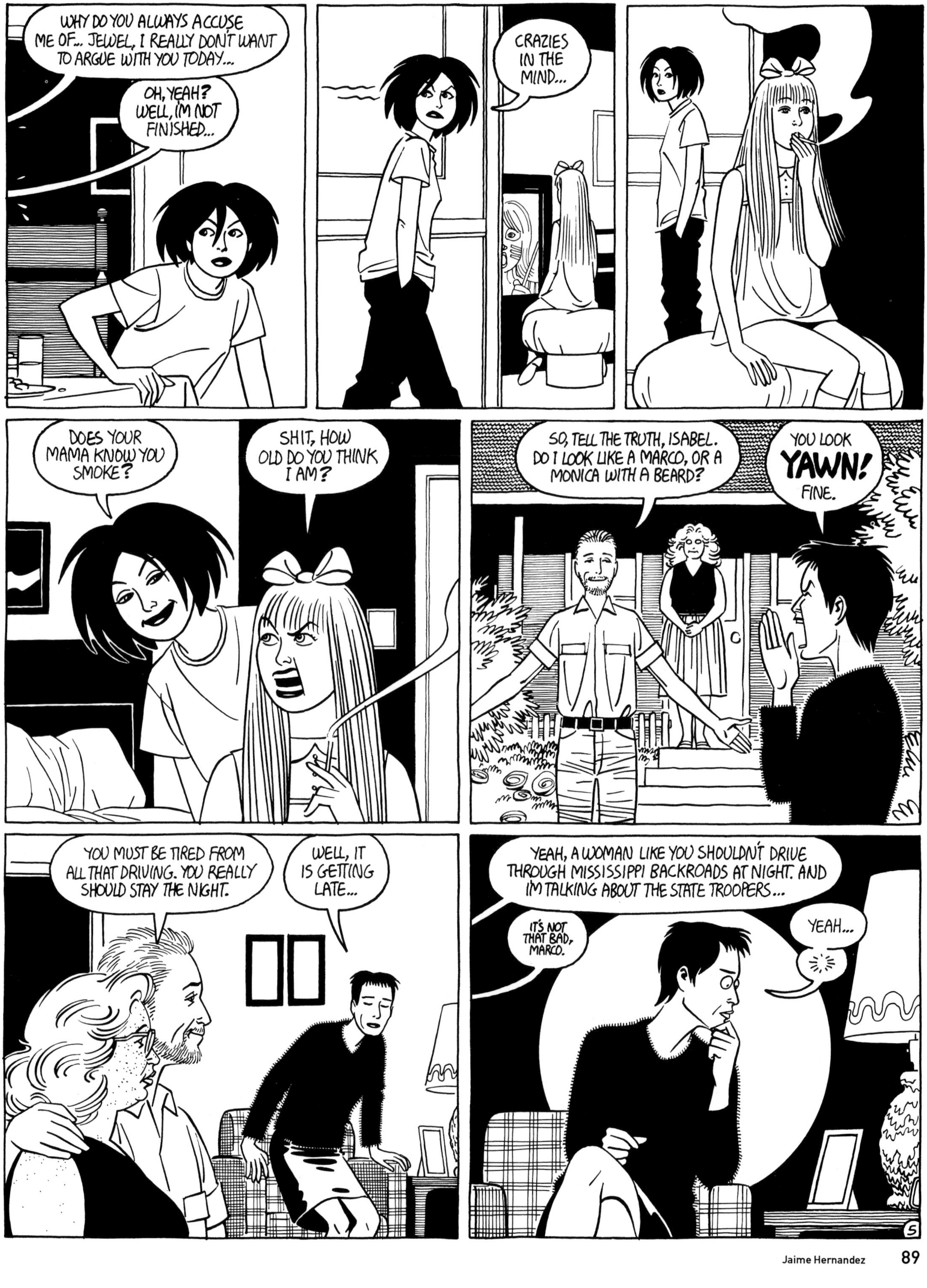
WHY DO YOU ALWAYS ACCUSE ME OF... JEWEL, I REALLY DON'T WANT TO ARGUE WITH YOU TODAY...
OH, YEAH? WELL, I'M NOT FINISHED...
CRAZIES IN THE MIND...
DOES YOUR MAMA KNOW YOU SMOKE?
SHIT, HOW OLD DO YOU THINK I AM?
SO, TELL THE TRUTH, ISABEL. DO I LOOK LIKE A MARCO, OR A MONICA WITH A BEARD?
YOU LOOK YAWN! FINE.
YOU MUST BE TIRED FROM ALL THAT DRIVING. YOU REALLY SHOULD STAY THE NIGHT.
WELL, IT IS GETTING LATE...
YEAH, A WOMAN LIKE YOU SHOULDN'T DRIVE THROUGH MISSISSIPPI BACKROADS AT NIGHT. AND I'M TALKING ABOUT THE STATE TROOPERS...
IT'S NOT THAT BAD, MARCO.
YEAH...
5

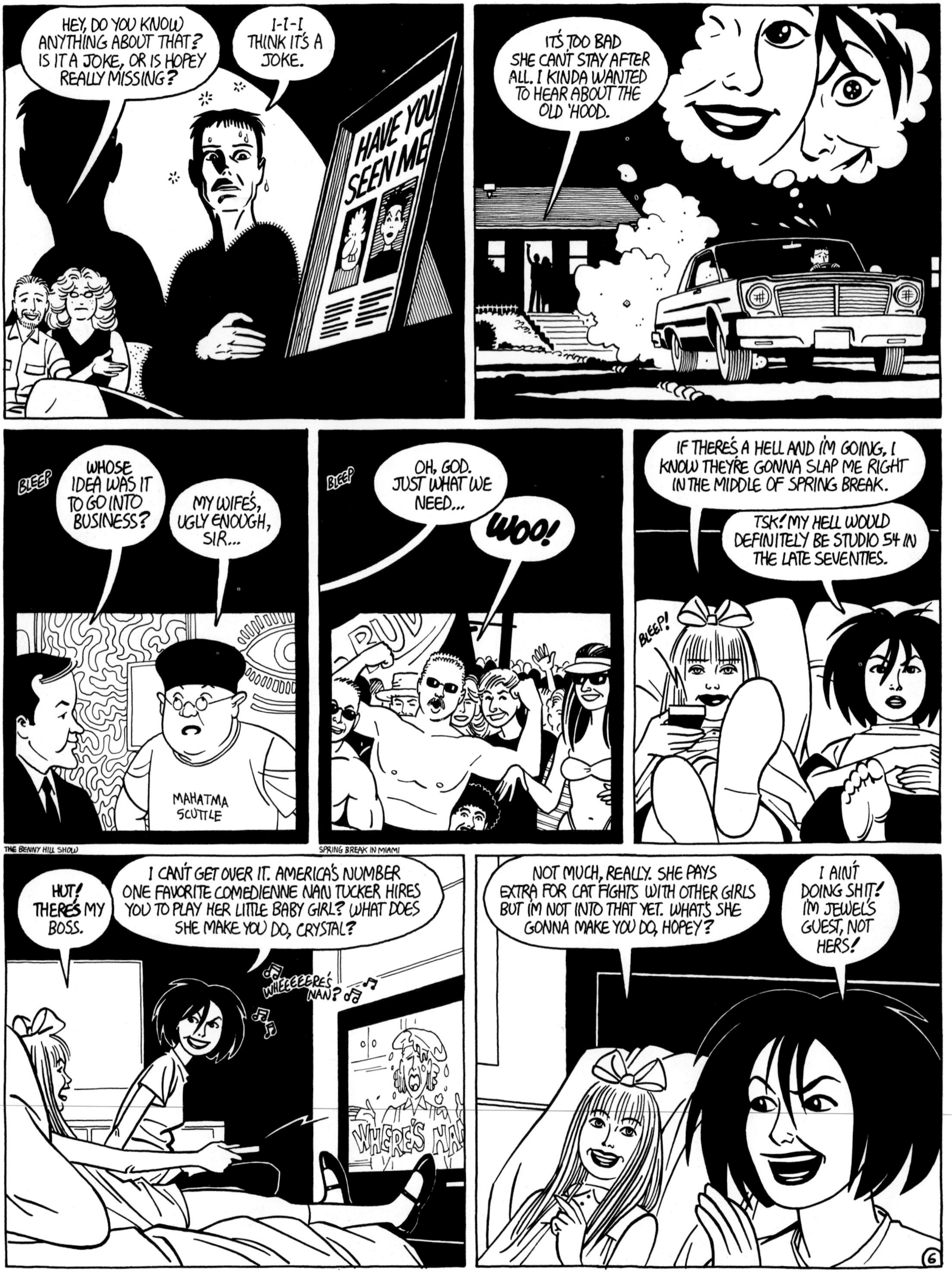
HEY, DO YOU KNOW ANYTHING ABOUT THAT? IS IT A JOKE, OR IS HOPEY REALLY MISSING?
I-I-I THINK IT'S A JOKE.
HAVE YOU SEEN ME
IT'S TOO BAD SHE CAN'T STAY AFTER ALL. I KINDA WANTED TO HEAR ABOUT THE OLD 'HOOD.
BLEEP
WHOSE IDEA WAS IT TO GO INTO BUSINESS?
MY WIFE'S, UGLY ENOUGH, SIR...
MAHATMA SCUTTLE
THE BENNY HILL SHOW
BLEEP
OH, GOD. JUST WHAT WE NEED...
WOO!
SPRING BREAK IN MIAMI
IF THERE'S A HELL AND I'M GOING, I KNOW THEY'RE GONNA SLAP ME RIGHT IN THE MIDDLE OF SPRING BREAK.
TSK! MY HELL WOULD DEFINITELY BE STUDIO 54 IN THE LATE SEVENTIES.
BLEEP!
HUT! THERE'S MY BOSS.
I CAN'T GET OVER IT. AMERICA'S NUMBER ONE FAVORITE COMEDIENNE NAN TUCKER HIRES YOU TO PLAY HER LITTLE BABY GIRL? WHAT DOES SHE MAKE YOU DO, CRYSTAL?
WHEEEEERE'S NAN?
WHERE'S NA
NOT MUCH, REALLY. SHE PAYS EXTRA FOR CAT FIGHTS WITH OTHER GIRLS BUT I'M NOT INTO THAT YET. WHAT'S SHE GONNA MAKE YOU DO, HOPEY?
I AIN'T DOING SHIT! I'M JEWEL'S GUEST, NOT HERS!
6

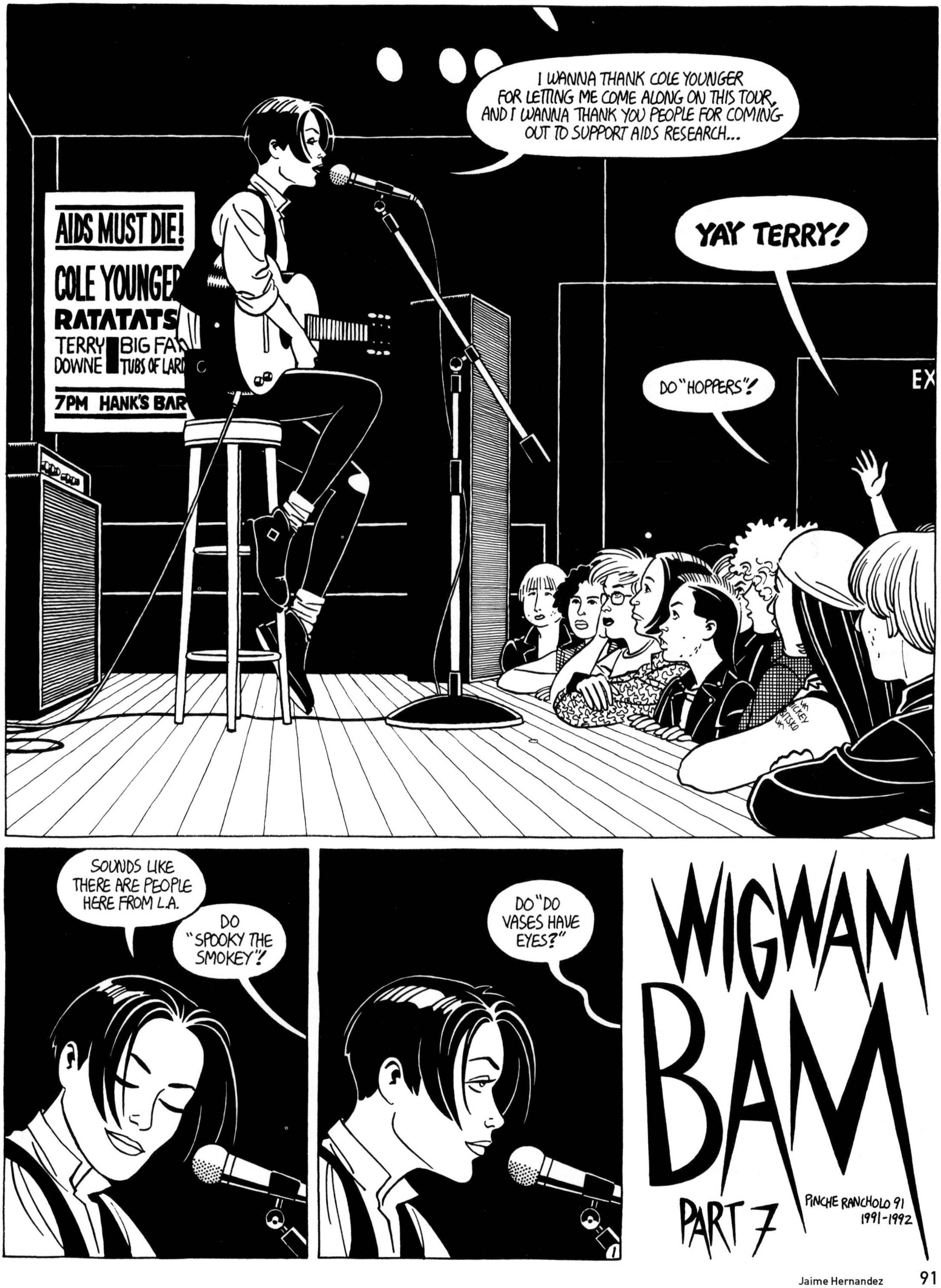
I WANNA THANK COLE YOUNGER FOR LETTING ME COME ALONG ON THIS TOUR, AND I WANNA THANK YOU PEOPLE FOR COMING OUT TO SUPPORT AIDS RESEARCH...
AIDS MUST DIE!
COLE YOUNGER
RATATATS
TERRY DOWNE
BIG FA
TUBS OF LAR
7PM HANK'S BAR
YAY TERRY!
DO "HOPPERS"!
SOUNDS LIKE THERE ARE PEOPLE HERE FROM L.A.
DO "SPOOKY THE SMOKEY"!
DO "DO VASES HAVE EYES?"
WIGWAM BAM
PART 7
PINCHE RANCHOLO 91
1991-1992

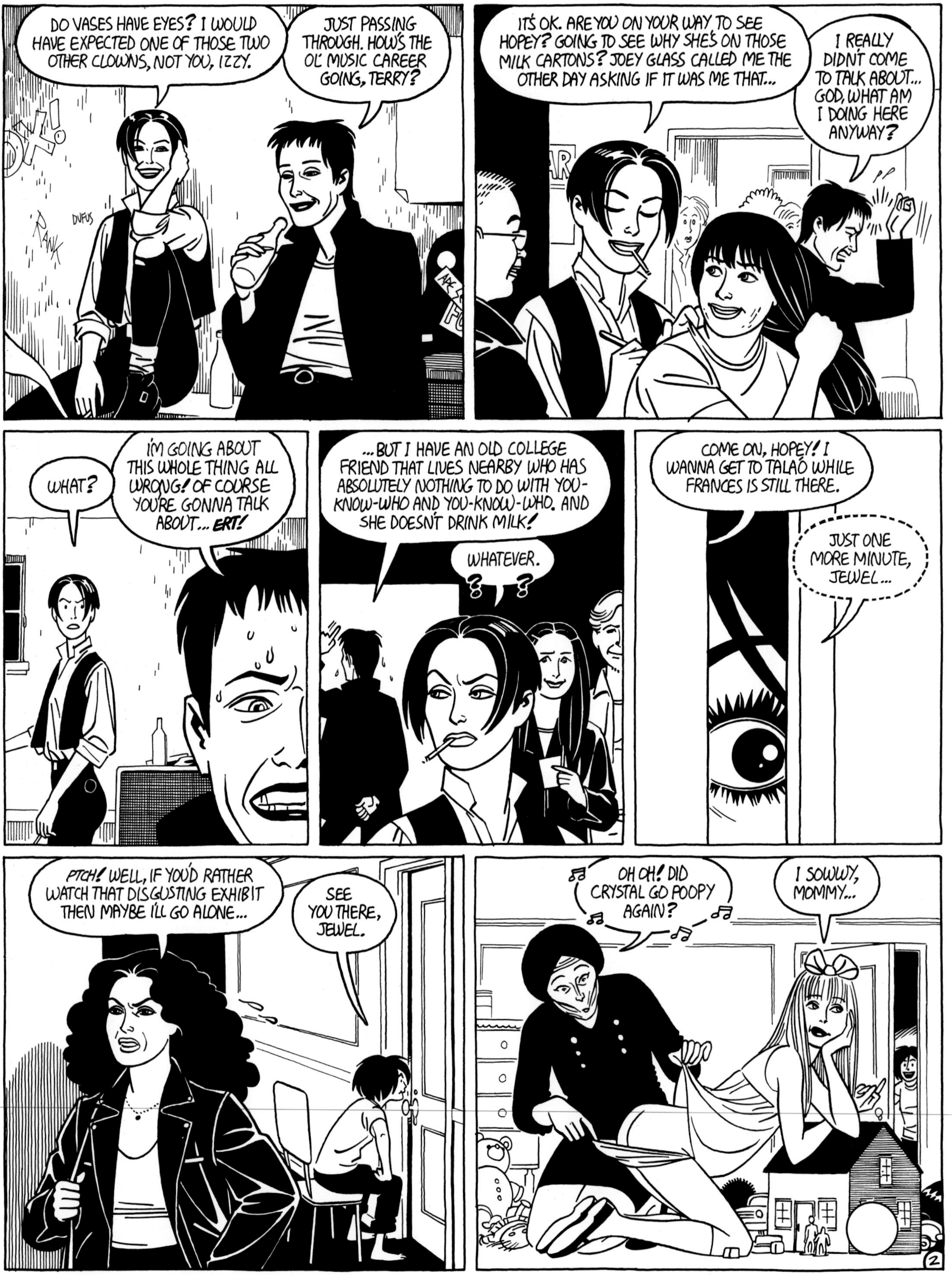
DO VASES HAVE EYES? I WOULD HAVE EXPECTED ONE OF THOSE TWO OTHER CLOWNS, NOT YOU, IZZY.
JUST PASSING THROUGH. HOW'S THE OL' MUSIC CAREER GOING, TERRY?
DUFUS
RANK
IT'S OK. ARE YOU ON YOUR WAY TO SEE HOPEY? GOING TO SEE WHY SHE'S ON THOSE MILK CARTONS? JOEY GLASS CALLED ME THE OTHER DAY ASKING IF IT WAS ME THAT...
I REALLY DIDN'T COME TO TALK ABOUT... GOD, WHAT AM I DOING HERE ANYWAY?
WHAT?
I'M GOING ABOUT THIS WHOLE THING ALL WRONG! OF COURSE YOU'RE GONNA TALK ABOUT... ERT!
...BUT I HAVE AN OLD COLLEGE FRIEND THAT LIVES NEARBY WHO HAS ABSOLUTELY NOTHING TO DO WITH YOU-KNOW-WHO AND YOU-KNOW-WHO. AND SHE DOESN'T DRINK MILK!
WHATEVER.
COME ON, HOPEY! I WANNA GET TO TALAÕ WHILE FRANCES IS STILL THERE.
JUST ONE MORE MINUTE, JEWEL...
PTCH! WELL, IF YOU'D RATHER WATCH THAT DISGUSTING EXHIBIT THEN MAYBE I'LL GO ALONE...
SEE YOU THERE, JEWEL.
OH OH! DID CRYSTAL GO POOPY AGAIN?
I SOWWY, MOMMY...
2

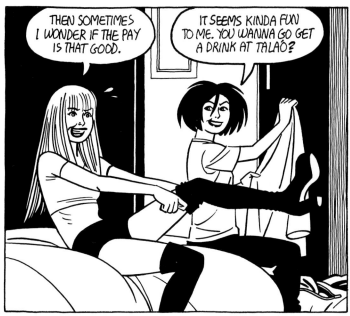

THEN SOMETIMES I WONDER IF THE PAY IS THAT GOOD.

IT SEEMS KINDA FUN TO ME. YOU WANNA GO GET A DRINK AT TALAO?

REMEMBER, I KINDA TOOK AN OATH TO MS. TUCKER THAT I DON'T TALK ABOUT MY JOB, IF YOU KNOW WHAT I MEAN...

DON'T WORRY ABOUT ME, CRYSTAL. MOM... UH, MUM'S THE WORD.

SAY NOPE TO HOPE, AND GAG TO MAG...

I WONDER IF IT'S AN EAST COAST THING NOT TO PUT NUMBERS ON YOUR HOUSE, OR IF I'M JUST SNOWBLIND.

ISABEL! THIS WAY!

I CAN'T BELIEVE IT'S YOU. WHAT'S IT BEEN, THIRTEEN YEARS?

B-B-BARB?

IT'S ME, BUT I GUESS I LOOK SOMEWHAT DIFFERENT TO YOU. I FINALLY GOT RID OF THE DOROTHY HAMMIL HAIRCUT, BUT THEN I ADOPTED HER THIGHS... THREE TIMES OVER, I'M AFRAID...

YOU KNOW, IT'S A REAL FUNNY COINCIDENCE THAT YOU CAME BY BECAUSE I WAS JUST IN YOUR NEIGHBORHOOD OUT IN CALIFORNIA LAST WEEK VISITING, BUT I DIDN'T KNOW HOW TO GET IN TOUCH WITH YOU. YOU'RE NOT LISTED, ARE YOU?

NNNNGHHH...

3

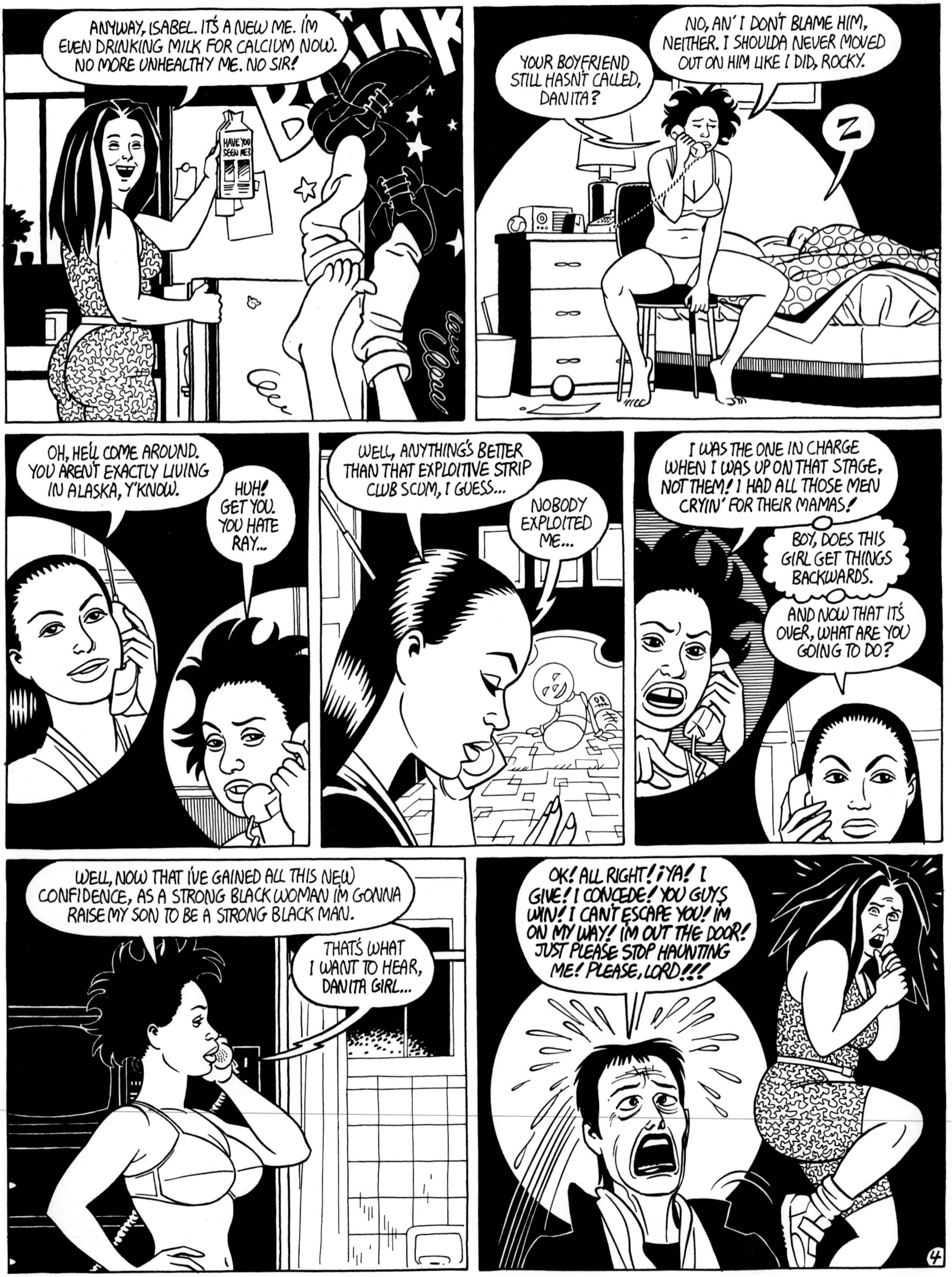
ANYWAY, ISABEL. IT'S A NEW ME. I'M EVEN DRINKING MILK FOR CALCIUM NOW. NO MORE UNHEALTHY ME. NO SIR!
HAVE YOU SEEN ME?
YOUR BOYFRIEND STILL HASN'T CALLED, DANITA?
NO, AN' I DON'T BLAME HIM, NEITHER. I SHOULDA NEVER MOVED OUT ON HIM LIKE I DID, ROCKY.
Z
OH, HE'LL COME AROUND. YOU AREN'T EXACTLY LIVING IN ALASKA, Y'KNOW.
HUH! GET YOU. YOU HATE RAY...
WELL, ANYTHING'S BETTER THAN THAT EXPLOITIVE STRIP CLUB SCUM, I GUESS...
NOBODY EXPLOITED ME...
I WAS THE ONE IN CHARGE WHEN I WAS UP ON THAT STAGE, NOT THEM! I HAD ALL THOSE MEN CRYIN' FOR THEIR MAMAS!
BOY, DOES THIS GIRL GET THINGS BACKWARDS.
AND NOW THAT IT'S OVER, WHAT ARE YOU GOING TO DO?
WELL, NOW THAT I'VE GAINED ALL THIS NEW CONFIDENCE, AS A STRONG BLACK WOMAN I'M GONNA RAISE MY SON TO BE A STRONG BLACK MAN.
THAT'S WHAT I WANT TO HEAR, DANITA GIRL...
OK! ALL RIGHT! ¡YA! I GIVE! I CONCEDE! YOU GUYS WIN! I CAN'T ESCAPE YOU! I'M ON MY WAY! I'M OUT THE DOOR! JUST PLEASE STOP HAUNTING ME! PLEASE, LORD!!!
4

FUCKIN' SHAME, HUH, DOYLE?

FUCKIN' SHAME, JOE.

Closed out of business

THAT PLACE MUST HAVE MEANT A LOT TO HIM, JOEY...

WELL, SURE, JANET. BUMPER'S WAS HIS HOME AWAY FROM... AH, HIS NEW GIRLFRIEND OUGHTA MAKE HIM FORGET REAL QUICK.

NAMI, DOYLE'S AT THE DOOR.

TSK! WELL, TELL HIM I'M NOT HERE, NOEL!

UCSB

SHE'S NOT HE... HUH?

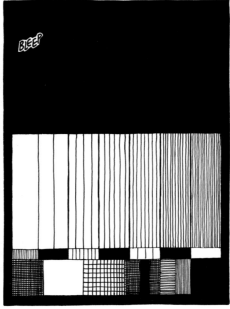

BLEEP!

⑤

Jaime Hernandez   95

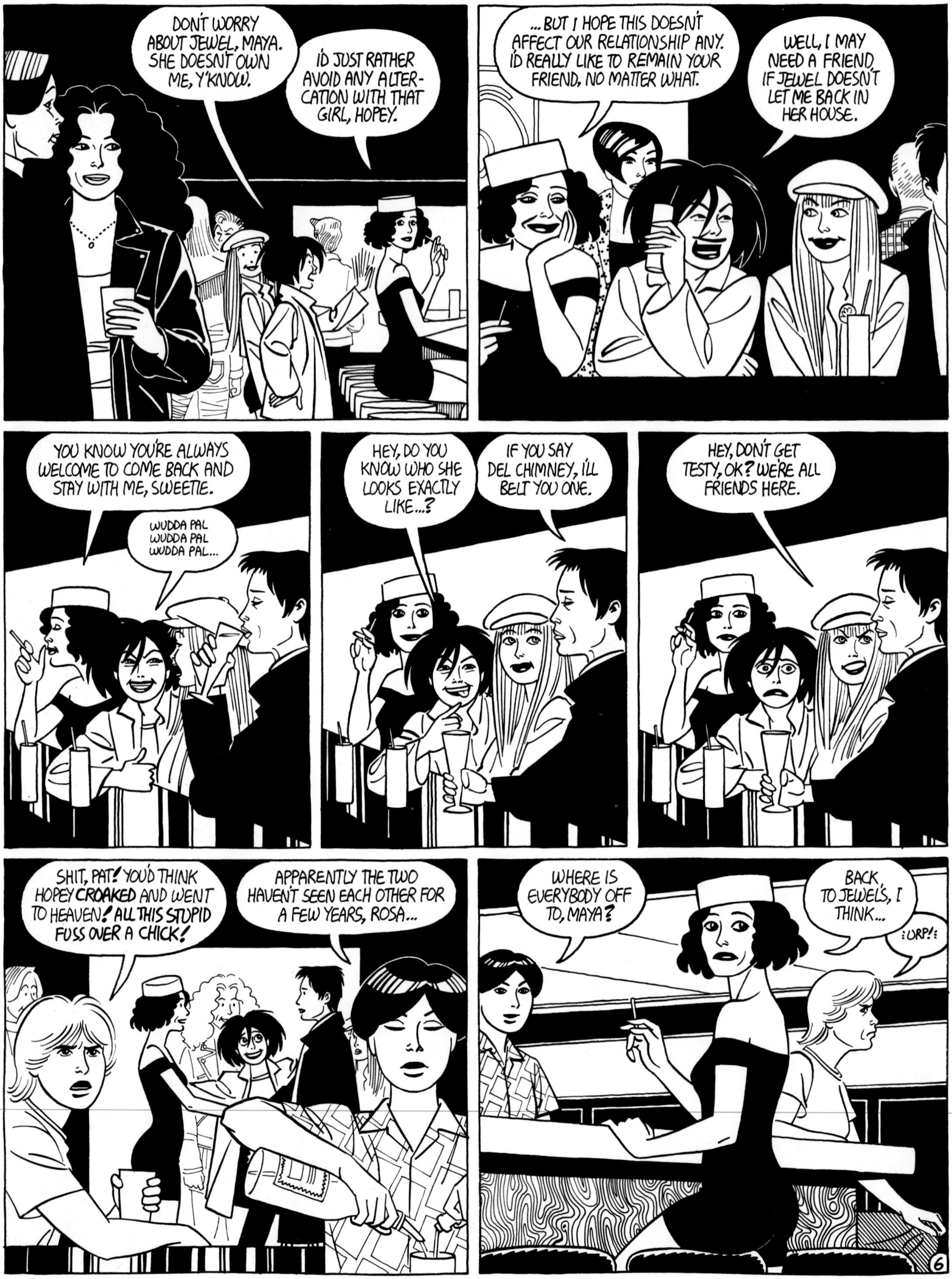
DON'T WORRY ABOUT JEWEL, MAYA. SHE DOESN'T OWN ME, Y'KNOW.
I'D JUST RATHER AVOID ANY ALTER-CATION WITH THAT GIRL, HOPEY.
...BUT I HOPE THIS DOESN'T AFFECT OUR RELATIONSHIP ANY. I'D REALLY LIKE TO REMAIN YOUR FRIEND, NO MATTER WHAT.
WELL, I MAY NEED A FRIEND, IF JEWEL DOESN'T LET ME BACK IN HER HOUSE.
YOU KNOW YOU'RE ALWAYS WELCOME TO COME BACK AND STAY WITH ME, SWEETIE.
WUDDA PAL WUDDA PAL WUDDA PAL...
HEY, DO YOU KNOW WHO SHE LOOKS EXACTLY LIKE...?
IF YOU SAY DEL CHIMNEY, I'LL BELT YOU ONE.
HEY, DON'T GET TESTY, OK? WE'RE ALL FRIENDS HERE.
SHIT, PAT! YOU'D THINK HOPEY CROAKED AND WENT TO HEAVEN! ALL THIS STUPID FUSS OVER A CHICK!
APPARENTLY THE TWO HAVEN'T SEEN EACH OTHER FOR A FEW YEARS, ROSA...
WHERE IS EVERYBODY OFF TO, MAYA?
BACK, TO JEWEL'S, I THINK...
URP!
6

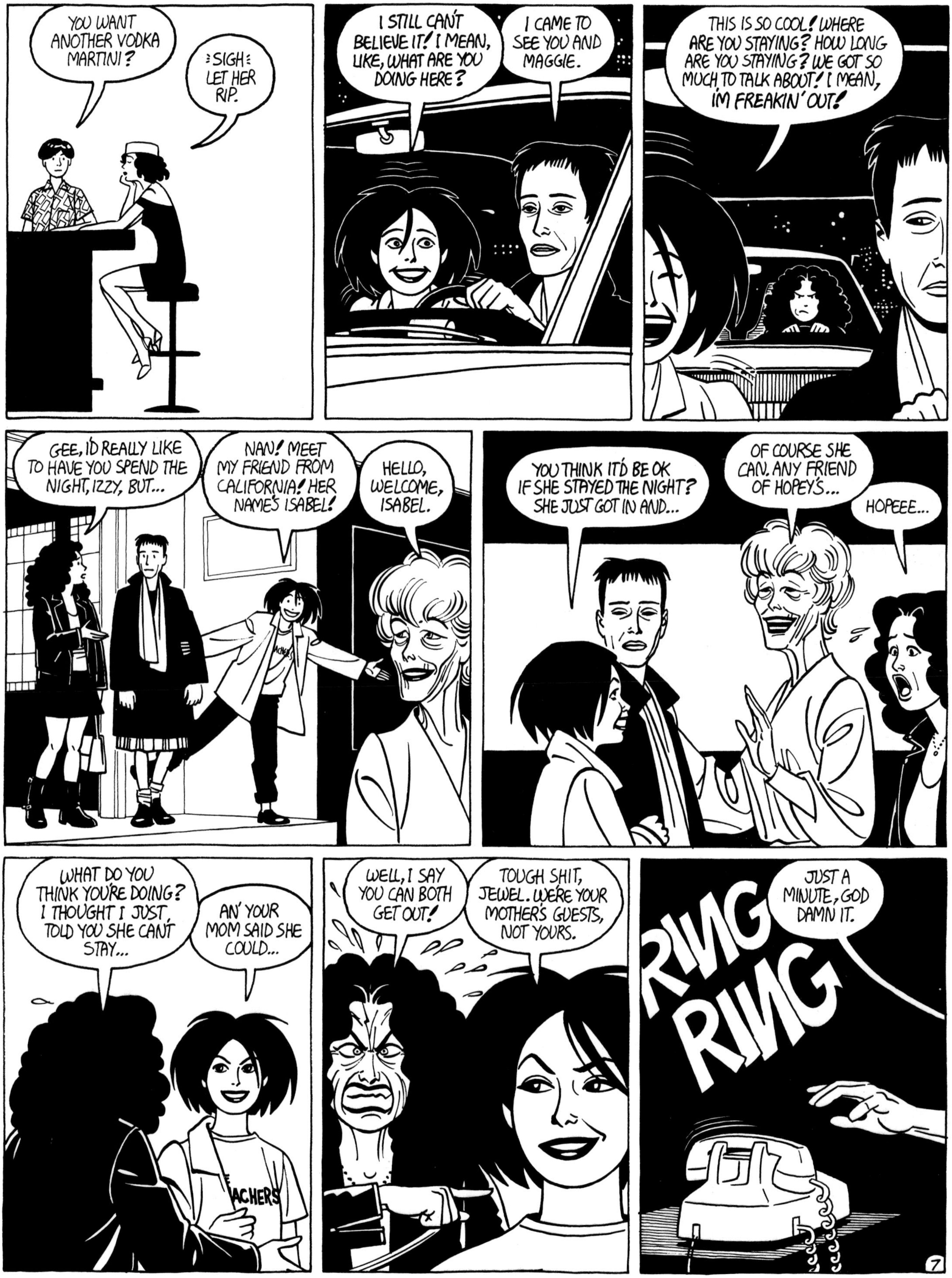
YOU WANT ANOTHER VODKA MARTINI?
SIGH LET HER RIP.
I STILL CAN'T BELIEVE IT! I MEAN, LIKE, WHAT ARE YOU DOING HERE?
I CAME TO SEE YOU AND MAGGIE.
THIS IS SO COOL! WHERE ARE YOU STAYING? HOW LONG ARE YOU STAYING? WE GOT SO MUCH TO TALK ABOUT! I MEAN, I'M FREAKIN' OUT!
GEE, I'D REALLY LIKE TO HAVE YOU SPEND THE NIGHT, IZZY, BUT...
NAN! MEET MY FRIEND FROM CALIFORNIA! HER NAME'S ISABEL!
HELLO, WELCOME, ISABEL.
YOU THINK IT'D BE OK IF SHE STAYED THE NIGHT? SHE JUST GOT IN AND...
OF COURSE SHE CAN. ANY FRIEND OF HOPEY'S...
HOPEEE...
WHAT DO YOU THINK YOU'RE DOING? I THOUGHT I JUST TOLD YOU SHE CAN'T STAY...
AN' YOUR MOM SAID SHE COULD...
WELL, I SAY YOU CAN BOTH GET OUT!
TOUGH SHIT, JEWEL. WE'RE YOUR MOTHER'S GUESTS, NOT YOURS.
RING RING
JUST A MINUTE, GOD DAMN IT.
7

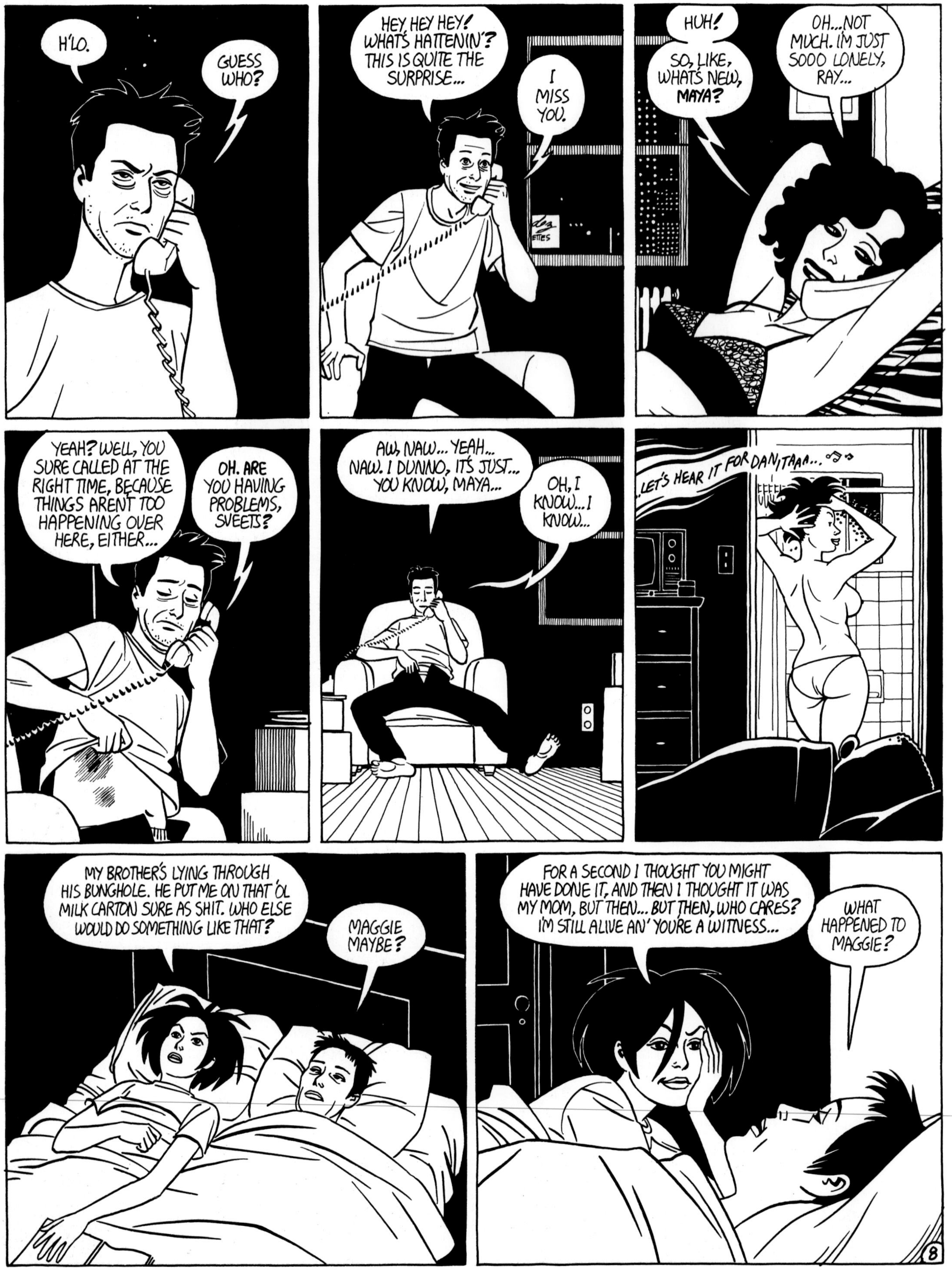
H'LO.
GUESS WHO?
HEY, HEY HEY! WHAT'S HATTENIN'? THIS IS QUITE THE SURPRISE...
I MISS YOU.
HUH!
SO, LIKE, WHAT'S NEW, MAYA?
OH... NOT MUCH. I'M JUST SOOO LONELY, RAY...
YEAH? WELL, YOU SURE CALLED AT THE RIGHT TIME, BECAUSE THINGS AREN'T TOO HAPPENING OVER HERE, EITHER...
OH. ARE YOU HAVING PROBLEMS, SWEETS?
AW, NAW... YEAH... NAW. I DUNNO, IT'S JUST... YOU KNOW, MAYA...
OH, I KNOW... I KNOW...
...LET'S HEAR IT FOR DANITAAA...
MY BROTHER'S LYING THROUGH HIS BUNGHOLE. HE PUT ME ON THAT 'OL MILK CARTON SURE AS SHIT. WHO ELSE WOULD DO SOMETHING LIKE THAT?
MAGGIE MAYBE?
FOR A SECOND I THOUGHT YOU MIGHT HAVE DONE IT, AND THEN I THOUGHT IT WAS MY MOM, BUT THEN... BUT THEN, WHO CARES? I'M STILL ALIVE AN' YOU'RE A WITNESS...
WHAT HAPPENED TO MAGGIE?
8

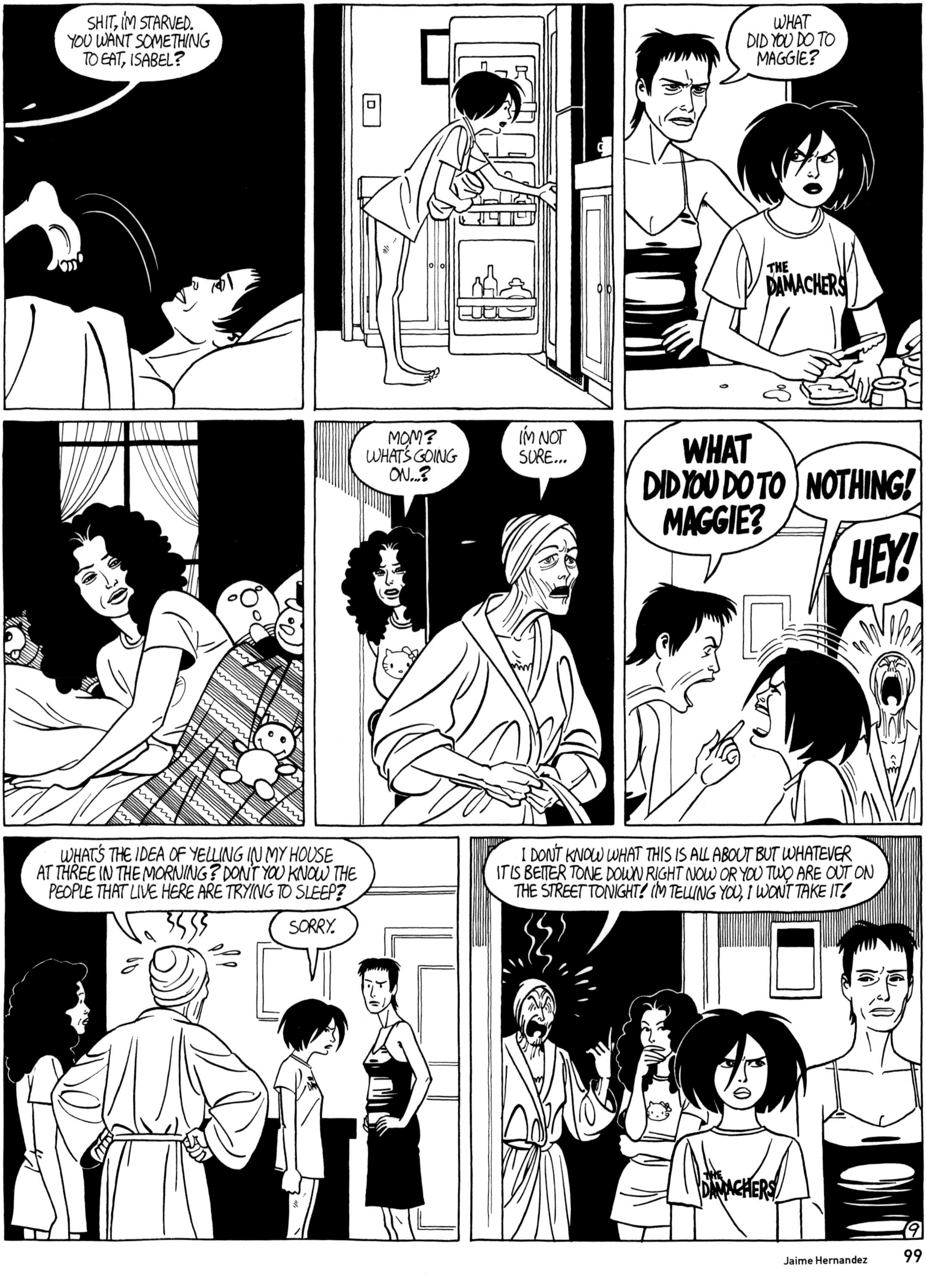
SHIT, I'M STARVED. YOU WANT SOMETHING TO EAT, ISABEL?
WHAT DID YOU DO TO MAGGIE?
THE DAMACHERS
MOM? WHAT'S GOING ON...?
I'M NOT SURE...
WHAT DID YOU DO TO MAGGIE?
NOTHING!
HEY!
WHAT'S THE IDEA OF YELLING IN MY HOUSE AT THREE IN THE MORNING? DON'T YOU KNOW THE PEOPLE THAT LIVE HERE ARE TRYING TO SLEEP?
SORRY.
I DON'T KNOW WHAT THIS IS ALL ABOUT BUT WHATEVER IT IS BETTER TONE DOWN RIGHT NOW OR YOU TWO ARE OUT ON THE STREET TONIGHT! I'M TELLING YOU, I WON'T TAKE IT!
THE DAMACHERS
9

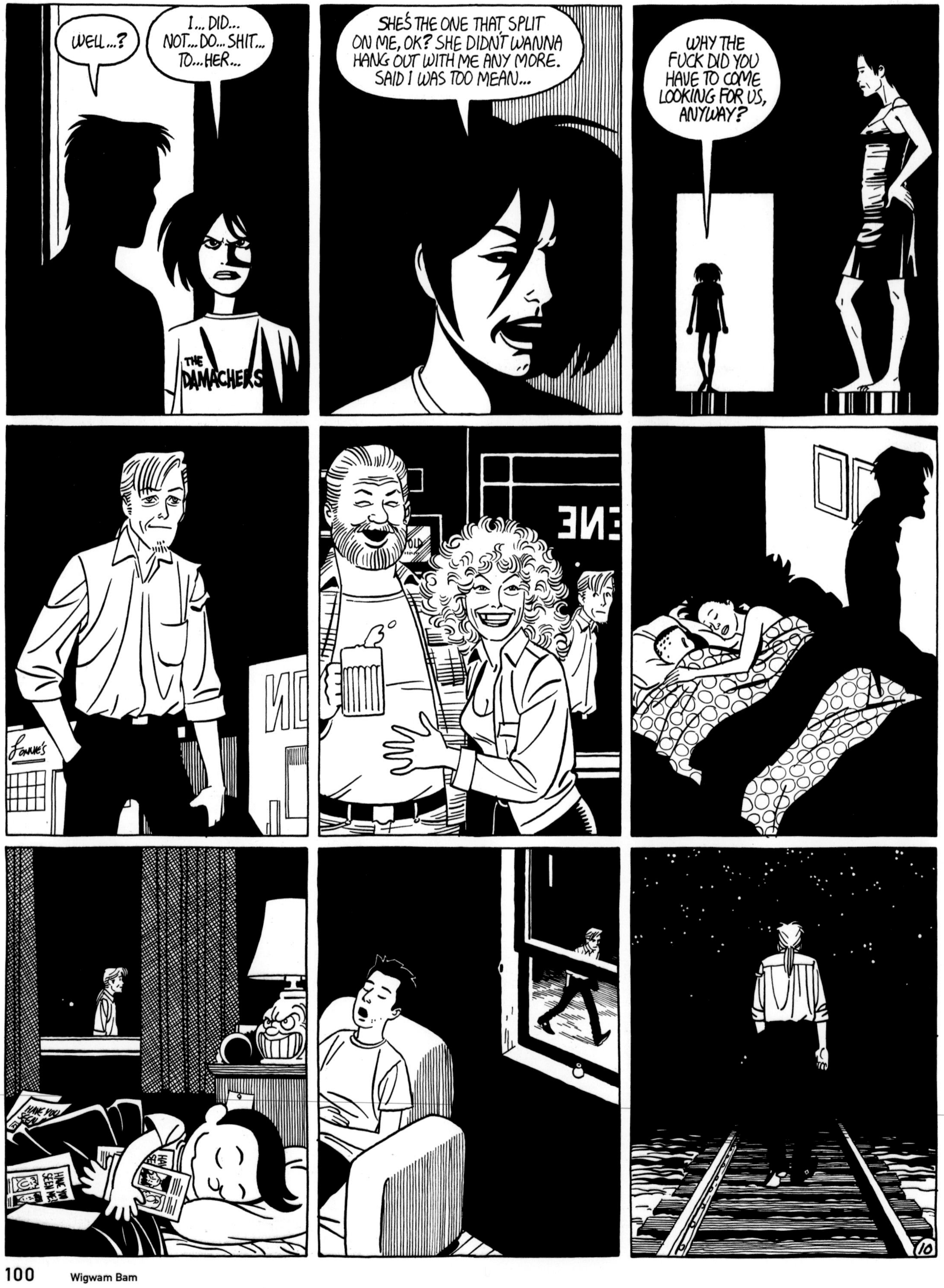
WELL...?
I... DID... NOT... DO... SHIT... TO... HER...
THE DAMACHERS
SHE'S THE ONE THAT SPLIT ON ME, OK? SHE DIDN'T WANNA HANG OUT WITH ME ANY MORE. SAID I WAS TOO MEAN...
WHY THE FUCK DID YOU HAVE TO COME LOOKING FOR US, ANYWAY?
HAVE YOU SEEN HER?

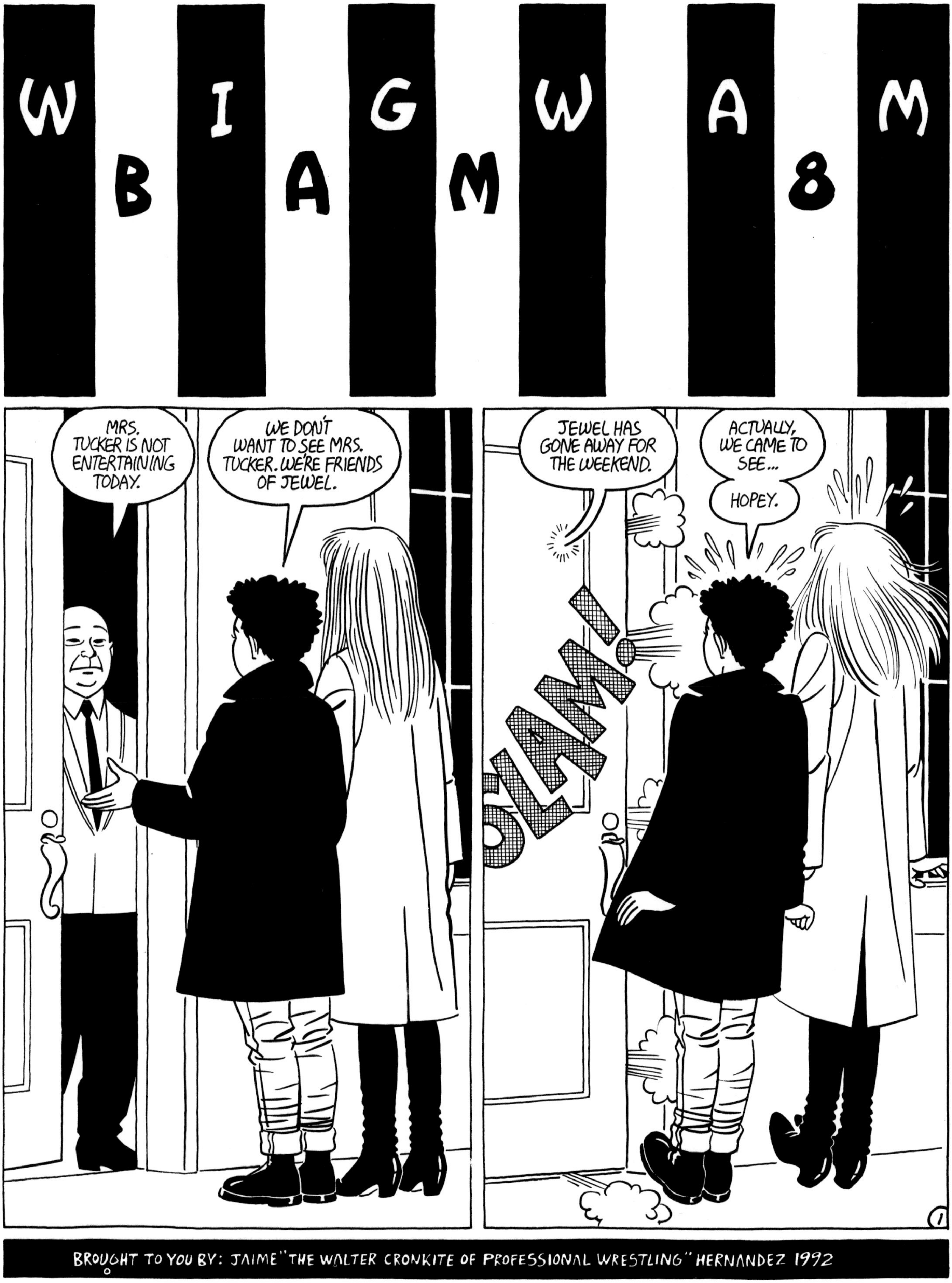
W B I A G M W A M 8 M
MRS. TUCKER IS NOT ENTERTAINING TODAY.
WE DON'T WANT TO SEE MRS. TUCKER. WE'RE FRIENDS OF JEWEL.
JEWEL HAS GONE AWAY FOR THE WEEKEND.
ACTUALLY, WE CAME TO SEE...
HOPEY.
SLAM!
1
BROUGHT TO YOU BY: JAIME "THE WALTER CRONKITE OF PROFESSIONAL WRESTLING" HERNANDEZ 1992

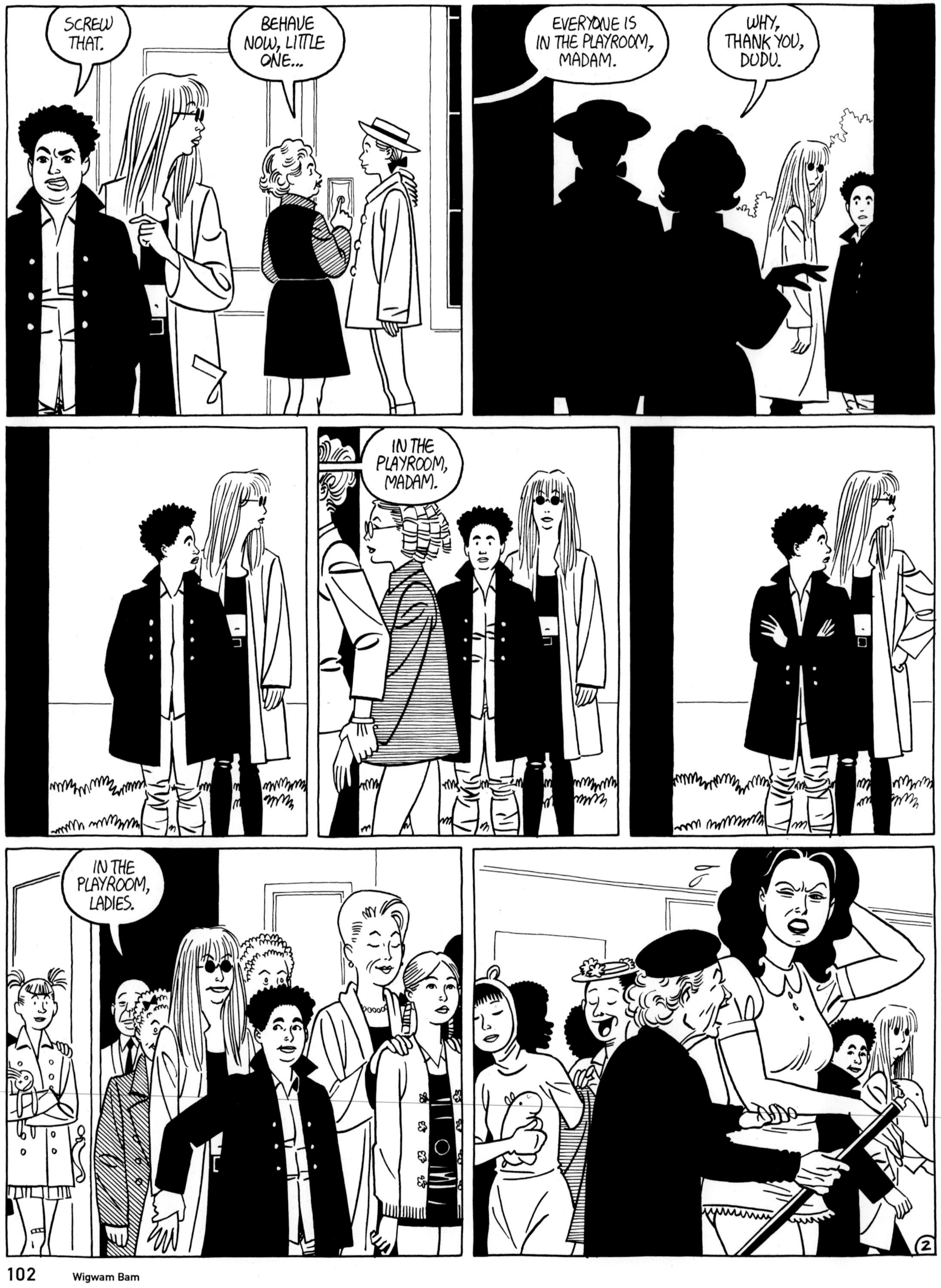
SCREW THAT.
BEHAVE NOW, LITTLE ONE...
EVERYONE IS IN THE PLAYROOM, MADAM.
WHY, THANK YOU, DUDU.
IN THE PLAYROOM, MADAM.
IN THE PLAYROOM, LADIES.
2

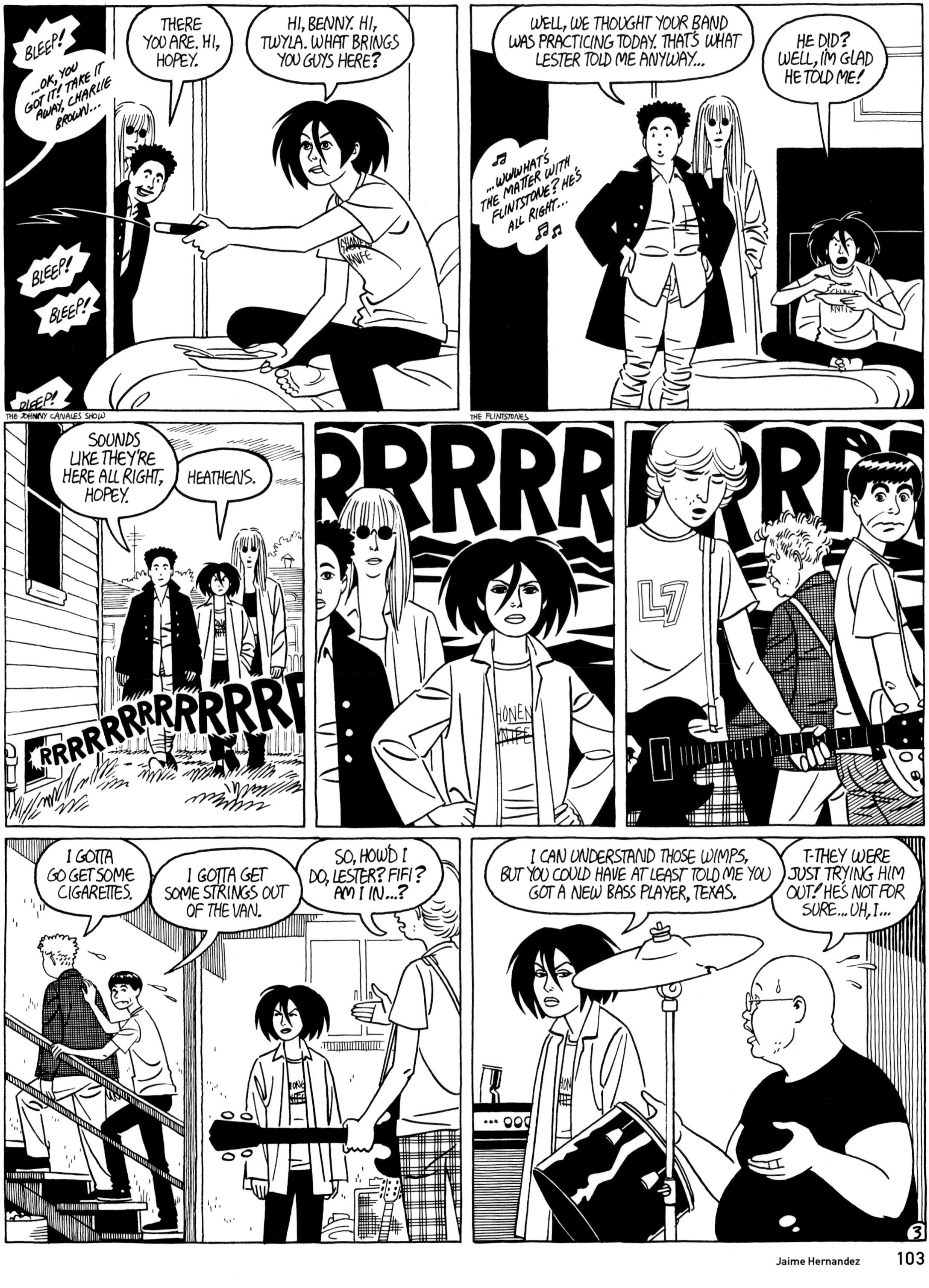
BLEEP!
...OK, YOU GOT IT! TAKE IT AWAY, CHARLIE BROWN...
THERE YOU ARE. HI, HOPEY.
HI, BENNY. HI, TWYLA. WHAT BRINGS YOU GUYS HERE?
BLEEP!
BLEEP!
BLEEP!
THE JOHNNY CANALES SHOW
WELL, WE THOUGHT YOUR BAND WAS PRACTICING TODAY. THAT'S WHAT LESTER TOLD ME ANYWAY...
HE DID? WELL, I'M GLAD HE TOLD ME!
...WWWHAT'S THE MATTER WITH THE FLINTSTONE? HE'S ALL RIGHT...
THE FLINTSTONES
SOUNDS LIKE THEY'RE HERE ALL RIGHT, HOPEY.
HEATHENS.
RRRRRRRRRRRRR
RRRRRR
L7
I GOTTA GO GET SOME CIGARETTES.
I GOTTA GET SOME STRINGS OUT OF THE VAN.
SO, HOW'D I DO, LESTER? FIFI? AM I IN...?
I CAN UNDERSTAND THOSE WIMPS, BUT YOU COULD HAVE AT LEAST TOLD ME YOU GOT A NEW BASS PLAYER, TEXAS.
T-THEY WERE JUST TRYING HIM OUT! HE'S NOT FOR SURE... UH, I...
3

YEAH, YEAH, RIGHT. LET'S GO, BENNY, TWYLA. BUNCHA FUCKIN' WIMPS...

LOOK, WHAT'S THE FUCKIN' DIFFERENCE? YOU DON'T TAKE THIS SHIT SERIOUSLY, ANYWAY! YOU'RE NEVER HERE! IT'S JUST NOT WORTH IT!!!!!

I SAY SCREW 'EM, HOPEY. YOU BELONG IN OUR BAND, THE DAMACHERS ANYWAY. WE DO TEN SHONEN KNIFE COVERS IN OUR SET AND OUR GUITAR SOLOS ARE TWO SECONDS LONG.

I'LL BE RIGHT BACK, LADIES.

BEHAVE NOW, CRYSTAL DARLING.

HOPEY? I THOUGHT YOU WENT TO EL SWANKOS WITH JEWEL...

NAH.

AND ISABEL? DID SHE LEAVE?

YEAH, THE DAY BEFORE YESTERDAY. SHE HAD TO GET BACK TO...WHATEVER.

YOU KNOW, WE DIDN'T EVEN GET TO CATCH UP ON STUFF. I MEAN, I ONLY HAVEN'T SEEN HER IN WHAT, A MILLION THOUSAND YEARS...

WE DIDN'T TALK ABOUT ME GETTING PREGNANT, OR HER LIVING IN THE NUTHOUSE, OR... WE DIDN'T EVEN GET TO...TALK ABOUT...

4

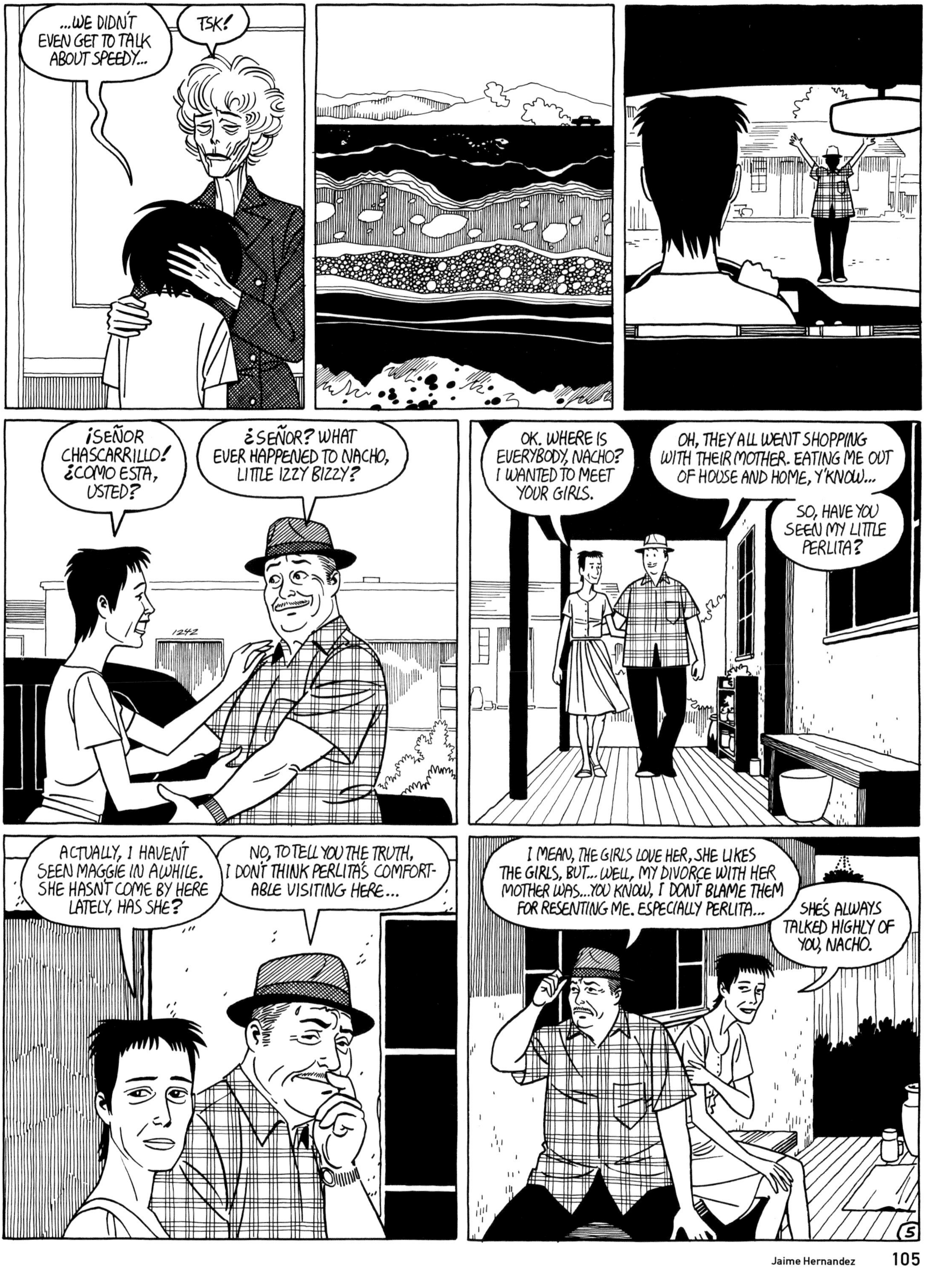
...WE DIDN'T EVEN GET TO TALK ABOUT SPEEDY...
TSK!
¡SEÑOR CHASCARRILLO! ¿COMO ESTA, USTED?
¿SEÑOR? WHAT EVER HAPPENED TO NACHO, LITTLE IZZY BIZZY?
1242
OK. WHERE IS EVERYBODY, NACHO? I WANTED TO MEET YOUR GIRLS.
OH, THEY ALL WENT SHOPPING WITH THEIR MOTHER. EATING ME OUT OF HOUSE AND HOME, Y'KNOW...
SO, HAVE YOU SEEN MY LITTLE PERLITA?
ACTUALLY, I HAVEN'T SEEN MAGGIE IN AWHILE. SHE HASN'T COME BY HERE LATELY, HAS SHE?
NO, TO TELL YOU THE TRUTH, I DON'T THINK PERLITA'S COMFORTABLE VISITING HERE...
I MEAN, THE GIRLS LOVE HER, SHE LIKES THE GIRLS, BUT... WELL, MY DIVORCE WITH HER MOTHER WAS...YOU KNOW, I DON'T BLAME THEM FOR RESENTING ME. ESPECIALLY PERLITA...
SHE'S ALWAYS TALKED HIGHLY OF YOU, NACHO.
5

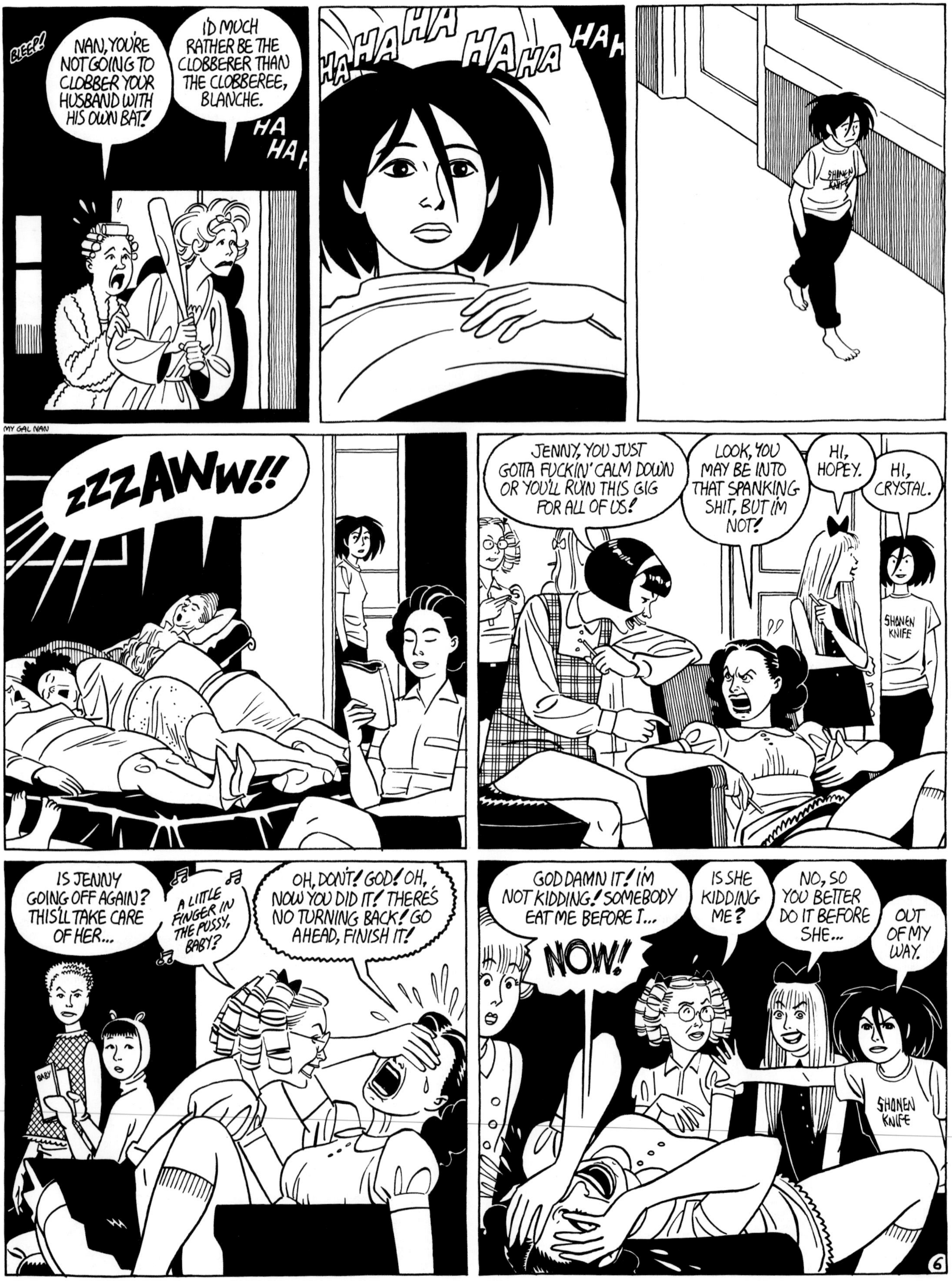
BLEEP!
NAN, YOU'RE NOT GOING TO CLOBBER YOUR HUSBAND WITH HIS OWN BAT!
I'D MUCH RATHER BE THE CLOBBERER THAN THE CLOBBEREE, BLANCHE.
HA HA
HA HA HA HA HA HA HA
MY GAL NAN
ZZZAWW!!
JENNY, YOU JUST GOTTA FUCKIN' CALM DOWN OR YOU'LL RUIN THIS GIG FOR ALL OF US!
LOOK, YOU MAY BE INTO THAT SPANKING SHIT, BUT I'M NOT!
HI, HOPEY.
HI, CRYSTAL.
SHONEN KNIFE
IS JENNY GOING OFF AGAIN? THIS'LL TAKE CARE OF HER...
A LITTLE FINGER IN THE PUSSY, BABY?
OH, DON'T! GOD! OH, NOW YOU DID IT! THERE'S NO TURNING BACK! GO AHEAD, FINISH IT!
BABY
GOD DAMN IT! I'M NOT KIDDING! SOMEBODY EAT ME BEFORE I...
NOW!
IS SHE KIDDING ME?
NO, SO YOU BETTER DO IT BEFORE SHE...
OUT OF MY WAY.
SHONEN KNIFE
6

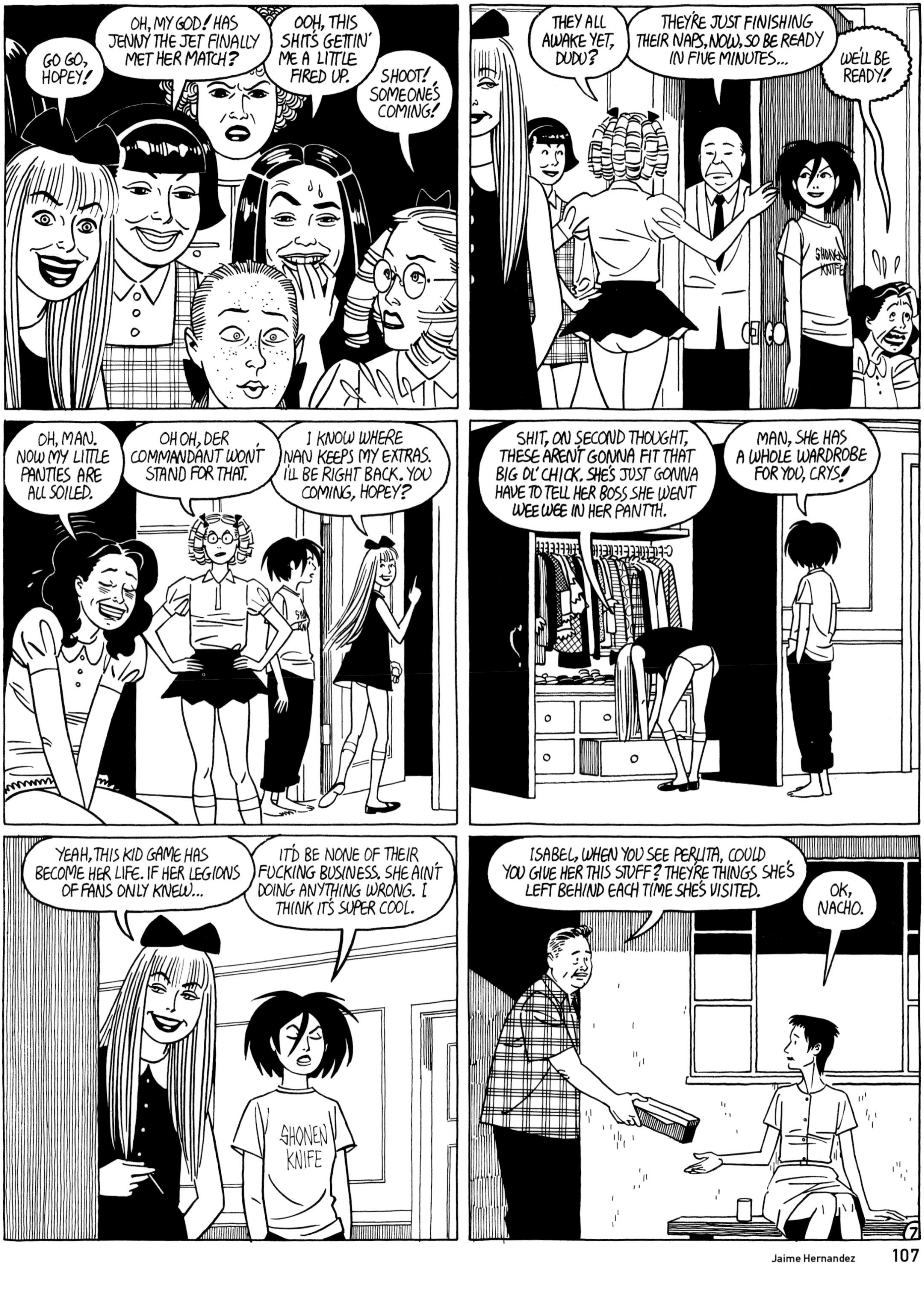
GO GO, HOPEY!
OH, MY GOD! HAS JENNY THE JET FINALLY MET HER MATCH?
OOH, THIS SHIT'S GETTIN' ME A LITTLE FIRED UP.
SHOOT! SOMEONE'S COMING!
THEY ALL AWAKE YET, DUDU?
THEY'RE JUST FINISHING THEIR NAPS, NOW, SO BE READY IN FIVE MINUTES...
WE'LL BE READY!
SHONEN KNIFE
OH, MAN. NOW MY LITTLE PANTIES ARE ALL SOILED.
OH OH, DER COMMANDANT WON'T STAND FOR THAT.
I KNOW WHERE NAN KEEPS MY EXTRAS. I'LL BE RIGHT BACK. YOU COMING, HOPEY?
SHIT, ON SECOND THOUGHT, THESE AREN'T GONNA FIT THAT BIG OL' CHICK. SHE'S JUST GONNA HAVE TO TELL HER BOSS SHE WENT WEE WEE IN HER PANTTH.
MAN, SHE HAS A WHOLE WARDROBE FOR YOU, CRYS!
YEAH, THIS KID GAME HAS BECOME HER LIFE. IF HER LEGIONS OF FANS ONLY KNEW...
IT'D BE NONE OF THEIR FUCKING BUSINESS. SHE AIN'T DOING ANYTHING WRONG. I THINK IT'S SUPER COOL.
SHONEN KNIFE
ISABEL, WHEN YOU SEE PERLITA, COULD YOU GIVE HER THIS STUFF? THEY'RE THINGS SHE'S LEFT BEHIND EACH TIME SHE'S VISITED.
OK, NACHO.
7

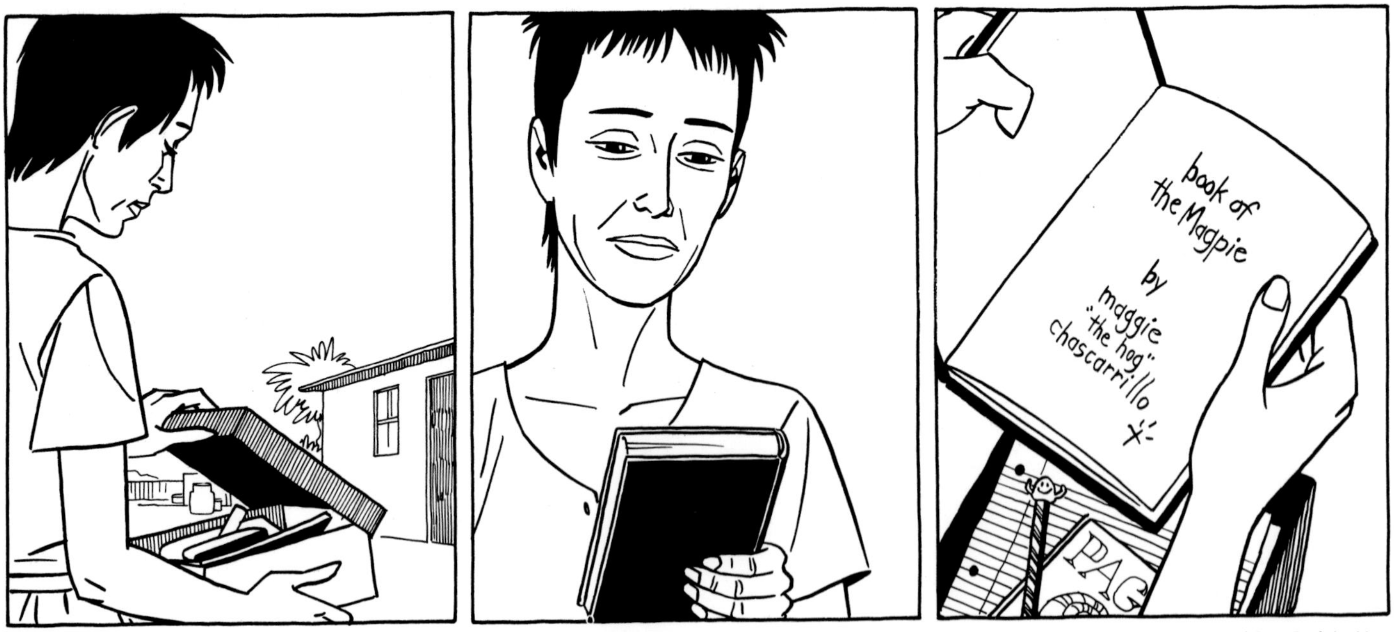
book of
the Magpie
by
maggie
"the hog"
chascarrillo

HERE I AM IN TEXAS VISITING DAD AND HIS FAMILY. HOPEY AND HER BAND HAVE BEEN ON THE ROAD FOR OVER TWO MONTHS NOW, SPEEDY'S BEEN DEAD FOR ALMOST TWO WEEKS AND I THINK RAY DOMINGUEZ HATES ME.

THINKING OF HOPEY AND SPEEDY HAS GOT ME THINKING ABOUT MY OLD VERY BEST FRIEND LETTY CHAVEZ. LIKE HOPEY, LETTY WAS A YEAR OLDER THAN ME, BUT SHE FLUNKED KINDERGARTEN, SO THAT'S WHY WE GREW UP SIDE BY SIDE LIKE THE BONNIE'S TWINS.

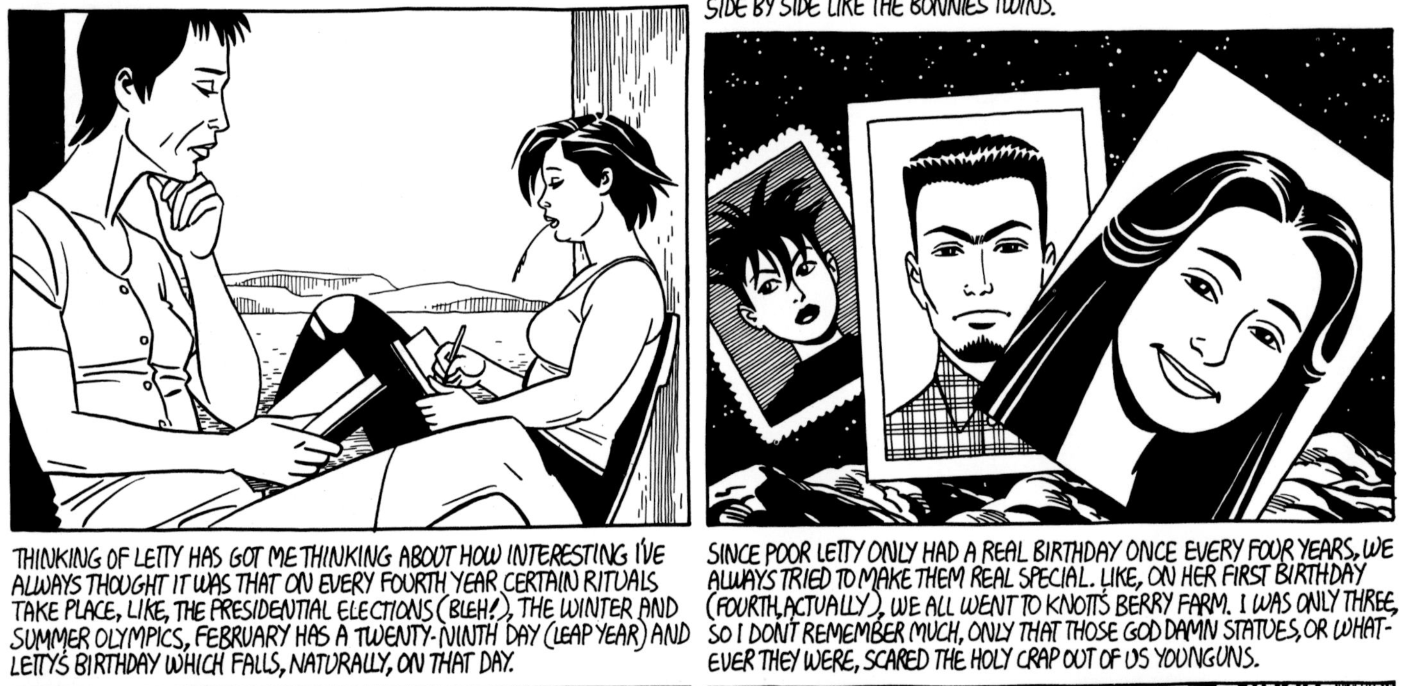

THINKING OF LETTY HAS GOT ME THINKING ABOUT HOW INTERESTING I'VE ALWAYS THOUGHT IT WAS THAT ON EVERY FOURTH YEAR CERTAIN RITUALS TAKE PLACE, LIKE, THE PRESIDENTIAL ELECTIONS (BLEH!), THE WINTER AND SUMMER OLYMPICS, FEBRUARY HAS A TWENTY-NINTH DAY (LEAP YEAR) AND LETTY'S BIRTHDAY WHICH FALLS, NATURALLY, ON THAT DAY.

SINCE POOR LETTY ONLY HAD A REAL BIRTHDAY ONCE EVERY FOUR YEARS, WE ALWAYS TRIED TO MAKE THEM REAL SPECIAL. LIKE, ON HER FIRST BIRTHDAY (FOURTH, ACTUALLY), WE ALL WENT TO KNOTT'S BERRY FARM. I WAS ONLY THREE, SO I DON'T REMEMBER MUCH, ONLY THAT THOSE GOD DAMN STATUES, OR WHATEVER THEY WERE, SCARED THE HOLY CRAP OUT OF US YOUNGUNS.

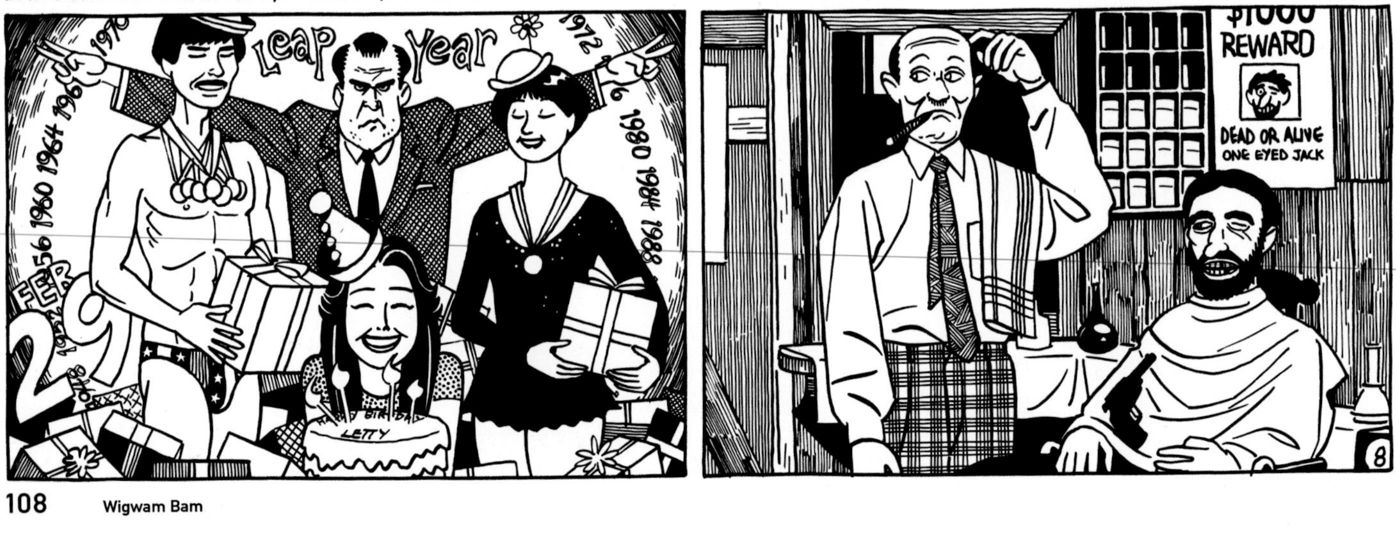
Leap Year
FEB 29
1960 1964
1972
1980 1984 1988
LETTY
REWARD
DEAD OR ALIVE
ONE EYED JACK
8

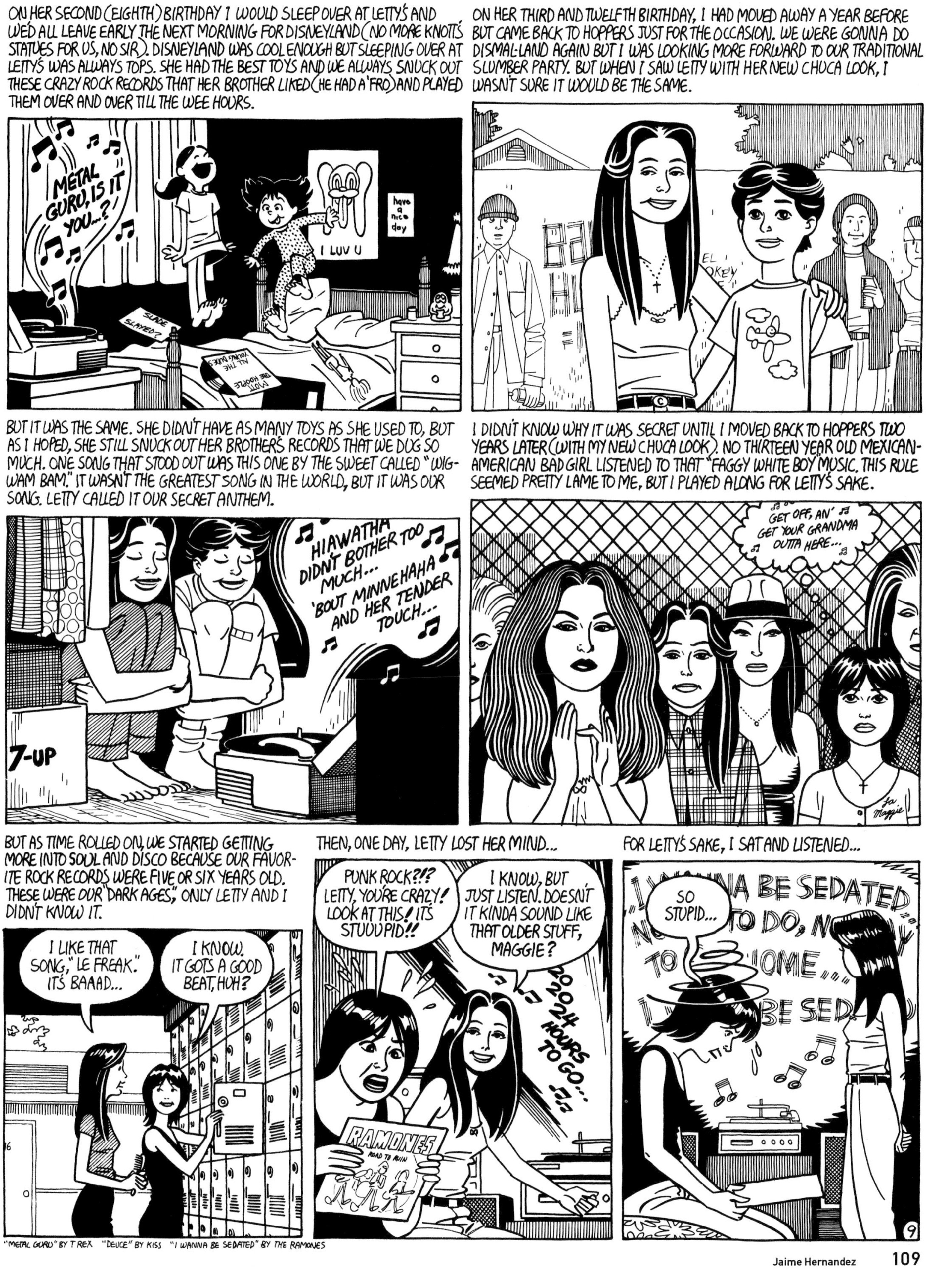

ON HER SECOND (EIGHTH) BIRTHDAY I WOULD SLEEP OVER AT LETTY'S AND WE'D ALL LEAVE EARLY THE NEXT MORNING FOR DISNEYLAND (NO MORE KNOTT'S STATUES FOR US, NO SIR). DISNEYLAND WAS COOL ENOUGH BUT SLEEPING OVER AT LETTY'S WAS ALWAYS TOPS. SHE HAD THE BEST TOYS AND WE ALWAYS SNUCK OUT THESE CRAZY ROCK RECORDS THAT HER BROTHER LIKED (HE HAD A 'FRO) AND PLAYED THEM OVER AND OVER TILL THE WEE HOURS.
METAL GURU, IS IT YOU...?
have a nice day
I LUV U
SLADE SLAYED?
MOTT THE HOOPLE ALL THE YOUNG DUDES
ON HER THIRD AND TWELFTH BIRTHDAY, I HAD MOVED AWAY A YEAR BEFORE BUT CAME BACK TO HOPPERS JUST FOR THE OCCASION. WE WERE GONNA DO DISMAL-LAND AGAIN BUT I WAS LOOKING MORE FORWARD TO OUR TRADITIONAL SLUMBER PARTY. BUT WHEN I SAW LETTY WITH HER NEW CHUCA LOOK, I WASN'T SURE IT WOULD BE THE SAME.
BUT IT WAS THE SAME. SHE DIDN'T HAVE AS MANY TOYS AS SHE USED TO, BUT AS I HOPED, SHE STILL SNUCK OUT HER BROTHER'S RECORDS THAT WE DUG SO MUCH. ONE SONG THAT STOOD OUT WAS THIS ONE BY THE SWEET CALLED "WIG-WAM BAM." IT WASN'T THE GREATEST SONG IN THE WORLD, BUT IT WAS OUR SONG. LETTY CALLED IT OUR SECRET ANTHEM.
HIAWATHA DIDN'T BOTHER TOO MUCH... 'BOUT MINNEHAHA AND HER TENDER TOUCH...
7-UP
I DIDN'T KNOW WHY IT WAS SECRET UNTIL I MOVED BACK TO HOPPERS TWO YEARS LATER (WITH MY NEW CHUCA LOOK). NO THIRTEEN YEAR OLD MEXICAN-AMERICAN BAD GIRL LISTENED TO THAT "FAGGY WHITE BOY" MUSIC. THIS RULE SEEMED PRETTY LAME TO ME, BUT I PLAYED ALONG FOR LETTY'S SAKE.
GET OFF, AN' GET YOUR GRANDMA OUTTA HERE...
La Maggie
BUT AS TIME ROLLED ON, WE STARTED GETTING MORE INTO SOUL AND DISCO BECAUSE OUR FAVORITE ROCK RECORDS WERE FIVE OR SIX YEARS OLD. THESE WERE OUR "DARK AGES," ONLY LETTY AND I DIDN'T KNOW IT.
I LIKE THAT SONG, "LE FREAK." IT'S BAAAD...
I KNOW. IT GOTS A GOOD BEAT, HUH?
THEN, ONE DAY, LETTY LOST HER MIND...
PUNK ROCK?!? LETTY, YOU'RE CRAZY! LOOK AT THIS! IT'S STUUUPID!!
I KNOW, BUT JUST LISTEN. DOESN'T IT KINDA SOUND LIKE THAT OLDER STUFF, MAGGIE?
20-20-24 HOURS TO GO...
RAMONES ROAD TO RUIN
FOR LETTY'S SAKE, I SAT AND LISTENED...
I WANNA BE SEDATED
SO STUPID...
9
"METAL GURU" BY T REX "DEUCE" BY KISS "I WANNA BE SEDATED" BY THE RAMONES

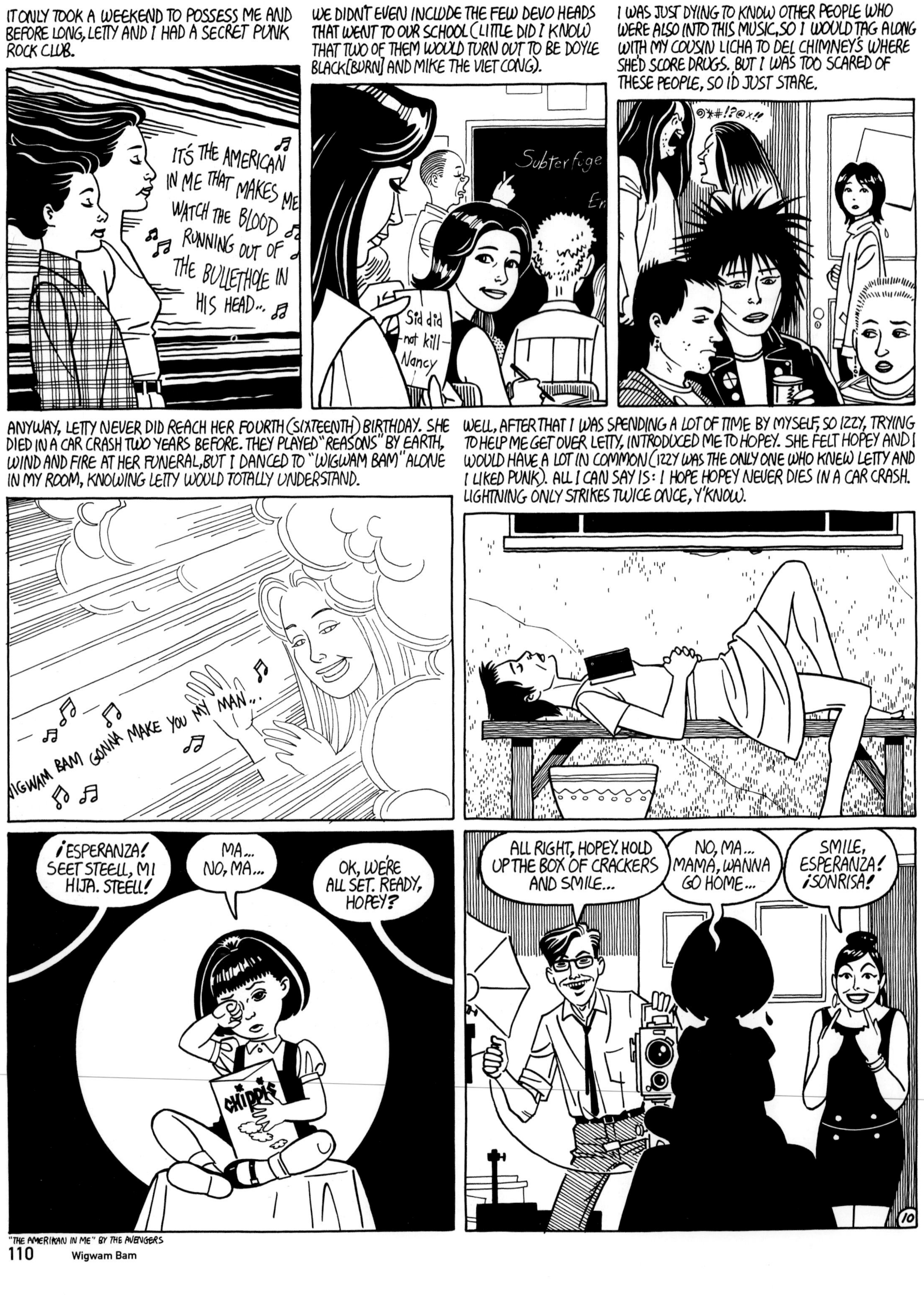
IT ONLY TOOK A WEEKEND TO POSSESS ME AND BEFORE LONG, LETTY AND I HAD A SECRET PUNK ROCK CLUB.
IT'S THE AMERICAN IN ME THAT MAKES ME WATCH THE BLOOD RUNNING OUT OF THE BULLETHOLE IN HIS HEAD...
WE DIDN'T EVEN INCLUDE THE FEW DEVO HEADS THAT WENT TO OUR SCHOOL (LITTLE DID I KNOW THAT TWO OF THEM WOULD TURN OUT TO BE DOYLE BLACK[BURN] AND MIKE THE VIET CONG).
Subterfuge
Sid did not kill Nancy
I WAS JUST DYING TO KNOW OTHER PEOPLE WHO WERE ALSO INTO THIS MUSIC, SO I WOULD TAG ALONG WITH MY COUSIN LICHA TO DEL CHIMNEY'S WHERE SHE'D SCORE DRUGS. BUT I WAS TOO SCARED OF THESE PEOPLE, SO I'D JUST STARE.
@*#!?@x!!
ANYWAY, LETTY NEVER DID REACH HER FOURTH (SIXTEENTH) BIRTHDAY. SHE DIED IN A CAR CRASH TWO YEARS BEFORE. THEY PLAYED "REASONS" BY EARTH, WIND AND FIRE AT HER FUNERAL, BUT I DANCED TO "WIGWAM BAM" ALONE IN MY ROOM, KNOWING LETTY WOULD TOTALLY UNDERSTAND.
WIGWAM BAM GONNA MAKE YOU MY MAN...
WELL, AFTER THAT I WAS SPENDING A LOT OF TIME BY MYSELF, SO IZZY, TRYING TO HELP ME GET OVER LETTY, INTRODUCED ME TO HOPEY. SHE FELT HOPEY AND I WOULD HAVE A LOT IN COMMON (IZZY WAS THE ONLY ONE WHO KNEW LETTY AND I LIKED PUNK). ALL I CAN SAY IS: I HOPE HOPEY NEVER DIES IN A CAR CRASH. LIGHTNING ONLY STRIKES TWICE ONCE, Y'KNOW.
¡ESPERANZA! SEET STEELL, MI HIJA. STEELL!
MA... NO, MA...
OK, WE'RE ALL SET. READY, HOPEY?
CHIPPIES
ALL RIGHT, HOPEY. HOLD UP THE BOX OF CRACKERS AND SMILE...
NO, MA... MAMA, WANNA GO HOME...
SMILE, ESPERANZA! ¡SONRISA!
10

"THE AMERIKAN IN ME" BY THE AVENGERS

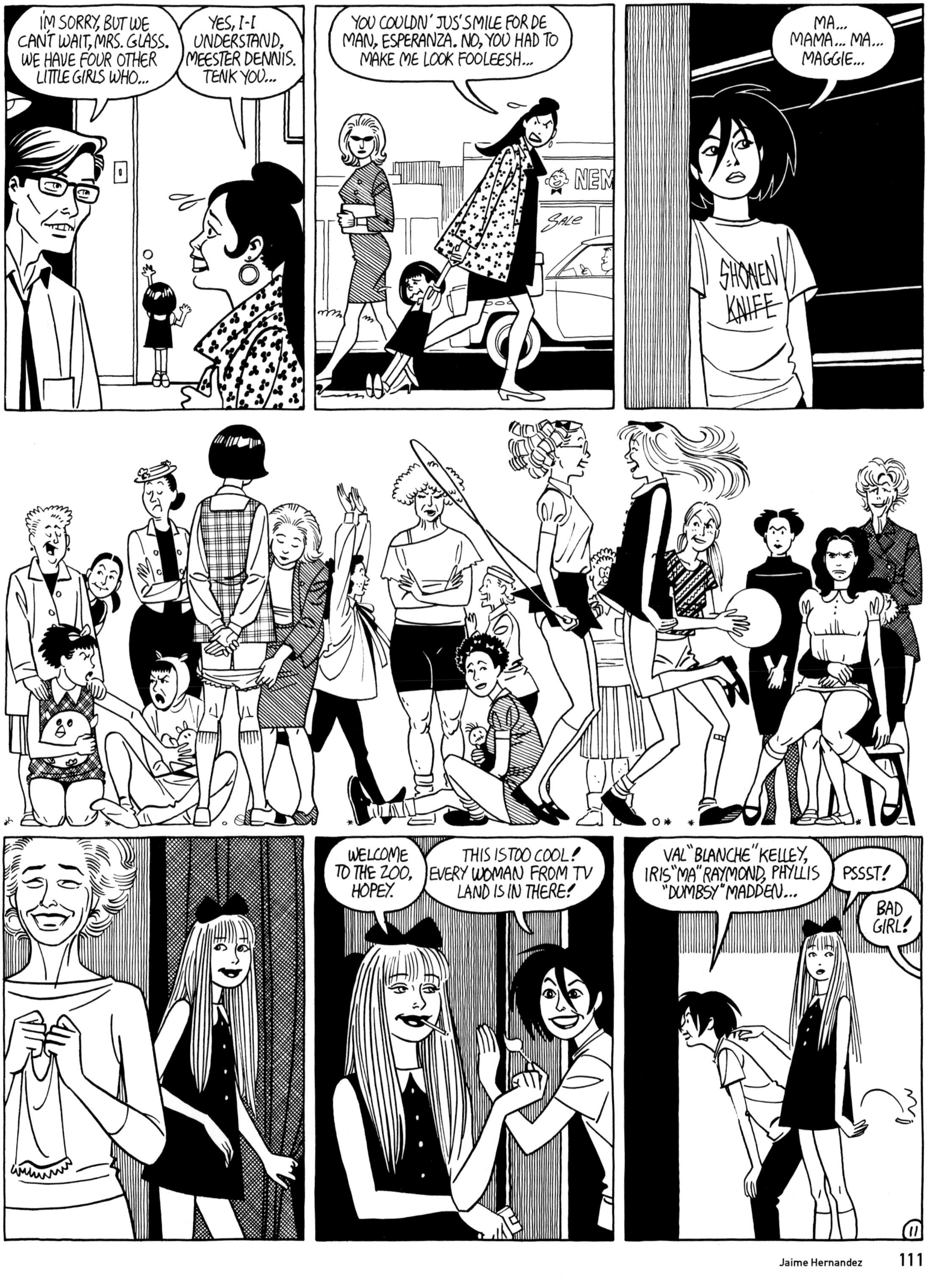
I'M SORRY, BUT WE CAN'T WAIT, MRS. GLASS. WE HAVE FOUR OTHER LITTLE GIRLS WHO...
YES, I-I UNDERSTAND, MEESTER DENNIS. TENK YOU...
YOU COULDN' JUS' SMILE FOR DE MAN, ESPERANZA. NO, YOU HAD TO MAKE ME LOOK FOOLEESH...
SALE
MA... MAMA... MA... MAGGIE...
SHONEN KNIFE
WELCOME TO THE ZOO, HOPEY.
THIS IS TOO COOL! EVERY WOMAN FROM TV LAND IS IN THERE!
VAL "BLANCHE" KELLEY, IRIS "MA" RAYMOND, PHYLLIS "DUMBSY" MADDEN...
PSSST!
BAD GIRL!
11

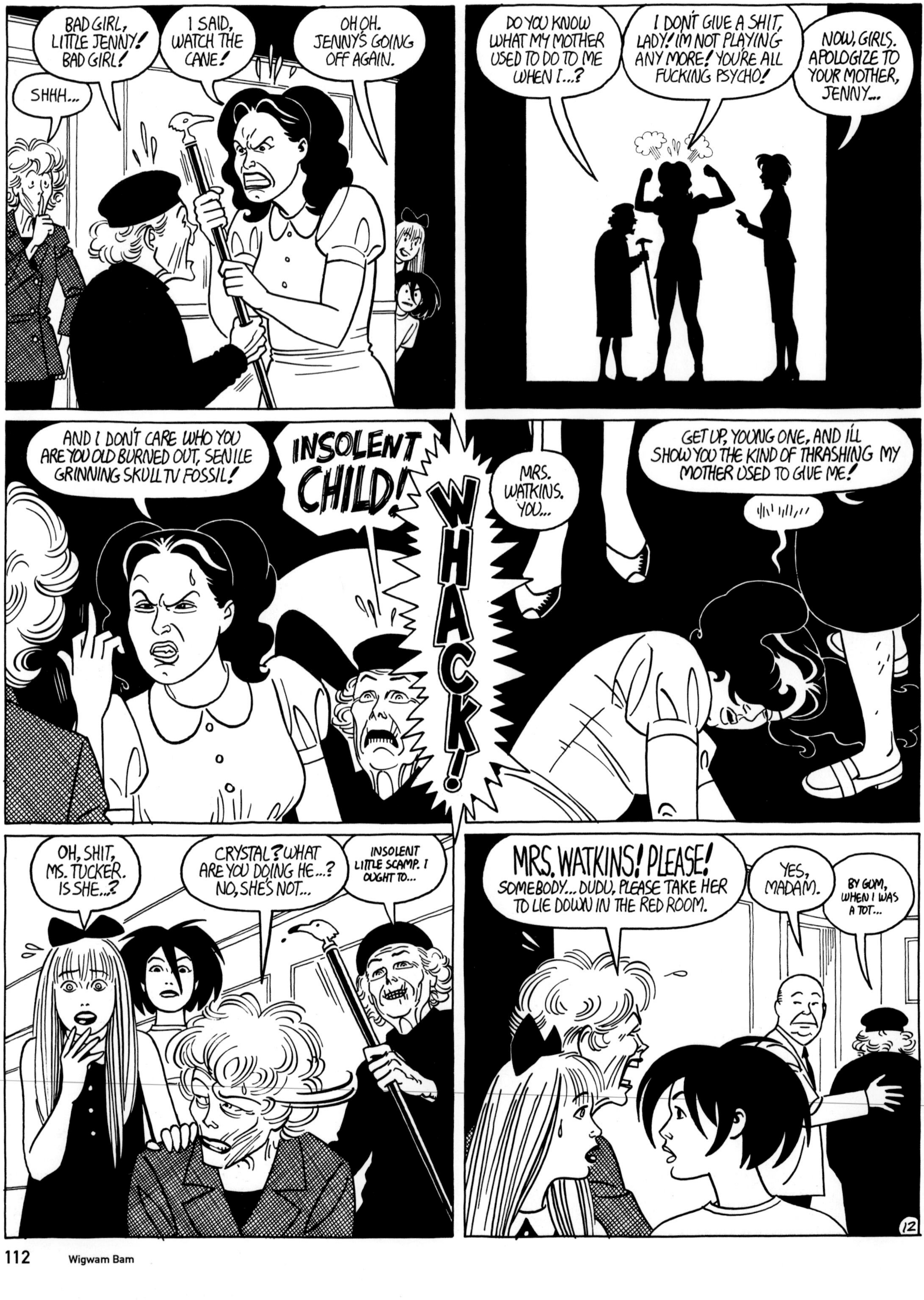
BAD GIRL, LITTLE JENNY! BAD GIRL!
SHHH...
I SAID, WATCH THE CANE!
OH OH. JENNY'S GOING OFF AGAIN.
DO YOU KNOW WHAT MY MOTHER USED TO DO TO ME WHEN I...?
I DON'T GIVE A SHIT, LADY! I'M NOT PLAYING ANY MORE! YOU'RE ALL FUCKING PSYCHO!
NOW, GIRLS. APOLOGIZE TO YOUR MOTHER, JENNY...
AND I DON'T CARE WHO YOU ARE YOU OLD BURNED OUT, SENILE GRINNING SKULL TV FOSSIL!
INSOLENT CHILD!
WHACK!
MRS. WATKINS. YOU...
GET UP, YOUNG ONE, AND I'LL SHOW YOU THE KIND OF THRASHING MY MOTHER USED TO GIVE ME!
OH, SHIT, MS. TUCKER. IS SHE...?
CRYSTAL? WHAT ARE YOU DOING HE...? NO, SHE'S NOT...
INSOLENT LITTLE SCAMP. I OUGHT TO...
MRS. WATKINS! PLEASE! SOMEBODY... DUDU, PLEASE TAKE HER TO LIE DOWN IN THE RED ROOM.
YES, MADAM.
BY GUM, WHEN I WAS A TOT...
12

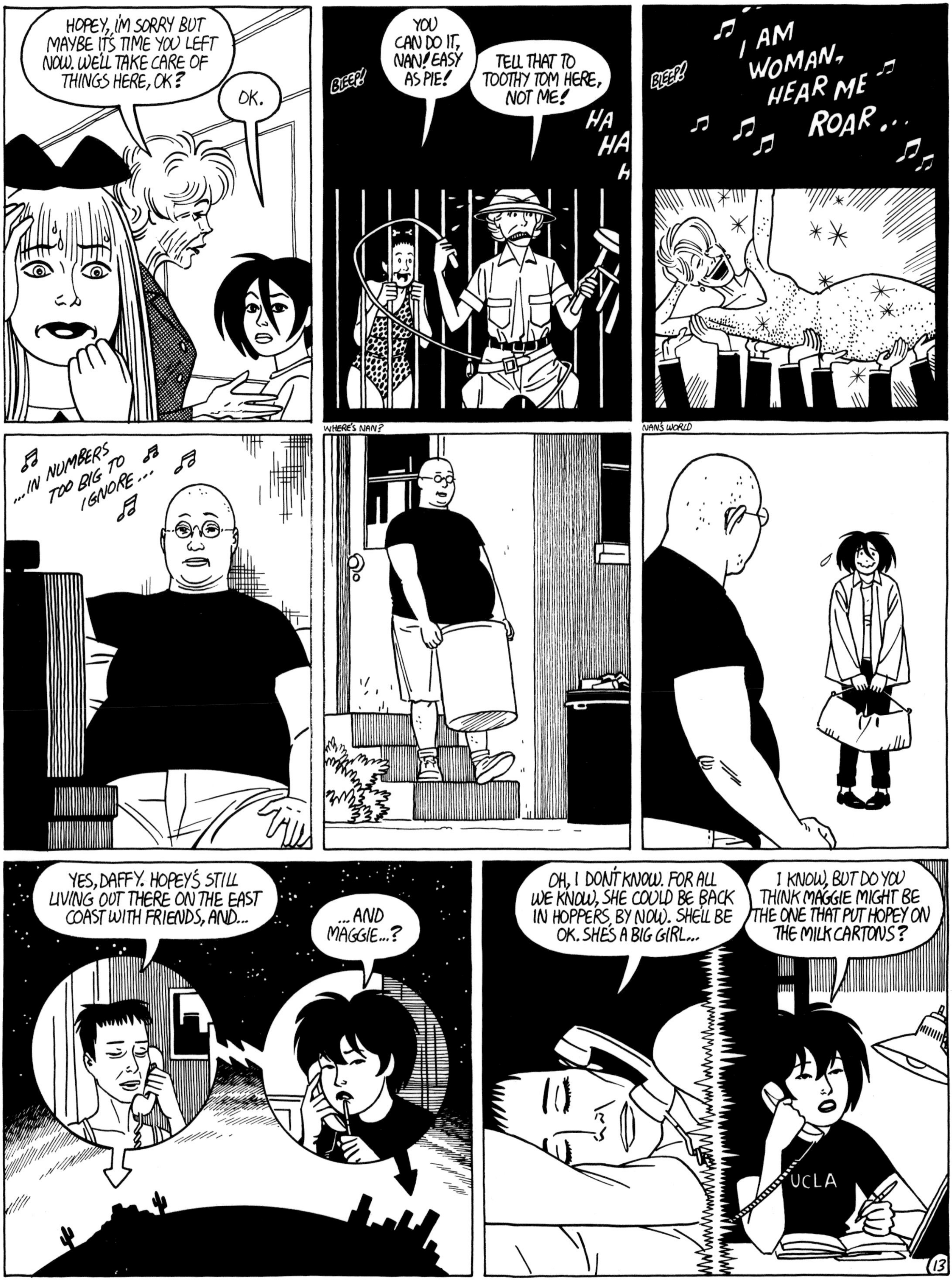
HOPEY, I'M SORRY BUT MAYBE IT'S TIME YOU LEFT NOW. WE'LL TAKE CARE OF THINGS HERE, OK?
OK.
BLEEP!
YOU CAN DO IT, NAN! EASY AS PIE!
TELL THAT TO TOOTHY TOM HERE, NOT ME!
HA HA H
WHERE'S NAN?
BLEEP!
I AM WOMAN, HEAR ME ROAR...
NAN'S WORLD
...IN NUMBERS TOO BIG TO IGNORE...
YES, DAFFY. HOPEY'S STILL LIVING OUT THERE ON THE EAST COAST WITH FRIENDS, AND...
...AND MAGGIE...?
OH, I DON'T KNOW. FOR ALL WE KNOW, SHE COULD BE BACK IN HOPPERS BY NOW. SHE'LL BE OK. SHE'S A BIG GIRL...
I KNOW, BUT DO YOU THINK MAGGIE MIGHT BE THE ONE THAT PUT HOPEY ON THE MILK CARTONS?
UCLA
13

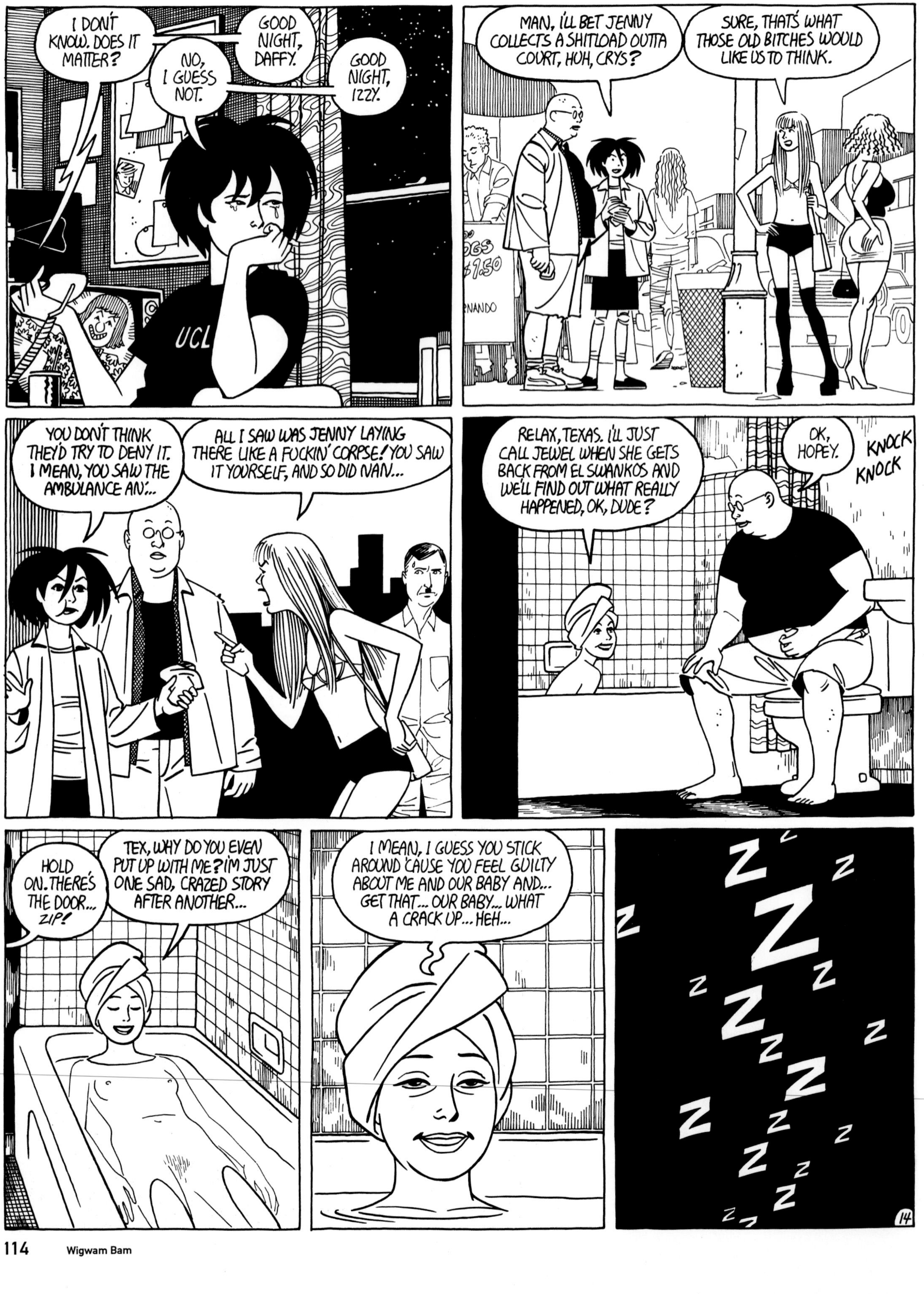
I DON'T KNOW. DOES IT MATTER?
GOOD NIGHT, DAFFY.
NO, I GUESS NOT.
GOOD NIGHT, IZZY.
UCL
MAN, I'LL BET JENNY COLLECTS A SHITLOAD OUTTA COURT, HUH, CRYS?
SURE, THAT'S WHAT THOSE OLD BITCHES WOULD LIKE US TO THINK.
DOGS $1.50
YOU DON'T THINK THEY'D TRY TO DENY IT. I MEAN, YOU SAW THE AMBULANCE AN'...
ALL I SAW WAS JENNY LAYING THERE LIKE A FUCKIN' CORPSE! YOU SAW IT YOURSELF, AND SO DID IVAN...
RELAX, TEXAS. I'LL JUST CALL JEWEL WHEN SHE GETS BACK FROM EL SWANKOS AND WE'LL FIND OUT WHAT REALLY HAPPENED, OK, DUDE?
OK, HOPEY.
KNOCK KNOCK
HOLD ON. THERE'S THE DOOR... ZIP!
TEX, WHY DO YOU EVEN PUT UP WITH ME? I'M JUST ONE SAD, CRAZED STORY AFTER ANOTHER...
I MEAN, I GUESS YOU STICK AROUND 'CAUSE YOU FEEL GUILTY ABOUT ME AND OUR BABY AND... GET THAT... OUR BABY... WHAT A CRACK UP... HEH...
Z Z Z
14

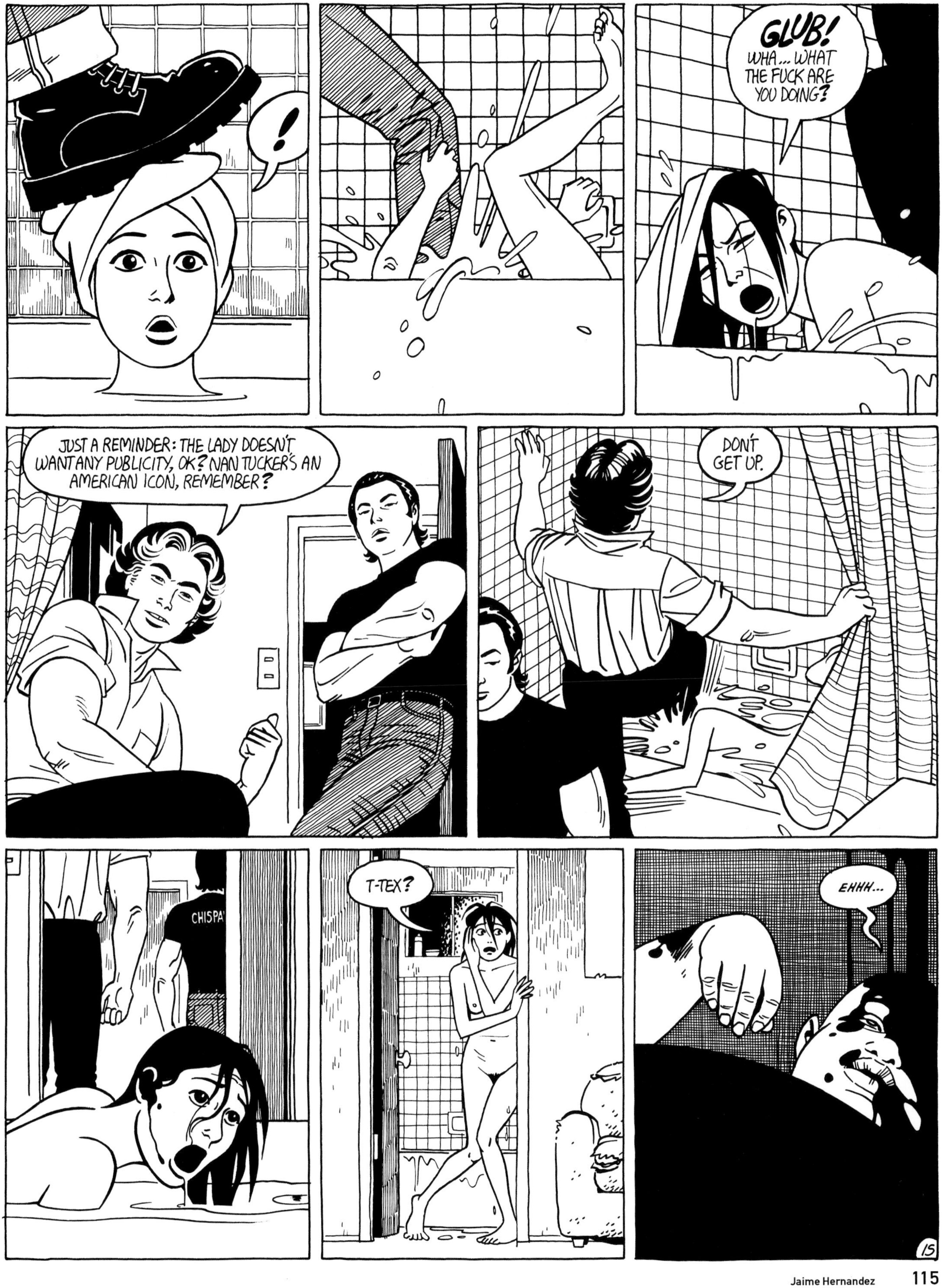
!
GLUB!
WHA... WHAT THE FUCK ARE YOU DOING?
JUST A REMINDER: THE LADY DOESN'T WANT ANY PUBLICITY, OK? NAN TUCKER'S AN AMERICAN ICON, REMEMBER?
DON'T GET UP.
CHISPA
T-TEX?
EHHH...
15

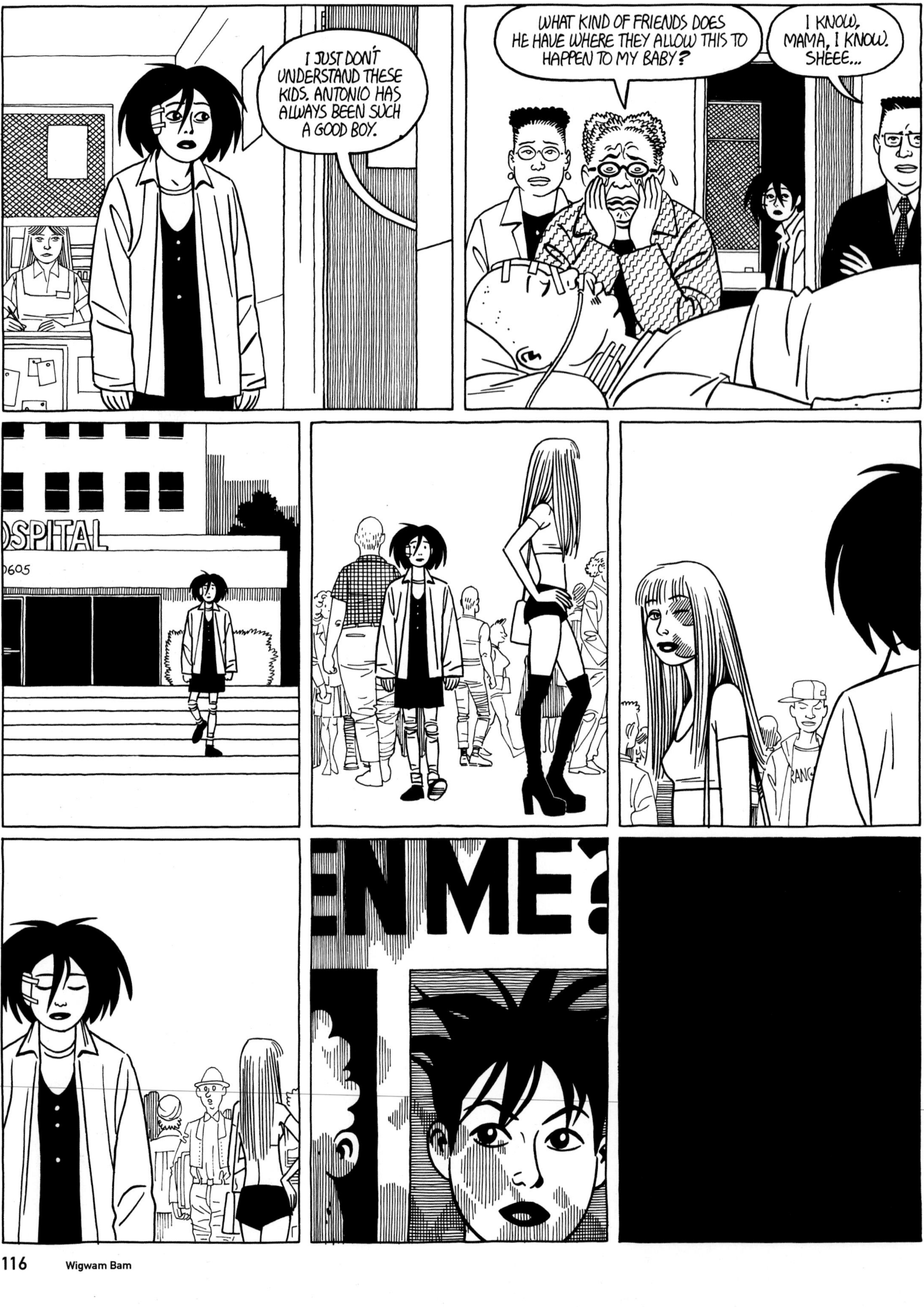
I JUST DON'T UNDERSTAND THESE KIDS. ANTONIO HAS ALWAYS BEEN SUCH A GOOD BOY.
WHAT KIND OF FRIENDS DOES HE HAVE WHERE THEY ALLOW THIS TO HAPPEN TO MY BABY?
I KNOW, MAMA, I KNOW. SHEEE...
OSPITAL
0605
RANG
EN ME?

epi logue

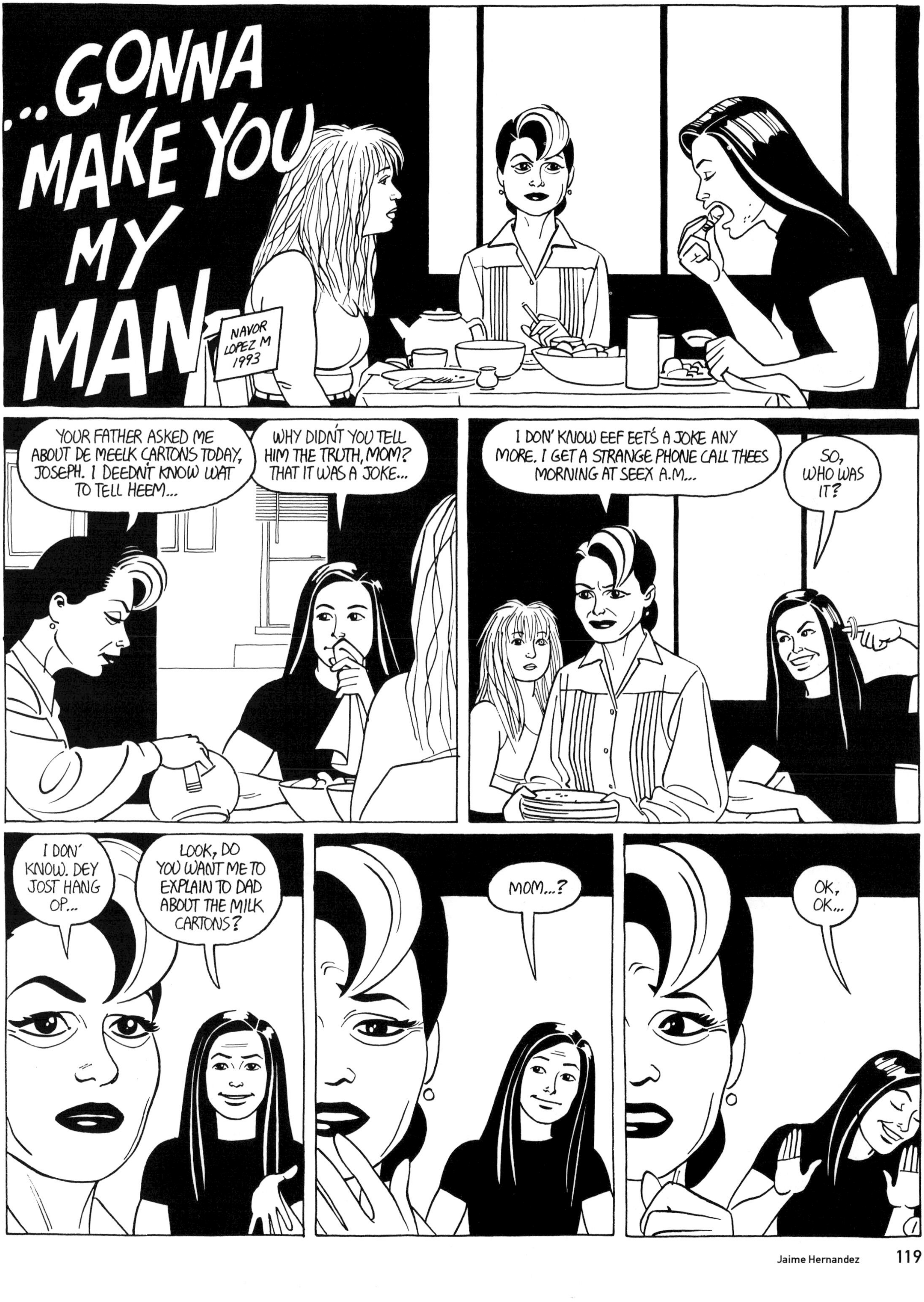
...GONNA MAKE YOU MY MAN
NAVOR LOPEZ M 1993
YOUR FATHER ASKED ME ABOUT DE MEELK CARTONS TODAY, JOSEPH. I DEEDN'T KNOW WAT TO TELL HEEM...
WHY DIDN'T YOU TELL HIM THE TRUTH, MOM? THAT IT WAS A JOKE...
I DON' KNOW EEF EET'S A JOKE ANY MORE. I GET A STRANGE PHONE CALL THEES MORNING AT SEEX A.M...
SO, WHO WAS IT?
I DON' KNOW. DEY JOST HANG OP...
LOOK, DO YOU WANT ME TO EXPLAIN TO DAD ABOUT THE MILK CARTONS?
MOM...?
OK, OK...

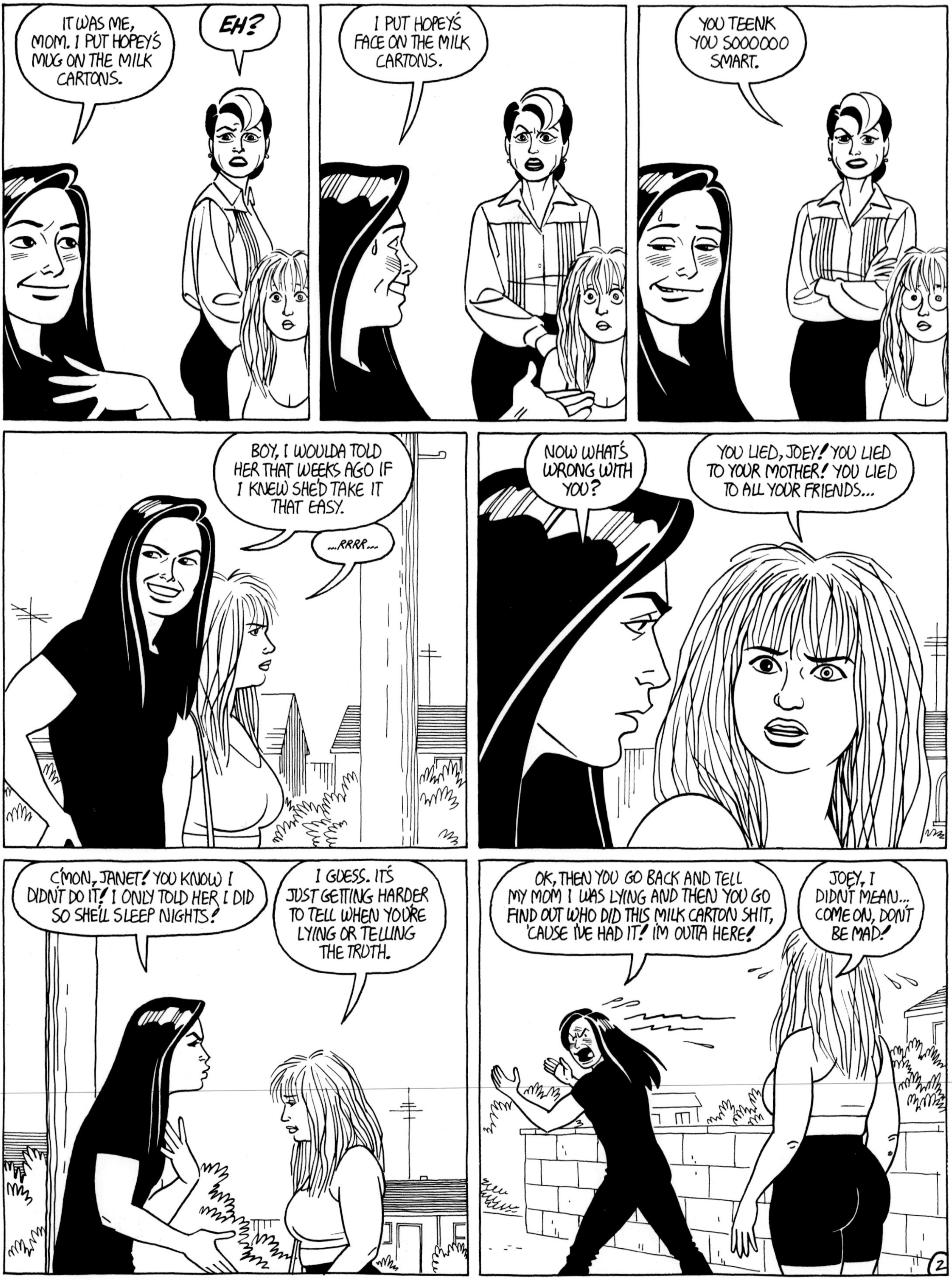
IT WAS ME, MOM. I PUT HOPEY'S MUG ON THE MILK CARTONS.
EH?
I PUT HOPEY'S FACE ON THE MILK CARTONS.
YOU TEENK YOU SOOOOOO SMART.
BOY, I WOULDA TOLD HER THAT WEEKS AGO IF I KNEW SHE'D TAKE IT THAT EASY.
...RRRR...
NOW WHAT'S WRONG WITH YOU?
YOU LIED, JOEY! YOU LIED TO YOUR MOTHER! YOU LIED TO ALL YOUR FRIENDS...
C'MON, JANET! YOU KNOW I DIDN'T DO IT! I ONLY TOLD HER I DID SO SHE'LL SLEEP NIGHTS!
I GUESS. IT'S JUST GETTING HARDER TO TELL WHEN YOU'RE LYING OR TELLING THE TRUTH.
OK, THEN YOU GO BACK AND TELL MY MOM I WAS LYING AND THEN YOU GO FIND OUT WHO DID THIS MILK CARTON SHIT, 'CAUSE I'VE HAD IT! I'M OUTTA HERE!
JOEY, I DIDN'T MEAN... COME ON, DON'T BE MAD!
2

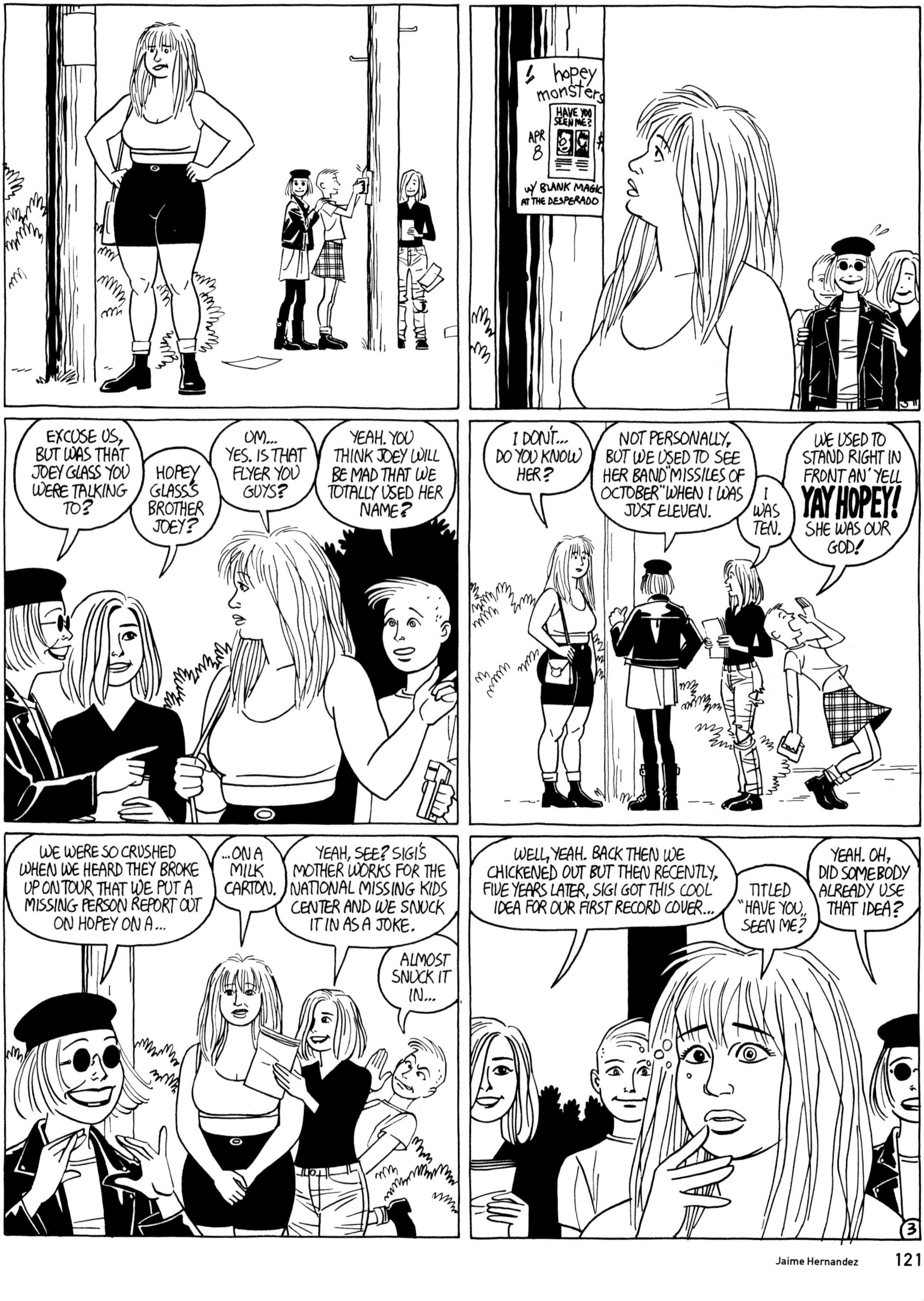

hopey monsters
HAVE YOU SEEN ME?
APR 8
w/ BLANK MAGIC AT THE DESPERADO
EXCUSE US, BUT WAS THAT JOEY GLASS YOU WERE TALKING TO?
HOPEY GLASS'S BROTHER JOEY?
UM... YES. IS THAT FLYER YOU GUYS?
YEAH. YOU THINK JOEY WILL BE MAD THAT WE TOTALLY USED HER NAME?
I DON'T... DO YOU KNOW HER?
NOT PERSONALLY, BUT WE USED TO SEE HER BAND "MISSILES OF OCTOBER" WHEN I WAS JUST ELEVEN.
I WAS TEN.
WE USED TO STAND RIGHT IN FRONT AN' YELL YAY HOPEY! SHE WAS OUR GOD!
WE WERE SO CRUSHED WHEN WE HEARD THEY BROKE UP ON TOUR THAT WE PUT A MISSING PERSON REPORT OUT ON HOPEY ON A...
...ON A MILK CARTON.
YEAH, SEE? SIGI'S MOTHER WORKS FOR THE NATIONAL MISSING KIDS CENTER AND WE SNUCK IT IN AS A JOKE.
ALMOST SNUCK IT IN...
WELL, YEAH. BACK THEN WE CHICKENED OUT BUT THEN RECENTLY, FIVE YEARS LATER, SIGI GOT THIS COOL IDEA FOR OUR FIRST RECORD COVER...
TITLED "HAVE YOU SEEN ME?"
YEAH. OH, DID SOMEBODY ALREADY USE THAT IDEA?
3

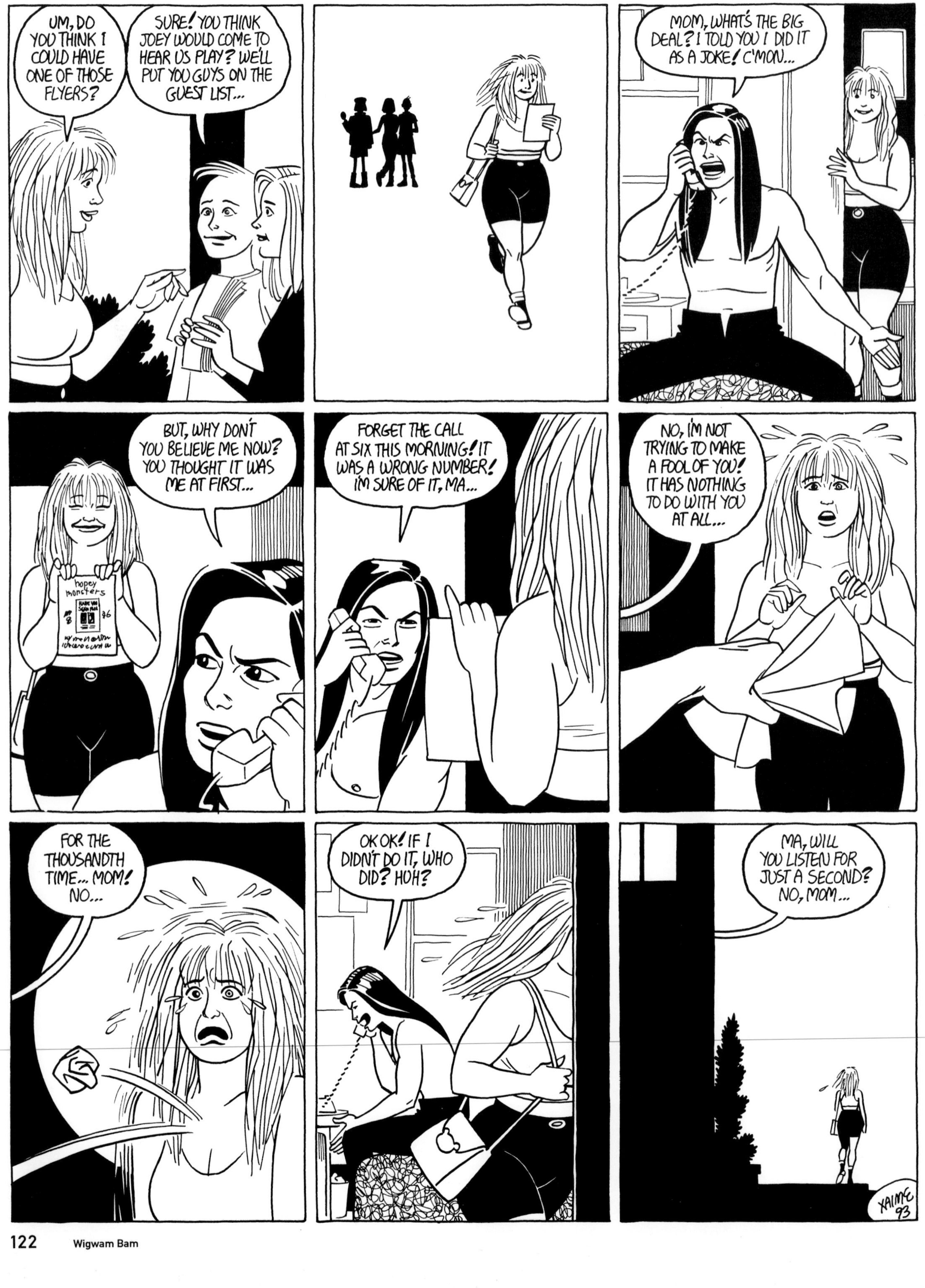
UM, DO YOU THINK I COULD HAVE ONE OF THOSE FLYERS?
SURE! YOU THINK JOEY WOULD COME TO HEAR US PLAY? WE'LL PUT YOU GUYS ON THE GUEST LIST...
MOM, WHAT'S THE BIG DEAL? I TOLD YOU I DID IT AS A JOKE! C'MON...
BUT, WHY DON'T YOU BELIEVE ME NOW? YOU THOUGHT IT WAS ME AT FIRST...
hopey monsters
FORGET THE CALL AT SIX THIS MORNING! IT WAS A WRONG NUMBER! I'M SURE OF IT, MA...
NO, I'M NOT TRYING TO MAKE A FOOL OF YOU! IT HAS NOTHING TO DO WITH YOU AT ALL...
FOR THE THOUSANDTH TIME... MOM! NO...
OK OK! IF I DIDN'T DO IT, WHO DID? HUH?
MA, WILL YOU LISTEN FOR JUST A SECOND? NO, MOM...
XAIME 93

SIDE BY SIDE LIKE THE BONNIE'S TWINS.

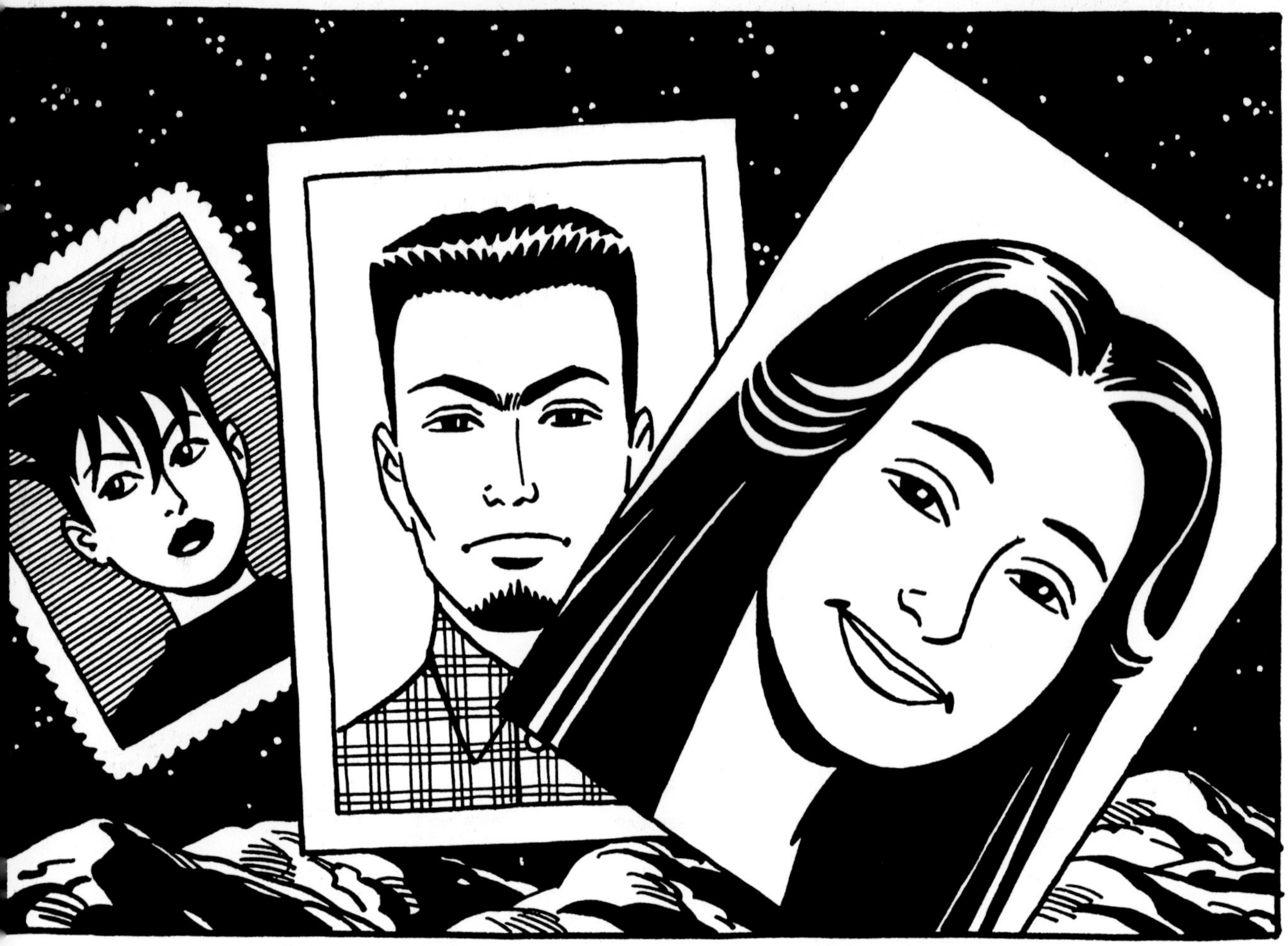

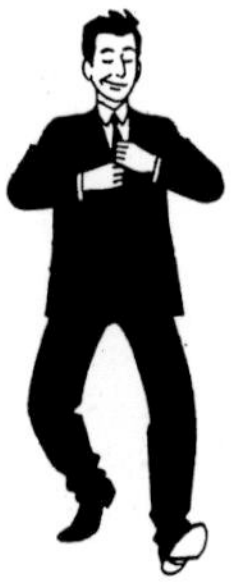

cover

gallery

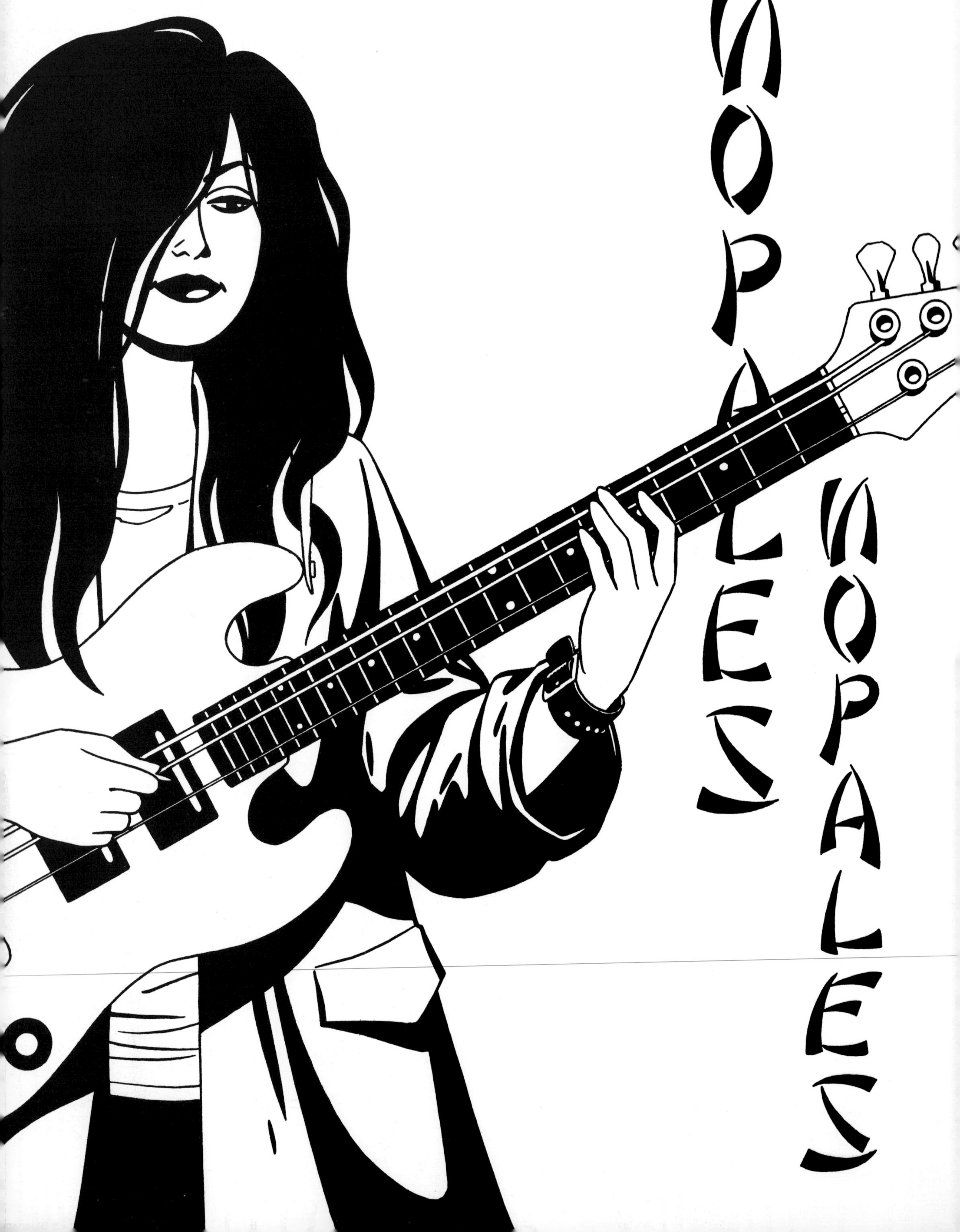
NOPALES
NOPALES
NOPALES

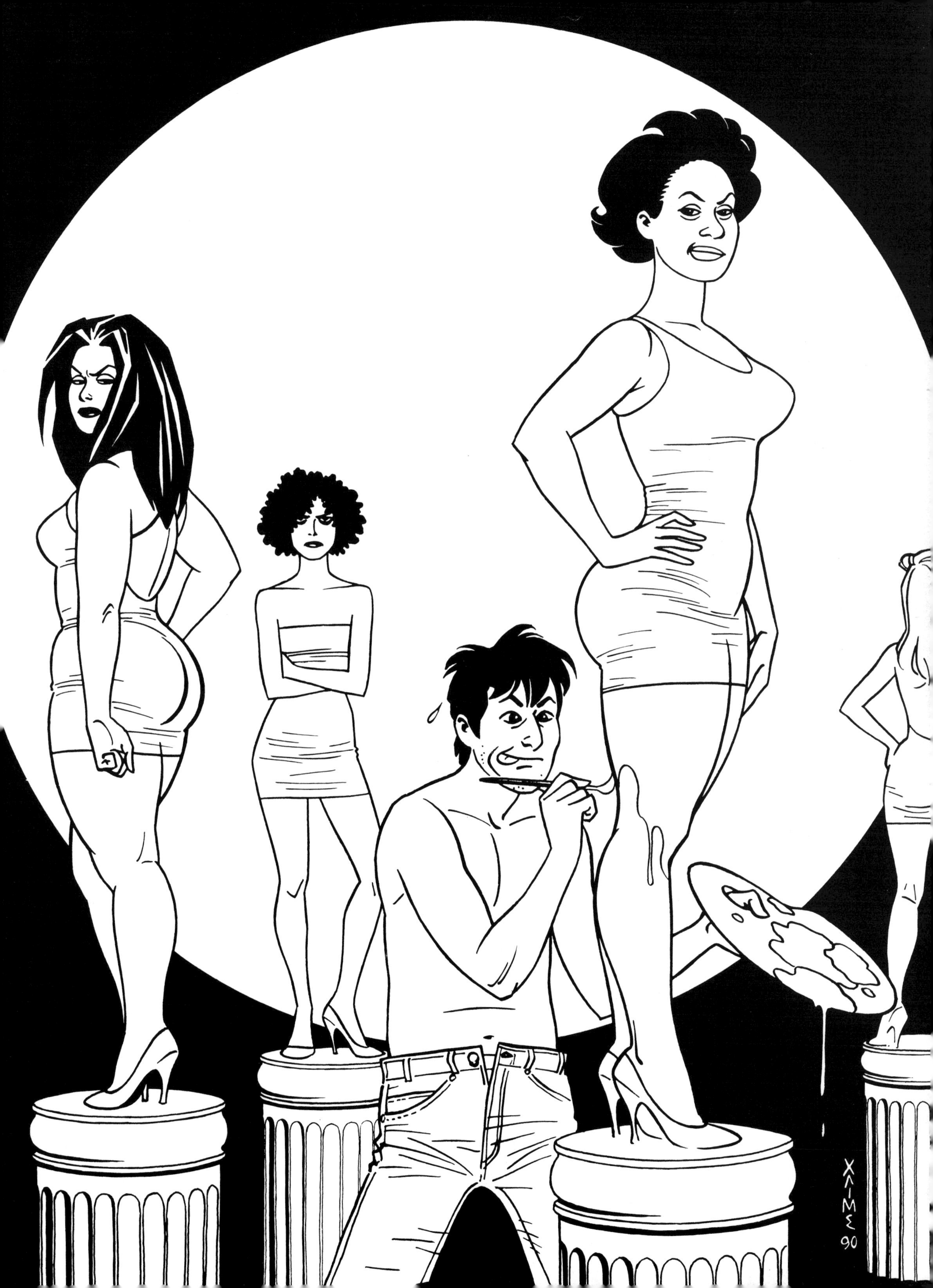
XAIME
90

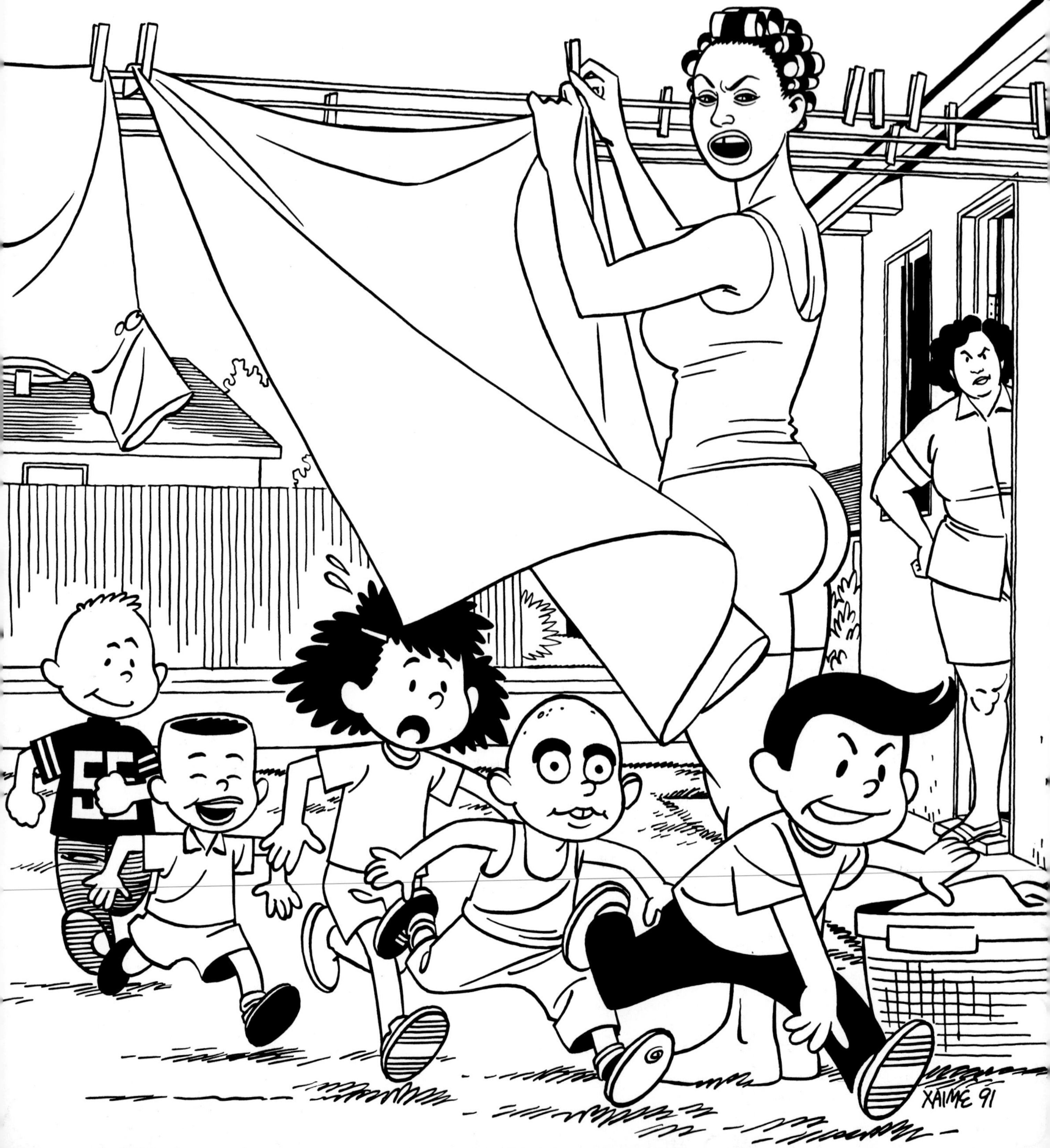
55
XAIME 91

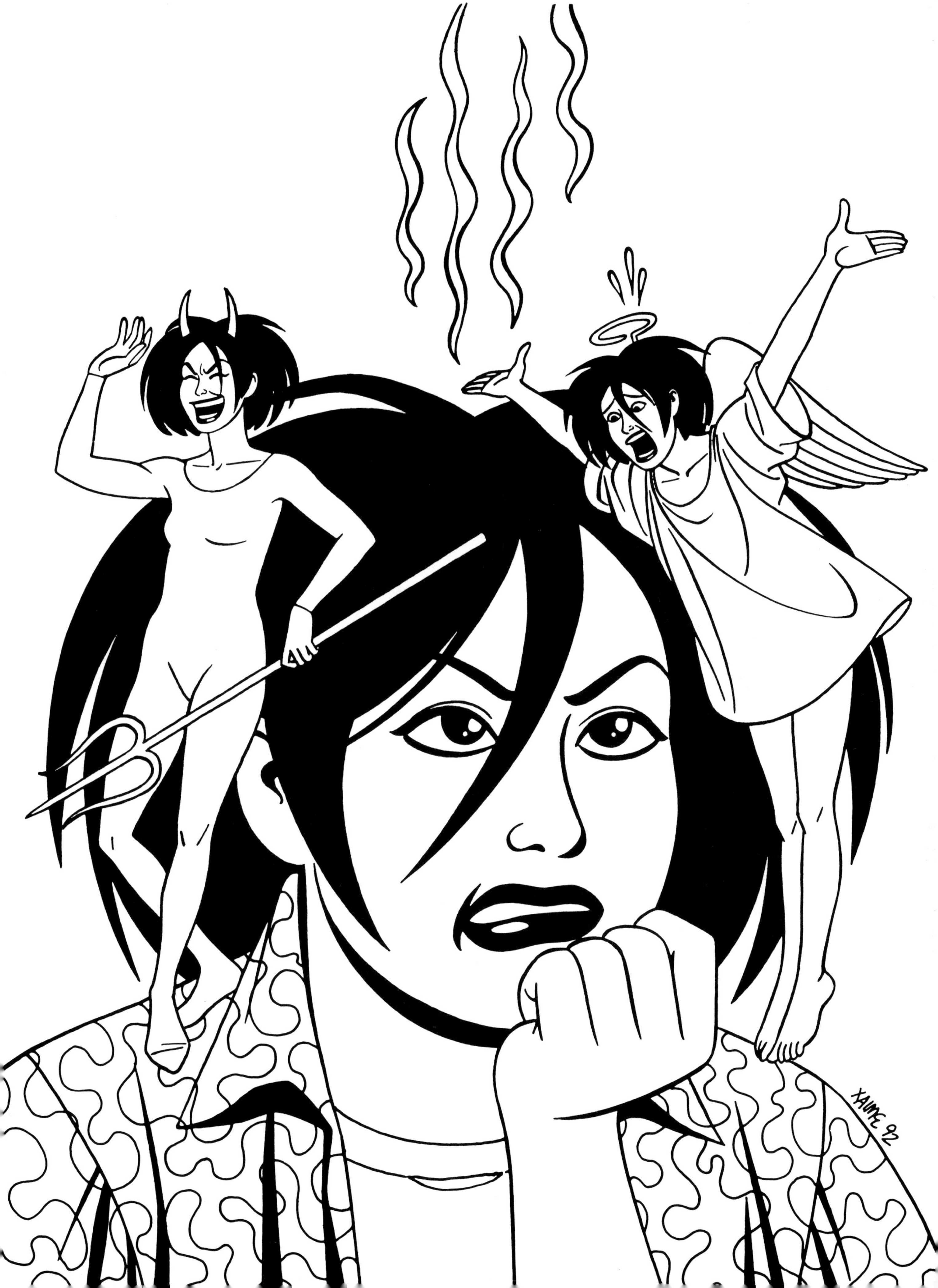
XAIME 92

Also available from
Fantagraphics Books:

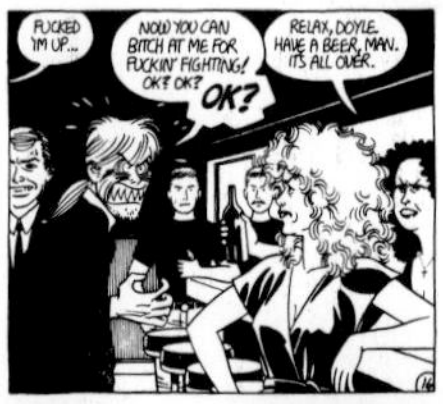
FUCKED 'EM UP...
NOW YOU CAN BITCH AT ME FOR FUCKIN' FIGHTING! OK? OK? OK?
RELAX, DOYLE. HAVE A BEER, MAN. IT'S ALL OVER.

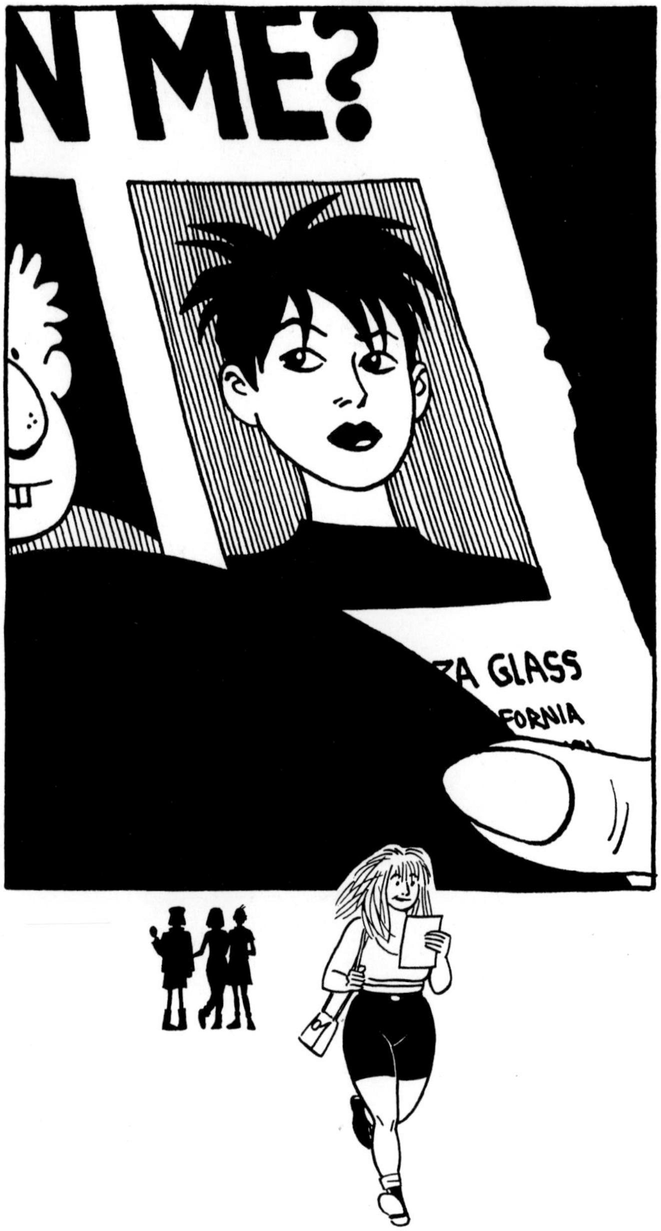
N ME?
ZA GLASS
FORNIA

LOVE & ROCKETS BOOK ONE
Music for Mechanics

LOVE & ROCKETS BOOK TWO
Chelo's Burden

LOVE & ROCKETS BOOK THREE
Las Mujeres Perdidas

LOVE & ROCKETS BOOK FOUR
Tears From Heaven

LOVE & ROCKETS BOOK FIVE
House of Raging Women

LOVE & ROCKETS BOOK SIX
Duck Feet

LOVE & ROCKETS BOOK SEVEN
The Death of Speedy

LOVE & ROCKETS BOOK EIGHT
Blood of Palomar

LOVE & ROCKETS BOOK NINE
Flies on the Ceiling

LOVE & ROCKETS BOOK TEN
Love & Rockets X

Love & Rockets Sketchbook
VOLUME ONE

Love & Rockets Sketchbook
VOLUME TWO

For a FREE full-color catalog
send your name and address to:

FANTAGRAPHICS BOOKS
7563 Lake City Way NE
Seattle WA 98115